95316

The "American Way"

THE "AMERICAN WAY"

*Family and Community in the
Shaping of the American Identity*

ALLAN CARLSON

ISI Books
Wilmington, Delaware

Cataloging-in-Publication Data:

The "American Way" : family and community in the shaping of the American identity / Allan Carlson. — Wilmington, DE : ISI Books, 2003.

     p. ; cm.
     Includes index.
     ISBN: 1-932236-11-2

     1. United States—Social life and customs. 2. United States—Civilization. 3. Idealsim, American. 4. National characteristics, American. I. Title.

E169.12 .C37 2003   2003109725
306/.0973—dc22   0309

Published in the United States by:

     ISI Books
     Post Office Box 4431
     Wilmington, DE 19807-0431

Cover design by Sam Torode
Book design by Kara Beer
Manufactured in the United States of America

To John Addison Howard

Contents

Preface

In the fall of 1999, the Wirthlin Worldwide polling organization conducted an international survey regarding social values. Nearly 2,900 randomly selected persons in five global regions responded to the following question: "If you could create society the way you think it should be, what would that society be centered around?" The choices offered were family, government, business, church, and individual.

The results were surprising. In the United States, fully 67 percent of persons chose "family" and another 20 percent chose "church." If we add these numbers together to form a kind of "communitarian index," the figure of 87 percent is as close to unanimous as polling usually gets.

The U.S. participants, moreover, chose "family" and "church" more than did those in any other region of the world. In Europe, for example, 58 percent of respondents chose "family" and only 4 percent chose "church." In the predominantly Islamic Middle East and North Africa, only 50 percent chose "family" and 16 percent their faith community.

Eight percent of Americans would build their ideal society around the individual, compared to 21 percent of Asians and 12 percent of Latin Americans. "Business" was the choice of a mere 3 percent in the

U.S., compared to 14 percent in Asia and 7 percent in the Islamic world. "Government" was the answer of just 2 percent of Americans, but a hefty 25 percent of Asians.[1]

In sum, nearly nine out of ten Americans in 1999 claimed to believe that the social order should be centered on families and religious communities, and Americans' overwhelming attachment to this ideal distinguished them from the rest of the world's peoples. Moreover, the Wirthlin poll occurred at the very height of the "dot.com" investment frenzy, at the apotheosis of the sex-scandal–scarred Clinton presidency, and in the wake of the notorious "me-decades" of the 1980s and 1990s. Some questions undoubtedly arise from this: How might the cultural analyst square this poll result with Calvin Coolidge's oft-cited aphorism that "the business of America is business"? Or with the supposed grounding of American political culture in Lockean individualism? Or with the contemporary claim that the essence of America lies in its commitment to "cultural diversity"?

Part of the answer can be found in the realization that for a long time now America's public leaders and intellectuals have trafficked in a distorted reading of the American past. In his provocative book, *The Myth of American Individualism*, political historian Barry Shain shows that "Americans in The Revolutionary era embraced a theory of the good life that is best described as reformed Protestant and communal." He explains that the American cause of 1776 had more to do with the retention of "familial independence" than it did dreams of personal liberation. The founding generation did not consist of the nascent individualists and proto-capitalists presumed in contemporary liberal and libertarian thought. Instead, they were a people bound by family, spiritual community, and social convention.[2]

This new study of the "American way" argues that "family" and "religiously-grounded community" also served in the twentieth century as the dominant imagery for American self-understanding, with important consequences. Now cast in the context of an industrial order, carefully cultivated concepts of "the American family" and "the American home" became powerful vehicles for the assimilation of new immigrants into national life. In the universality of maternal love and family affections, nation-builders found powerful emotions that united an otherwise diverse and polyglot people. In doing so, they pushed aside rival visions of American self-understanding: a racialist Anglo-Saxonism and a "cultural pluralism" that celebrated ethnic and lifestyle

diversity. These same architects of twentieth-century ideals of citizenship and nationhood then erected a distinctive social welfare system
that was intended both to reflect and reinforce "the traditional American family." These policies contributed in turn to the historically unique
revitalization of marriage and fertility in the U.S. during the middle
decades of the twentieth century. The same images of social rebirth
and family strength undergirded much American policy in the Cold
War against communism. When, somewhat later, "the American family" system came under critical assault and exhibited signs of profound
distress, American foreign policy began to unravel as well: a relationship more than coincidental. Some coherence was regained only when
national leaders tentatively restored the rhetorical bond between nation and family. And with the United States of America now sitting
astride the globe as the last superpower, the metaphors of "the American home" and "the natural community" have gained new and even
more urgent import.

  This book examines six episodes in the crafting of a family- and
community-centered national identity. The first chapter explores the
ideas of early twentieth-century American preeminent nation-builder,
Theodore Roosevelt. T.R. emerges as the first American president to
grapple with the challenges of modernity as they confronted the family; the first to articulate a family-centric worldview; and the first to
link the stable, child-rich family with American patriotism. Chapter 2
uses the story of the German-Americans, America's largest ethnic
group, to dissect the crisis over immigrant assimilation in the early decades of the twentieth century and the resolution found in a common
celebration of home and motherhood. The third chapter shows how a
remarkable group of women, labeled here the "maternalists", successfully turned the New Deal into a policy vehicle to promote "the traditional American family," which is built on the bread-winning father
and the homemaking mother. Chapter 4 traces how the imagery of
"family" and "faith" were used by master promoter and publisher
Henry Luce to shape a portrait of "the New America" that defined, in
turn, "the American Century." Chapter 5 underscores how the chief
architects of American foreign policy between 1946 and 1965 all presumed the existence of a family-centered, religious people at home,
who provided a stable base for their "grand designs" abroad. It also
describes how mounting perceptions of disorder at home subsequently
led to foreign policy failure. The final chapter explores the collapse of

maternalist ideals in the mid-1960s and emphasizes the internal weaknesses that made this end likely. The chapter also describes the tentative recovery of a family-centered national identity during the presidency of Ronald Reagan. The volume concludes with a reformulation of the language of "family," "community," and "nationhood" that might be more appropriate for the new circumstances of the twenty-first century.

o o o o o o o o o

Expressions of gratitude are in order. Archivists in a number of locations graciously assisted in the crafting of this work. These research centers included: the Lyndon B. Johnson Presidential Library (Austin, Texas); the John F. Kennedy Presidential Library (Boston); the Caroliniana Collection at the University of South Carolina (Columbia); the Time, Inc. Archives (New York); the Archives of Princeton University; the Max Kade Institute for German-American Studies (Madison, Wisconsin); and the Wisconsin State Historical Society. My colleagues John Howard, Bryce Christensen, and Bill Kauffman read chapters and offered valuable comments and cautions. Heidi Gee managed the word processing chores. Barry Shain of Colgate University gave the project a special boost at a critical time. The Earhart Foundation of Ann Arbor, Michigan, provided a generous grant for research, travel, and time. And the Pew Charitable Trusts encouraged the work through this author's involvement in Pew's remarkable "Nature of the Human Person" project.

1
Home and Nation: The Family Politics of Theodore Roosevelt

I do not wish to see this country a country of selfish prosperity where those who enjoy the material prosperity think only of the selfish gratification of their own desires, and are content to import from abroad not only their art, not only their literature, but even their babies.
— Theodore Roosevelt, 1911

With regard to the family, Theodore Roosevelt can be called the first "modern" American president. He grappled openly with a range of new social and cultural issues surrounding the home, and was the first president to describe in philosophical terms the importance of family life to national life. He was the first to document and analyze an emerging crisis among American families and the first to understand the vast import of feminism, and to embrace it—albeit on his own terms. Roosevelt was also the first president to understand the powerful challenges to family life lurking within the new biological sciences.

How might we explain this interest? To begin with, Theodore Roosevelt had an amazing intellect, which embraced a vast range of subjects. He may have been the greatest mind ever to inhabit the White House (with the ritual "possible exception" of Jefferson). He was a voracious reader, reading at least one book a day, even during his Presidency (from 1901 to 1909) and over five hundred a year. "Reading with me is a disease," he reported. Roosevelt was a prolific writer as well, and produced an amazing body of writing between his graduation from Harvard in 1880 and the middle year of his presidency (1905) alone. The contemporaneous Elkhorn Edition of *The Works of Theodore*

Roosevelt, which already numbered 23 volumes by 1905, covered history, natural history, political philosophy, biography, and essays. Critics considered two of his works, *The Naval War of 1812* and the four-volume *Winning of the West*, as definitive on their subjects. Roosevelt's published book reviews numbered over one thousand. His memory amazed all those who met him.[1]

Roosevelt was also a student of numbers, particularly census numbers. He pored over U.S. Census reports from 1890, 1900, and 1910, commenting frequently on the strong evidence of mounting family decay. There was much to worry about. Between 1890 and 1910, the number of divorced Americans rose threefold. Among 35- to 44-year-olds, the increase was even greater. The U.S. birthrate fell by over 30 percent between 1880 and 1920, with the decline particularly sharp in Roosevelt's native Northeast. Indeed, when combined with high immigration, the low fertility there caused the proportion of "native stock" to fall from 67 percent in 1880 to only 56 percent by 1910. In the nation as a whole, the number of children under five years of age per 1000 women between the ages 20 and 44 had tumbled from 1,295 in 1820 to 631 by 1910, figures reflecting a dramatic retreat from child-bearing. Among New England women in the latter year, the figure was only 482.[2]

Finally, Theodore Roosevelt was a conscious nation builder, working to intellectually construct an American identity, a type of nationalism suitable to a country leaving its frontier phase and moving out into the world. He toyed, at times, with a concept of America as an "ethnic nation," much like those found in Western Europe. On other occasions, he defined *Americanism* as a set of philosophical or political ideals, to which persons of any ethnicity might adhere. Yet neither resolution seemed satisfactory to him. Roosevelt's focus on family questions actually represented a bold attempt to craft a third form of American identity, one built around social and biological imperatives.

BURDEN OF THE "R" WORD

Oddly, little recent attention has been paid to Roosevelt's treatment of the family. His biographers, including Edmund Morris, largely ignore it. And while writers on the ideological Left do sometimes draw a quote or two from Roosevelt, it is inevitably to brand him (and, implicitly, subsequent family advocates) as racist.

The problem derives from Roosevelt's own language, in which he regularly used the word *race* and phrases such as *race suicide* in his commentaries on family matters. To read Roosevelt correctly, the reader must first understand what he meant by this terminology.

The twentieth century—from the "race politics" of the National Socialists in Germany during the 1930s and 1940s to the "race struggles" in America during the 1960s—has endowed the word *race* with a great ideological and moral burden. Yet a century ago, the term carried a very different set of meanings. It was, for example, commonly viewed as interchangeable with the words *nation* or *people. Race* conveyed the sense of a group with a common history, a common culture, and a yearning for a common destiny. Some saw it as designating a citizenry with "a certain homogeneity because of common laws, institutions, customs, or loyalty." Others understood *race* as meaning the sharing of a common ancestor. While it is true that "scientific" conceptions of *race* were also extant (as a "genetically distinctive population within a species"), there were frequent literary uses as well. Oscar Wilde called imagination "the result of heredity. It is simply concentrated *race-memory*." William James described how "*race* heritage forms in its totality a monstrously unwieldy mass of learning." Citizenship, nationality, genetic similarity, a people, heritage, a common history—all these were conflated with the word *race*,[3] without the negative connotations of superiority or oppression attached.

For example, Roosevelt frequently used the term, *race*-suicide. But to this phrase he attached a very specific meaning: "the gradual extinction of a people through a tendency to restrict voluntarily the rate of population growth." His concerns were the causes and the demographic consequences of birth control; but the term *race-suicide*—loaded as it now is with mid–twentieth-century baggage with which Roosevelt was never confronted—is now off-putting. To understand Roosevelt's comments on family, it seems that we almost need a translator.

Roosevelt did occasionally convey a desire to preserve the line of those with whom he shared genetic traits. But when doing so, he usually used a word other than race. For example, in his 1917 book on domestic American politics, *The Foes of Our Own Household*, Roosevelt quoted from a letter he had sent to a woman in poverty who had complained of her burden of six children and his opposition to birth control. "I do not want to see us Americans forced to import our babies from abroad," he wrote. "I do not want to see the *stock* of people like yourself and my family die out."[4]

But at the philosophical level, Roosevelt regularly opposed the social Darwinism of the scientific racists and their argument that natural selection and conflict improved "the race." To the contrary, he maintained, "the rivalry of natural selection works against progress. Progress is made in spite of it." Cooperation and acts of altruism marked those communities that truly moved forward, he said. Indeed, in opposition to "survival of the fittest," Roosevelt posited maternal love as the true source of progress:

> A more supreme instance of unselfishness than is afforded by motherhood cannot be imagined, and when [the author under review] implies...that there is no rational sanction for the unselfishness of motherhood, for the unselfishness of duty, or loyalty, he merely misuses the word rational.[5]

One finds further evidence of Roosevelt's relatively liberal views on race in his frequent condemnation of peoples—including his own ethnic stock—who voluntarily failed to reproduce. In the same review dismissing social Darwinism, Roosevelt wrote: "When a people gets to the position even now occupied by the mass of the French and by sections of the New Englanders, where the death rate surpasses the birthrate, then that *race* [people] is not only fated to extinction but *it deserves* extinction."[6] He denounced the much ballyhooed "Puritan conscience" as "so atrophied, so diseased and warped" as to be unable to recognize its own self-destruction. Roosevelt instead threw in his lot with the "new" immigration of his time: "The New England of the future will belong, and ought to belong, to the descendents of the immigrants of . . . today, because the descendants of the Puritans have lacked the courage to live."[7] Looking elsewhere, he pointed to the absurdly low birthrate of Australia—"a continent which could support . . . tenfold the present population"—and predicted the doom of the "White Australia" policy. As he explained: "no race [people] can hold a territory save on condition of developing and populating it."[8] Any people who practiced "the base and selfish doctrine" of the two-child system deserved extinction in order to give "place to others with braver and more robust ideals."[9] Roosevelt even saw miscegenation or interracial marriage—the bête noire of the true racist—as one positive solution to fertility decline. If healthy men and women failed to marry

and bear children, he wrote, "the result must necessarily be race deterioration, unless the race is partly *saved* by the infusion into it of *blood
of other races* that have not lost the virile virtues."[10]

Roosevelt became on occasion even more explicit. While touring
in South America, he praised the vitality of the people he met: "The
families are large. The women, charming and attractive, are good and
fertile mothers in *all* classes of society." The South American peoples,
he continued, "have far more to teach than to learn from the English-
speaking countries" regarding their public obligations and family responsibility. Indeed, Roosevelt even predicted with accuracy the demographic future of California and the American Southwest: "The nineteenth century saw a prodigious growth of the English-speaking, relative to the Spanish speaking, population . . . The end of the twentieth
century will see this completely reversed."[11]

Roosevelt also wove these views into his effort to understand and
shape the American identity. In the process, he linked the ideals of the
Founders to the familial obligations of the living. In his review of the
book *Racial Decay* by Octavius Beale, Roosevelt wrote: "I, for one,
would heartily throw in my fate with the men of *alien stock* who were
true to *the old American principles* rather than with the men of the old
American stock who were traitors to the old American principles."[12]
Before an audience of liberal Christian theologians in 1911, he was
even more blunt about the bond between procreation and Americanism:

> If you do not believe in your own stock enough to wish to see
> the stock kept up, then you *are not good Americans*, you are
> *not patriots*; and . . . I for one shall not mourn your extinc-
> tion; and in such event I shall welcome the advent of a new
> race that will take your place, because you will have shown
> that you *are not fit to cumber* the ground.

Roosevelt called this "the most essential and the least pleasant truth
that I have to tell you."[13]

A VISION OF FAMILISM

Like many philosophers, Roosevelt built his social vision in reaction to
the cultural, demographic, and political developments of his time (these
will be discussed later). But Roosevelt also turned his analysis into a

positive philosophy of family life that is rich in content and argumentation.

To begin with, he repeatedly emphasized the centrality of the child-rich family to the very existence of the American nation: "it is in the life of the family, upon which in the last analysis the whole welfare of the Nation rests. . . . The nation is nothing but the aggregate of the families within its borders."[14] Elsewhere, he wrote that "[e]verything" in the American civilization and nation "rests upon the home."[15] He labeled the family relation "as the most fundamental, the most important of all relations."[16] A nation existed only as its "sons and daughters thought of life not as something concerned only with the selfish evanescence of the individual, but as a link in the great chain of creation and causation," a chain forged by the "vital duties and the high happiness of family life."[17]

Roosevelt viewed family as the essential wellspring of citizenship, and in it he saw signs of hope for America:

> [I]n all the world there is no better and healthier home life, no finer factory of individual character, nothing more representative of *what is best and most characteristic in American life*, than that which exists in the higher type of family; and this higher type of family is to be found everywhere among us.[18]

He specifically praised the large families still evident in the American South and Middle West. In Roosevelt's view, good American citizenship rested on "the building up of the kind of character which will make the man a good husband, a good father, a good son; which will make the woman a good daughter when she is young and a good wife and mother as she grows older."[19] Underscoring the common grounding of citizenship and Americanism upon a great chain of being, Roosevelt stressed that "no other success in life, not being President, or being wealthy, or going to college, or anything else, comes up to the success of the man and woman who can feel that they have done their duty and that their children and grandchildren rise up to call them blessed."[20] Accordingly, the birth control issue became for him "the most serious of all problems, for it lies at the root of, *and indeed itself is, national life.*"[21]

At times Roosevelt subordinated all other public questions to the issue of family formation. It was "useless" to devote time and resources to education "if there are not going to be enough children to educate."[22]

"Reform" made no sense if there was no one to reform. He declared that "no piled-up wealth, no splendor of material growth, no brilliance of artistic development" would be of any value or meaning to the nation unless its men and women were "able and willing to bear, and to bring up as they should be brought up, healthy children, sound in mind, body, and character; and numerous enough" for the nation to grow.[23] Indeed, procreation was so fundamental to national life that Roosevelt gave a preference to illegitimacy or out-of-wedlock birth over sterility: "after all, such vice may be compatible with a nation's continuing to live; and while there is life, even a life marred by wrong practices, there is chance of reform."[24] Or as he stated elsewhere, "while there is life, there is hope, whereas nothing can be done with the dead."[25]

Accordingly, Roosevelt elevated motherhood to the most important of human tasks. His language here was strong and specific. No nation, he insisted, "can exist at all" unless the average woman is "the home-keeper, the good wife, and unless she is the mother of a sufficient number of healthy children" to keep the nation "going forward." The "indispensable work for the community" was not that of careers, industry, or research; it was "the work of the wife and mother."[26] The "woman's work in the home" was "more important" than any man's endeavors. "She does play a greater part."[27]

Roosevelt did, however, emphasize that motherhood should not be coerced: "The imposition on any woman of excessive childbearing is a brutal wrong."[28] But all Americans have it as "their prime duty...to leave their seed after them to inherit the earth."[29] He summoned all healthy women to bear at least four children, and hoped for even more. There were practical advantages to fertility as well; as he reported, "the health of the mother is best, and the infant mortality lowest, in families with at least six children."[30] More commonly, Roosevelt praised the heroism of childbearing: "The birthpangs make all men the debtors of all women." American sympathies and support were due, above all, "to the struggling wives among those whom Abraham Lincoln called *the plain people* . . . ; for the lives of these women are often led on the lonely heights of quiet, self-sacrificing heroism."[31] True heroes were those women who "walked through the valley of the shadow to bring into life the babies they love."[32] Like the bravest of soldiers, the good mother "has gladly gone down to the brink of the chasm of darkness to bring back the children in whose hands rests the future of the years."[33]

Roosevelt sought to elevate the place or status of fatherhood, as well. On the one hand, he defined the father's task as one of bread-winning: "The primary task of the man is to earn his own livelihood and the livelihood of those dependent on him." The man must also do his business well to support his family, so "that the nation may continue to exist." But Roosevelt insisted that this task be seen in the wider context of building the good home: "The primary work of the average man and the average woman—and of all exceptional men and women whose lives are to be really full and happy—must be the great primal work of *home-making* and *home-keeping*."[34] (Note here that the father was the true "home-maker" in Roosevelt's usage.) Addressing both men and women, Roosevelt emphasized that no "career" could ever be more than a poor substitute "for *the career of married lovers* who bring into the world, and rear as they should be reared, children sufficiently numerous" to move the nation forward.[35]

The good marriage, Roosevelt argued, was a full partnership, in which "each partner is honor bound to think of the rights of the other as well as of his or her own."[36] The way for men to honor "this indispensable woman, the wife and the mother," was to insist on her treatment as "the full equal of her husband."[37] Regarding the rearing of offspring, "[t]here must be *common* parental care for children, by both father and mother."[38] Roosevelt's view of marital partnership, though, went beyond the vision of shared tasks and responsibilities. On the emotional and spiritual side, he said that a true marriage would be "a partnership of the soul, the spirit and the mind, no less than of the body."[39] The "highest ideal of the family" could be obtained "only where the father and mother stand to each other as lovers and friends."[40] On the practical and material side, Roosevelt believed in early marriage as a counter to temptations toward vice.[41] More profoundly, he believed that the successful marriage, "the partnership of happiness," must also be "a partnership of work."[42] Anticipating the future insights of microeconomists, Roosevelt understood that the strong family must be a true economic unit. "Our aim," he wrote, "must be the healthy economic interdependence of the sexes." Attempts to craft the "economic independence" of the sexes would create "a false identity of economic function" and result in national ruin.[43]

While avoiding some of the excesses of so-called agrarian fundamentalism, Roosevelt still saw country life and farm life as intimately connected with healthy family life. Fertility was higher in the countryside than in the cities, in some regions nearly twice as high. This meant that "nearly half the children of the United States are born and brought up on farms." History taught that "the permanent greatness of any state" depended primarily on "the character of its country popula-tion."[44] The small landowner, "the men who own their little homes . . . the men who till farms, the men of the soil, have hitherto made the foundation of lasting national life in every state." It had been the man born and raised in the country who had been "most apt to render the services which every nation most needs." Among American statesmen, "it is extraordinary to see how large a proportion started as farm boys." In sum, "the best crop" on American farms "is the crop of children; the best products of the farm are the men and women raised thereon." Family life and farm life were deeply intertwined; renewing families depended in part on renewing rural community.[45]

These views coalesced in Roosevelt's mind so that he nearly equated American nationalism with adequate procreation. "I do not wish to see this country a country of selfish prosperity," Roosevelt told the Protestant theologians, "where those who enjoy the material pros-perity think only of the selfish gratification of their own desires, and are content to import from abroad not only their art, not only their literature, but even their babies."[46] It was "utterly futile," he wrote else-where, "to make believe that fussy activity for somebody else's babies atones for failure of personal parenthood." Instead, in "the name of the larger Americanism," in "fealty to the highest American ideal," he summoned women in particular to "dare to live nobly and bravely" by bearing more children. The American nation needed "the positive preaching of birth encouragement" so that it might live into the fu-ture.[47]

FOES OF THE FAMILY

Such appeals came in the face of grave challenges to the family, forces or "foes" that Roosevelt sought to identify and understand. At the most fundamental level, he explained, stood the complex effects of industri-alism. The "substitution in a time of profound peace of a factory-town population for an agricultural population" had a "far more calami-tous" impact on the nation than any war. "Uncontrolled industrial-ism" tore through family life in many ways. Most directly, Roosevelt noted that the annual death toll in American industries outnumbered "the deaths in the bloodiest battle of the Civil War."[48] In broader terms, the "ruin of motherhood and childhood by the merciless exploitation of the labor of women and children" should be considered a capital crime. He believed that these "grave dangers" of industrialism should be countered by sheltering the home from its influences. Above all, "the service of the good mother" in the home was worth "infinitely" more to society "than any possible service the woman could render by any other, and necessarily inferior, form of industry."[49]

More specifically, Roosevelt condemned the practice of "willful sterility in marriage." Birth control was "the capital sin" against civilization, a practice that meant national death.[50] It was a puzzle, he said, that birth control should be most widespread in the very places where "abounding vigor" was so strikingly displayed: Canada, Australia, New Zealand, and the United States. In these lands, there was "no warrant whatever in economic conditions for a limitation of the birth rate"; and yet, fertility was in decline.

Roosevelt searched for the causes of this problem. Importantly, he refused to indict "the growth of independence among women" as a factor. The women of France, he reasoned, had gone the furthest in birth limitation, despite the fact that their legal status was inferior to that of American women. Rather, Roosevelt pointed beyond the broad effects of industrialism to the power of wrong ideas. He cited "the profound and lasting damage unwittingly done by Malthus" in his pessimism over population growth "and, to a less extent, by John Stuart Mill" in his open advocacy for birth limitation.[51] He also blamed the "blatant sham reformers who, in the name of the new morality, preach the old, old vice and self-indulgence." These "most foolish of all foolish people who advocate a profoundly immoral attitude toward life" in the name of "reform" through "birth control" were in fact the real problem. Claiming to deal with pathologies, they themselves represented the true "pathological condition."[52]

Of course, Roosevelt acknowledged that some couples were denied "the supreme blessing of children." These couples were due "respect and sympathy."[53] And he admitted that there was a "submerged tenth" of society, the poorest of the poor, whose lives were constantly on the brink of disaster. Urging them to bear more children made little sense. But for the great majority, the 90 percent, "the real danger" was "not lest they have too many children, but lest they have too few."[54] Among this group, the deliberate rejection of childbearing merited only contempt. The behavior derived, he suggested, "from viciousness, cold-ness, shallow-heartedness, self-indulgence, or mere failure to appreci-ate aright the difference between the all-important and the unimpor-tant." While laying blame on both deliberately childless men and women, he offered a special comment on the latter: "The existence of women of this type forms one of the unpleasant and unwholesome features of modern life."[55]

Elsewhere, he pointed to "love of ease" and "striving after social position" as lying behind the birth control mentality.[56] The New En-gland conscience now condoned "frightful and fundamental immoral-ity," which twisted sexual conduct "into improper channels." Roosevelt rejected the counterargument often heard at the women's colleges that a higher "quality" of children made up for a slackened quantity. "When quantity falls off, thanks to willful sterility," he retorted, "the quality will go down too." And so the American pioneers who wrote "the tre-mendous epic that tells of the conquest of a continent" saw their sons and daughters in "fear of all work and risk." These descendents were willing "to let the blood of the pioneers die out" on the land because they shrank "from the most elemental duties of manhood and wom-anhood."[57]

A certain sort of feminism also stood as a foe of the family. But Roosevelt embraced feminism of another sort early on, a philosophi-cal loyalty from which he never wavered.

As a young scholar at Harvard in 1880, Roosevelt wrote his se-nior thesis on the "Practicality of Giving Men and Women Equal Rights." To the disgruntlement of his professors, who thought that the essay showed softness, the college senior argued:

> A cripple or a consumptive in the eye of the law is equal to the
> strongest athlete or the deepest thinker, and the same justice
> should be shown to a woman whether she is or is not the equal
> of man. . . . As regards the laws relating to marriage there
> should be the most absolute equality preserved between the
> sexes.[58]

Indeed, Roosevelt went on to suggest that wives should keep their own last names, and that the word "obey" in the wedding vows should be pledged equally by bride and groom. According to biographer Edmund Morris, Roosevelt would for the whole of his life "remain acutely aware of the needs and sensibilities of women."

In fact, Roosevelt was what some historians would later call a *social feminist*, and others a *maternalist*. The formula here was quite simple, and repeated frequently in his work: "We believe in equality of right, not in identity of functions." In this sense, Roosevelt welcomed recent changes in the legal status of women. He dismissed the outcry against "unwomanly" activities such as higher education as "nonsense": "[t]he woman is entitled to just as much education as the man." And he called it "common sense" to allow women to pursue careers in areas where they were capable: "There is a real need for a certain number of women doctors and women lawyers."[59] Nothing should preclude women from following opportunities and leading lives of "full and varied interest, which of necessity means a life in which work worth doing is well done." In science, he added, women had already proved themselves, and he heaped praise on Lauri Bassi, an eighteenth-century Italian physicist, as an example.[60]

But the key to his position was the fact that Professor Bassi was also the mother of twelve children: "She never permitted her extraordinary scientific and literary work to conflict with her domestic duties." So, despite the higher learning and the possibility of pursuing a career, the true and good woman would still be focused first on the home and children. As Roosevelt summarized in a 1912 essay: "I believe in woman's rights. I believe even more earnestly in the performance of duty by both men and women." Indeed, he reasoned, all rights depended on accepting an accompanying duty or responsibility, a view he elaborated in his review-essay on women in science. "Neither woman nor man can shirk duties under penalty of eventually losing rights, for the possession of the right should be conditioned upon the performance of the duty." Since equality of rights did not mean identify of function, he concluded that in any "healthy community," the "prime duty of the woman will ever be that of the wife and mother."[61]

Consistent with this view, Roosevelt took a middle position on giving the vote to women: "I am rather tepidly in favor of woman's suffrage." Whenever forced to take sides, he supported it. He regularly suggested that the matter be decided by referenda among women themselves: if they chose to acquire the vote, then let them have it. However, Roosevelt also emphasized that the issue of woman's voting was not "a thousandth or a millionth part as important as the question of keeping, and where necessary reviving among the women . . . the realization that their great work must be done in the home."[62]

While a fervent social feminist, Roosevelt was also a strident critic of the liberal or equity feminists of his day, who wanted full equality in functions as well as in rights. He blasted as fools those "professional feminists" and "so called woman's rights women" who labeled wives and mothers at home as "parasite" women. A woman keeping a home is not a parasite on society, he rebutted. "She *is* society." He mocked the president of a women's college who had argued in a well-publicized speech that it was better to bear one child brought up in the proper way than to improperly rear several. This speaker was "not only unfit to be at the head of a female college, but is not fit to teach the lowest class of a kindergarten." Roosevelt also pointed to "the most pitiable showing by the graduates of the women's colleges": the average product of Smith or Vassar bore only 0.86 children during her lifetime. "Do these colleges teach 'domestic science,'" he asked? If so, "what is it that they teach? There is something radically wrong with the home training and the school training that produces such results."[63] Advocates urging women to cease viewing their primary duties as those of wives and mothers were, he concluded, "not only foolish but *wicked*."[64]

Easy divorce stood as another family foe in Roosevelt's analysis. He saw the effects of divorce made manifest in "sinister fashion" in the 1900 census. The statistics were "fairly appalling," he told The National Congress of Mothers in 1905. To them he argued that "easy divorce is now, as it ever has been, a *bane* to any nation, a *curse* to society, a *menace* to the home, an *incitement* to married unhappiness, and to immorality." Easy divorce stood as "an evil thing for men, and a still more hideous evil for women." When the 1910 census showed still another leap in the divorce rate, Roosevelt reiterated the devilish nature of the problem: "Multiplication of divorces means that there is something rotten in the community, that there is some principle of evil at work." He warned that unless the development was counteracted, "wide-spread disaster" would follow.[65]

Science unguided by principle also threatened the family. Eugenics was the fashionable "new science" of the early twentieth century, promising as it did an improvement of the human species through controlled breeding. Roosevelt was not immune to its allure, but he repeatedly cautioned that it not be made an excuse for inhuman abuses. He admitted that "the great problem of civilization" was "to secure a relative increase of the valuable as compared with the less valuable" portion of the population. But he refused to accept arguments that "value" could be determined along racial or ethnic lines. Moreover, he recoiled from the use of "negative" measures such as forced sterilization to prevent the "less valuable" from breeding. Roosevelt reasoned: "Except in a small number of cases, the state can exercise little active control against the perpetuation of the unfit." Rather, the emphasis should be placed on "getting desirable people to breed." And he cast the net of the "desirable" quite widely: "I am speaking of the ordinary, every day Americans, the decent men and women who do make good fathers and mothers, and who ought to have good-sized families."[66]

AN "AMERICAN" FAMILY POLICY

Roosevelt's identification of the foes of the family, tied to his positive vision of the good home, guided his formulation of a comprehensive—and sometimes surprising—family policy. Although deploring birth control, he never called for its legal prohibition. Love and a sense of duty, not coercion, he thought, should be the weapons of choice in fighting its spread. Yet he did craft a sexual policy in other areas. For example, he considered prostitution terrible and degrading, a sign of moral disorder. As a response, he endorsed the idea already adopted in Great Britain of flogging the male offenders, pimps and clients alike.[67]

Turning to rural policy, he urged that the U.S. Department of Agriculture be redirected so that it balanced economic goals with an equal attention to "agriculture for its social results." This meant support "for the best kind of life on the farm for the sake of producing the best kind of men." Progressive taxation should be used to break up the great landed estates, in order to turn tenant farmers into landowners. The state should mobilize investment capital for small farmers, and favor farm-produce cooperatives through law. Regarding rural women, the first priority should be to end their lives of drudgery. Extension programs should guide them into focusing on home-keeping, rather than on grueling field work. Rural schools should aim at turning the girls into "first class farmers' wives."[68]

More broadly, Roosevelt argued that "[m]otherhood should be protected." Mothers and children "should not be allowed to work in any way that interferes with home duties." In line with the maternalist program of mothers' pensions, Roosevelt also urged that widowed and deserted young mothers receive aid sufficient to keep them at home with their children. He was aware of the possible moral hazards of such assistance, and cautioned that aid should not be given in ways that encouraged men to shirk their paternal duties. Indeed, Roosevelt thought the law should be especially severe in collecting child support from fathers who did not marry the mothers of their children. In addition, he praised the German welfare system, which provided health care to ordinary families, and thought it ought to be adopted in the United States.[69]

Roosevelt also saw the unique social-policy potential of differential taxation. Unmarried men, he argued, ought to pay "a far heavier share of taxation than at present."[70] Elsewhere, he urged that both income tax and inheritance tax rates "should be *immensely heavier* on the childless and on families with one or two children, while there should be an equally heavy discrimination in reverse, in favor of families with over three children." More specifically, he argued that no reduction in tax rate should be the consequence of mere marriage. Rather, married taxpayers should receive an exemption of $500 (current value equal to approximately $10,000) for each of their first two children, and $1,000 (current value approximately $20,000) for each subsequent child.[71]

The concept of a "family wage" also appealed to Roosevelt. He believed that private employers should recognize their obligation to support the fathers they employed as heads of households, providing them with wages sufficient to sustain the home. Meanwhile, the state should always give preference to the parents of large families (in an interestingly gender-neutral way): "In all public offices in every grade the lowest salaries should be paid the man *or woman* with no children, or only one or two children, and a marked discrimination made in favor of the man *or woman* with a family of over three children."[72]

In retrospect, there is a serious weakness in Roosevelt's family advocacy. He built his case for marriage and high fertility, as well as his condemnation of birth control, on strictly secular grounds. He cast the creation of a family as a duty to the nation, not as a consequence of fidelity to God's will for humankind. The inadequacy of this foundation, though, would only become apparent at a later time.

Indeed, Roosevelt's ideas would be highly influential in shaping American social policy in the period from 1915 to 1960. Through the work of Roosevelt's friend, Liberty Hyde Bailey of Cornell University, the USDA did shift its emphasis toward agriculture's social consequences, seeking for the next twenty-five years to undergird the family farm.[73] Projects ranged from the Homemaker and 4-H Clubs created by extension agents for the retraining of wives and children to the sub-sidization of Subsistence Homestead settlements in the 1930s. Federal tax policy in the 1940s came to reflect Roosevelt's ideas about generous child exemptions, finally reaching the $500 per child figure in 1948 (cur-rent value approximately $7,500). Employment patterns after World War II favored family wages for fathers.[74] Numerous state and local governments also crafted wage policies that rewarded families with children, some of whose rules were to be found as recently as 1960. Moreover, there is evidence to suggest that these measures played a role in turning around marriage, birth, and divorce rates in America. The U.S. marriage rate began to climb again in 1934; and the birth rate began rising a year later, eventually becoming the Baby Boom of 1945 to 1963. Even the divorce rate began falling in 1947, a decline that con-tinued into the early 1960s.

The sense of nationhood that Roosevelt sought to build, resting on a vision of political ideals linked to social ideals centered on the child-rich family, seemed finally to have emerged during the early pe-riod of the Cold War. One suspects that at the height of this period of family renewal, circa 1957, the old Roughrider, even in his long sleep in a New York cemetery, might have smiled.

2

Hyphenates, *Hausfraus*, and Baby-Saving: The Peculiar Legacy of German America

The alternative before Americans is Kultur Klux Klan or Cultural Pluralism.
— Horace Kallen, 1924

Approached from the neighborhood and family and met squarely, the problem of Americanization can be solved adequately.
— Frances Kellor, 1918

"There is disloyalty active in the United States and it must be crushed," declared President Woodrow Wilson before hundreds of thousands of Americans at a "preparedness" rally held in Washington, D.C., on Flag Day, June 14, 1916. The disloyalty he spoke of came from a minority "who are trying to levy a species of political blackmail, saying 'do what we wish in the interest of foreign sentiment, or we will wreak our vengeance at the polls.'" Wilson predicted that the American nation "will teach these gentlemen once and for all that loyalty to this flag is the first test of tolerance in the United States."[1]

Speaking in the Midwest on the same day, former President Theodore Roosevelt was less circumspect about the identity of the disloyal: "No good American . . . can have any feeling except scorn and detestation for those professional German-Americans who seek to make the American President in effect a viceroy of the German Emperor." Roosevelt blasted that "adherence to the politico-racial hyphen which is the badge and sign of moral treason."[2]

One day later the Democratic Party, during its convention in the heavily German-American city of St. Louis, adopted a platform plank on "Hyphenates" and "Americanism." Together, these stood as "the supreme issue of the day," the document declared. Anyone "actuated

by the purpose to promote the interests of a foreign power in disregard of our own country's welfare" created "discord and strife" among Americans; obstructed "the whole sum process of unification;" was "faithless to the trust . . . of [U.S.] citizenship;" and stood as "disloyal to his country." Any "division" of Americans into antagonistic racial groups destroyed "that complete . . . solidarity of the people and that unity of sentiment and national purpose so essential to the perpetuity of the nation and of its free institutions." In his reelection campaign, President Wilson pledged to make "anti-hyphenism" the leading issue. Meanwhile, convention officials in St. Louis distributed new campaign buttons to the party faithful, featuring a picture of the president above two words cast in bold letters: America First.[3]

Held during the third year of the Great War in Europe, the American election of 1916 became—at least at the level of rhetoric and domestic politics—a form of civil war. The supposed "German-American threat" to national unity betokened a crisis in American self-understanding. For 125 years, from 1790 to 1915, the dominant view of immigration had been positive and welcoming. There was an implicit faith in the power of American institutions to tolerate difference and to craft a minimum degree of unity. The purest expression of this embrace of difference came in a 1915 essay written by the Jewish-American writer Horace Kallen, in which he made the case for "cultural pluralism" in the United States. Wartime, however, brought to the fore both demands for "100% Americanism" and an openly racialist Anglo-Saxonism. This racialism demanded immigration restrictions and forced assimilation into the English language and American customs; the institutions of German America became its first foe. Between 1916 and 1924, the conflict between these rival visions of America was intense. Yet quietly and unexpectedly another vision of American identity also took form. With roots in both the folkways of German America and the ideology of the Settlement House movement, this vision of American unity rested on a new communitarianism that focused on "natural" structures such as the family, and gave particular attention to the mother's role in the home and the defense of infant life. When the more visible contestants, the "cultural pluralists" and the "Anglo-Saxonists," faded after 1925, the family-centered vision of America remained a viable, compelling moral and political force, with direct consequences for the American identity during the next forty years.

CULTURAL PLURALISM, INFORMAL AND FORMAL

At the founding of the new American Republic, most persons saw the American identity in abstract, ideological terms. For obvious and personal reasons, ethnic considerations among the Anglo-American revolutionaries drew little attention. America stood as the "asylum of liberty," "the new order for the ages," where the ideals of freedom, equality, and republicanism governed. American nationality stood open to anyone who desired to adhere to these principles. As Philip Gleason writes, the naturalization policy adopted in 1790, "bespoke great confidence in the power of American principles, institutions, and environment" to transform immigrants quickly into acceptable Americans, without systematic coercion.[4]

John Higham emphasizes how, into the early twentieth century, a deep faith in the resilience of America and of the assimilation process held sway. Moreover, "the American people did not really demand a high level of national solidarity. They had enough already for their individualistic purposes." Nativist episodes such as the anti-Catholic "Know Nothing" movement and reactions to the 1886 Haymarket Riot (sparked by a bomb thrown by a German-born anarchist) were the short-lived exceptions. Most of the time, a "loose-knit, flexible society" and a common interest in commerce seemed adequate for a nation facing few external dangers.[5]

Some saw the Americanization process in more active terms. They mused about a "melting pot" wherein the best traits of foreign-born and native-born alike would fuse into a new and distinct "American way". The image first appeared in the late eighteenth century through Michel-Guillaume Jean de Crevecoeur's *Letters from an American Farmer*:

> What then is the American, this new man? . . . *He* is an American, who, leaving behind him all his ancient prejudices and manners, receives new ones from the new mode of life he has embraced. . . . Here individuals are *melted* into a new race of men.

The term surfaced again in Israel Zangwell's famed 1909 play, *The Melting Pot*. It showed the fire of the American experience burning off human impurities, fusing all the best elements of each immigrant "race" into "a new and superior American nationality." The old identities could not survive this change. As Frederick Kapp's history of the Germans in colonial New York concludes: "he who emigrates gives up his father-land and is lost to it. . . . Therefore either German or American: The German-American is only a transitional figure, who disappears in the second generation."[6]

The "melting pot" concept, though, seemed inadequate to others as an explanation of the American reality. Historian Frederick Jackson Turner emphasized "the primacy of geography over race and culture," and suggested that the development of distinctive sectional or regional identities formed the American present and future.[7] The continuation of dozens of distinct immigrant communities into the early twentieth century—Little Italies, "Andersonvilles," "Micktowns"—suggested still another vision of the American identity. Rather than a "melting pot" or an ideological union, America could be considered a federation of nationalities, where hyphenization was permanent, where diversity and harmony coexisted, where, in the words of Horace Kallen, America stood as "a multiplicity in a unity, an orchestration of mankind."

Kallen was the most compelling advocate for this view of cultural pluralism. The son of Jewish immigrant parents, Kallen attended Harvard University where he became an early Zionist and an active member of the Intercollegiate Menorah Association. From one of his teachers, Barrett Wendell, he adopted the argument that America had begun as "another Israel" and that the early Puritans were in fact largely Jewish in blood—an argument that convinced him that one could re-main fully Jewish while still belonging to America. From William James he adopted a view of pluralism that gave legitimacy to the idea that one could balance independent loyalties within one's personality.[8]

In February 1915, the venerable *Nation* magazine carried a two-part article by Kallen entitled "Democracy versus the Melting Pot: A Study of American Nationality." Kallen wrote in reaction to a book by Edward Alsworth Ross, *The Old World in the New*, which focused on the issue of the declining birthrate among old-stock Anglo-Americans. Kallen quoted from Ross's book: "A nation may reason: why burden ourselves with the rearing of children? Let them perish unborn in the womb of time. The immigrants will keep up the population. A people that has no more *respect for its ancestors* and no more *pride of race* than this deserves the extinction that surely awaits it." Taking vehe-ment exception to his own characterization of the argument, Ross went on to call for restrictions on immigration. For his part, Kallen picked up on the italicized phrases, noting that such language was found "wherever Americans of British ancestry congregate thoughtfully." By implication, he deplored this evidence of racialism among Anglo-Americans as a negation of the ideals of democracy and equality.[9]

At a deeper level, though, Kallen actually shared aspects of the racialist worldview of Ross. The young Jewish-American held that ethnic or racial characteristics were natural or innate, deeply rooted, and unalterable. This made the "melting pot" a myth. While one might choose one's profession, one's citizenship, or even one's religion, ethnicity was an unalterable inheritance. Even intermarriage would accomplish nothing: an Irishman would always be an Irishman; a Jew always a Jew.[10]

From this, Kallen drew a portrait showing America to be a grand ethnic mosaic. In American cities, "[p]robably 90 percent" of the population was "either foreign-born or of foreign stock." Such towns were "aggregations" of peoples, not unities. City life revolved around the incidental cooperation of these ethnic enclaves and a common commitment to commercial endeavors; it did not rest on "a unity of heritage, mentality, and interest." Only "South of Mason and Dixon's line" did a unity among "the descendants of the native white stock, often degenerate and backward, prevail among the whites." Elsewhere, "the older America, whose voice and whose spirit was New England, is gone beyond recall." Attempts at "Americanization" through "adoption of English speech, of American clothes and manner" collapsed in futility against the sturdier and more natural reality of true nations: the Creoles of the South, the French-Canadians of the North, the "intensely national Irish," the "universally separate Jews," the dour Scandinavians of the Middle West.

Where Ross saw the Poles as "a backward people, prolific, brutal, priest-ridden," Kallen praised their distinctive qualities: "What troubles Mr. Ross…is not really inequality; what troubles [him] is difference." Kallen underscored how true Americanization "liberated nationality." In truth, America was no longer a federation of states: it had become "a great republic consisting of a federation or commonwealth of nationalities." To force unity on this grand diversity of peoples would require draconian measures: "the complete nationalization of education," the abolition of all private and parochial schools and of the teaching of languages other than English, and a strict focus on instruction in history and literature from an English perspective. But these acts, Kallen asserted, would undermine both liberty and democracy.

Properly understood, America was "a democracy of nationalities, cooperating voluntarily and autonomously in the enterprise of self-realization through the perfection of men *according to their kind*." America's shared political-economic system allowed "the realization of the distinctive individuality of each nation that composes it."[11]

In subsequent essays, Kallen drew out the implications of his argument. He underscored how the great immigrant influx between 1866 and 1914 had "irrevocably" built "a new America, an America of new institutions, new stocks, new ideals, with a wider and more varied cultural inheritance and therefore cultural prospect." The distinctive phrase of the American idiom, "make good," underscored how "values accrue to persons and institutions by achievement, not inheritance." The old America had been agrarian, where landlords and freeholders held onto a liberty rooted in land, localism, and statehood. But the Civil War gave birth to "a different type of liberty," one "progressively industrial and commercial," where growing economic interdependence "led to the conception of subordination of political rights to changing economic needs," and the transfer of political authority from local to centralized government. Kallen celebrated this "Americanization of Capitalism" as wholly compatible with a mosaic of ethnicities. "Big business is an amiable monster," he wrote, making possible "the spontaneous self-rooting and automatic growth of differentiated communities" across the continent. He underscored "the *natural* hyphenization of the American citizen." American democracy involved "*not* the elimination of differences, but *the perfection and conservation of differences. It aims, through union, not at uniformity, but variety.*"[12]

This cultural liberty, Kallen insisted, extended beyond matters of language, food, and customary celebrations: "Free enterprise for the mind is the ineluctable precondition of every other variety of free enterprise." Freedom of conscience presupposed freedom of religion, and "all cults and denominations" had found ways to live together peacefully in America, an "unprecedented" development in the "war of faiths which marks the long history of Judeo-Christianity." Kallen extended this cultural pluralism to embrace moral and familial matters as well. He mocked efforts by "the evangelical church" to govern "familial mores" and "familial habits." Human nature, he insisted, had "no inevitabilities, no rigidities"; instead, it was "variable." The intent of the

"American Idea" was "to keep the ways of life equally open to the enterprise of whoever in good faith freely chooses to seek his or her spiritual or material fortune upon them." "[B]elieving Americans" knew
that there was no fixed social order; no one form of home or family.
Americanization meant learning how to live with diverse styles of life;
"Americanism . . . denote[s] the union of the diverse."[13]

THE GERMAN-AMERICANS

In his celebration of cultural pluralism in America, Kallen's most frequent example of success was German America. German immigrants
and their descendants had spread throughout, and now dominated,
the upper Mississippi and Ohio River Valleys. Over large parts of Ohio
and Indiana, study of the German language was required for young
students. In Wisconsin, "the fragrance of *Deutschthum* ['German-ness']
pervades the life of the whole state." Efficient, centralized governance
existed there, along with a strong reform-socialist presence. German
was the overwhelmingly predominant "foreign" language in the public
schools and universities. Throughout Middle America, German hymns
rang out in churches, complemented by singing societies, "cooking"
institutions, a massive German press, German theaters, and widespread
club life. The German-Americans created Germanic museums, erected
monuments to German heroes, and exchanged professors with their
homeland. Moreover, "they are organized into a great national society,
The German-American [National] Alliance, which is dedicated to the
advancement of German culture and ideals. They encourage and make
possible a close and more intimate contact with the fatherland."[14]

Indeed, the remarkable rise and apparent durability of German
America deserves close examination. The first German-speaking immigrants arrived in America in 1683; and a modest but steady stream
followed in the eighteenth century, settling most often in the Delaware
Valley and Pennsylvania. The early nineteenth century witnessed several abortive attempts to craft a "New Germania" resting on a pure
German culture, in Missouri, Wisconsin, and Texas. The failed liberal
revolutions of 1848 in several German states brought a wave of new
immigrants to America. These '48ers were well educated and highly
idealistic, and included distinguished statesmen such as Carl Schurz
(Major General in the Civil War, Senator from Wisconsin, Minister to
Spain, and Secretary of the Interior). The number of Germans enter-

ing the United States surged after 1850. In fact, during the 1860s, over one-third of all immigrants were German and even by the 1880s the proportion remained high (27.5 percent). From 1840 to 1900, six million Germans landed on American soil. Although the number of new immigrants fell off sharply after 1893, the German element in the United States remained massive. During the period Between 1850 and 1900, Germans never constituted fewer than 25 percent of all foreign-born persons in America, and between 1880 and 1920, they were—at 30 percent—the largest single ethnic group among first-generation American immigrants. The German-Americans were heavily concentrated on farms in the greater Mississippi Valley and in 1900, 11 percent of all American farms were owned by the German-born, with family-centered production—"labor rich, cash poor"—as the rule. Meanwhile, in urban areas, German-Americans in 1900 constituted over half of the inhabitants of St. Louis, Baltimore, Milwaukee, Cincinnati, Newark, Jersey City, Louisville, Indianapolis, and Columbus, and they were the largest single immigrant group in both New York and Chicago.[15]

How well did they embody Kallen's vision of a distinct and impermeable ethnic culture? Most historians concur that the large majority of German-Americans in 1900 were rapidly assimilating into American society. According to David Detjen, the Germans were "better attuned to the environment they were entering in America" than any other immigrant group. Enthusiastic about democracy, they rapidly learned to handle the prevailing political order. Once they mastered the English language, they were quick to leave the "Little Germany" ghettoes. After the immigrant boats from Bremen and Hamburg ceased arriving in significant numbers, even the massive German press began to decline. As late as 1892, there were 727 German-language newspapers in the United States (including six dailies in Milwaukee alone). By 1904, though, the number had already fallen by 25 percent. The 1900 census showed that German-Americans were the most likely of all immigrant groups to become naturalized: over 90 percent of German-born persons had at least applied for citizenship. German-American rhetoricians described Germans as the *most* assimilable of peoples. According to the speaker at the 1890 "German-American Day" rally in Milwaukee, the German is fit to become an American "because all the qualities for making one are born in him . . . integrity, straight forwardness, trustworthiness, and enthusiasm. . . . [The German] loves the country that sustains him and is always ready to protect it." Viewed from this perspective, the genial melting pot seemed to be doing its work, fating German America for a quiet obsolescence.[16]

But other forces were pushing for something closer to Kallen's vision. Some in the German-American community did not completely submit to Americanization. At the most benign level, they remained attached to their German ways of expressing the "joy of living," evidenced in boisterous songs, beer gardens, and elaborate celebrations at Christmas and Easter. But among a significant minority, there was a certain "mental reservation" about "full immersion into American culture." Conservative German-American Lutherans, for example, held strong beliefs in Bible-centered education and in the preservation of German as a church and family language. Eschewing the secular public schools, they built their own: some 2,100 of them existed by 1900. German Catholics, holding similar views, built their own schools as well.

Among the more secular German-Americans, the growing power of Imperial Germany and the high prestige attached to early–twentieth-century German achievements in music, science, education, and industry sparked a greater interest in the "old Fatherland." As a prominent German-American from Cincinnati, Carl Ruemelin, explained: "We did not wish to establish here a mere New Germany, nor . . . did we wish simply to disappear into America. . . . [W]e have succeeded in remaining honorably German without . . . being untrue to our new Fatherland." An editor at the *Omaha Bee* cast the formula this way: "Germania our Mother, Columbia our Bride." Such expressions were as music to Kallen's ears. Only a few, such as the editor Emil Preetorius, prophesied "that the cultural juggling act" performed by many German-Americans "would collapse if the United States and Germany [ever] went to war."[17]

The rallying point for this rejuvenated German America was the *Deutsche-Amerikanischer National-Bund*, or the German-American National Alliance. Founded in 1899, it followed by two years the creation of the Pan-German Alliance in Berlin, an ultranationalist organization designed to rally expatriate Germans around the globe in support of the Fatherland. The stated purposes of the German-American National Alliance were actually Kallen-like: to increase the feeling of unity among the German element of the United States; to pursue worthy aims (such as promotion of the German language) that did not run counter to good U.S. citizenship; to oppose nativistic influences and support further immigration; and to cultivate a spirit of friendship "between America and the Fatherland." At another level, the Alliance represented an effort to unite the "Church Germans"—Catholic, Calvinist, and Lutheran—with the secular "Club Germans" active in the singing societies and athletic clubs. Historian Carl Wittke saw the Alliance as an effort "to preserve a German *Lebensanschauung*. It opposed prohibition, feminism, Puritanism, and 'all follies which threaten personal liberty.'"[18]

Formally, the Alliance was a loose union of 6,500 distinct German-American organizations. While claiming to eschew politics, the political potency of the Alliance became evident in 1907 when the U.S. Congress took the unusual step of granting it a Congressional Charter, a privilege reserved to only a handful of organizations, such as the Boy Scouts. As an advocate of immigrant rights and a distinctive culture, the Alliance might be seen as *La Raza* of its day. Appearing before the Prussian Diet in early 1914, the German-American poet and editor George Viereck claimed that the German-American National Alliance was "the most widespread German body the world has ever seen." Membership that year was two million and in the critical year of 1916, the Alliance would claim three million members.[19]

Peering deeper into the Alliance's activities, though, one sees more complex aims. First, the German-language press actively promoted the Alliance as a way to boost its flagging readership. Second, and more important, the Temperance campaign of the early twentieth century can be seen as an indirect challenge by old-stock Americans to German culture and style of life. Detjen emphasizes how "the Prohibition movement gave German-Americans a common foe, which created a solidarity within the German-American community that had never existed before."[20] The German-dominated brewing industry gave lavish financial support to the Alliance as a way to fight Prohibition: "The Anti-Saloon League did more to build the Alliance than did German politicians in the Reich or the lovers of German culture in America," writes historian Lavern Rippley.[21] The Alliance's president Charles Hexamer, the American-born son of a '48er, claimed that German America would survive "only if we stand together and conquer the dark spirit of . . . Prohibition just as Siegfried slew the dragon."

At its best, the Alliance's campaign against Prohibition can be seen as a defense of personal and cultural liberty. But, more dangerously, the Alliance also began to project an attitude of cultural superiority, particularly within its secular wing. The increasing "glory of the German Reich" in the years after 1900 gave evidence of "the greatness of the German language" and of the culture of Goethe and Schiller, Beethoven and Bach. This pride, claims Detjen, "also encouraged a sense of aloofness from . . . those aspects of American society and culture that German-Americans found vulgar."[22] The rhetoric of German-American leaders grew more pointed. In a 1902 speech to a rally in Madison Square Garden, Dr. Hexamer declared that

> we are all patriotic Americans. . . . But with just cause we are
> also proud of our ancestry, for we spring from a great race. A
> race that defeated the Romans, and crushed the Old World
> Empire, . . . produced a Kant, a Fichte, a Hegel, . . . a
> Schopenhauer, . . . gave the world the most exalted results of
> modern thought—German philosophy, liberated youth from
> the shackles of scholastic instruction, . . . [and gave human-
> ity] those astounding triumphs of modern science.

He emphasized that while the Puritan New Englanders were persecuting Quakers and burning witches, it was "our forefathers at Germantown [Pennsylvania]" who in 1688 "drew up a remonstrance against slavery—the first of all such protests."[23]

These German-American claims centered on *Kultur*. In an official 1911 history of its early years, the Alliance stated that its "lofty" purpose was to bring German idealism to a crass American people: "It feels that its duty is to remedy to the best of its ability the lack of ideals; to fill the hollowness and shallowness of purely materialistic prosperity with the solid happiness and real contentment of purely cultural achievement." Dr. Hexamer explained that "it is German culture which has advanced more than any other," and that the "German-American idea will grow and blossom into one of the tenets of the American Nation enhancing its ideals and culture for the good of America."[24] Writing in the *Pan-German Gazette* that same year, Robert Thiem was more expansive, arguing that "the Germanization of America has gone ahead too far to be interrupted. . . . In a hundred years the American people will be conquered by the victorious German spirit so that it will present an enormous German empire."[25] While English was the American language for commerce, German should be seen as the new American "language of culture." "Consider, you German pioneers, that we are giving this people here the best thing that there is on earth—Germanic culture."[26] Indeed, the more chauvinistic of the German-Americans were projecting "their heritage as a counter-culture to the dominant one," creating a most volatile situation.[27] Such phrases and goals would soon come back to haunt and hurt their creators.

THE CRISIS OF 1914–1917

War exploded across Europe in August 1914. Following the German invasion of Belgium, Great Britain joined France and the Russian Empire in alliance against the German and Austro-Hungarian empires. The loyalties of German-Americans, and the identity of America itself, were quickly put to the test.

With the United States formally neutral (although soon selling war materiel and lending money to Britain and France), reason prevailed for a time. Theodore Roosevelt actually published a book in 1916 in which he labeled attempts to paint the Kaiser as a bloodthirsty devil "an absurdity." He sympathized with the German position and heaped praise on Kaiser Wilhelm II: "[A]s so often before in his personal and family life, he and his family have given honorable proof that they possess the qualities that are characteristic of the German people." The Germans, "from the highest to the lowest, have shown a splendid patriotism." Roosevelt continued: "they themselves are fighting, each man for his own hearthstone, for his own wife and children, and all for the future existence of the generations yet to come." The Germans, claimed Roosevelt, were "not merely brothers; *they are largely ourselves*," a point that underscored his call for a peace without victors.[28]

The war of 1914 gave another rejuvenating jolt to German America. No one seriously argued for American entry into the conflict in support of Germany. Instead, German-Americans showed solidarity with the Old Fatherland by opposing American aid to the British and French. Some joined antiwar groups and most advocated strict neutrality. They called for an embargo on all arms sales and opposed U.S. loans to Britain and France. Congressman Richard Bartholdt of Missouri introduced a bill which prohibited the export of all war materiel, warning his colleagues that Germany and Austria claimed the kinship of twenty-five million Americans "who cast at least five million votes." German-language newspapers and churches collected two million signatures favoring an embargo, which were received by Con-

gress with a few Anglophile mutters about "a close resemblance to treason."[29]

A second priority for German-Americans was countering British
war propaganda. The main vehicle for this was the *Fatherland*, a newspaper founded in 1914 (with $100,000 in support from Germany itself)
and edited by the clever publicist George Viereck. After only two
months, circulation had soared past the 100,000 mark. Arguing that it
fought for the true interests of America, the *Fatherland* claimed to give
a fair hearing to the German side of the war, to offer unbiased report-
ing on military campaigns, and to correct "misstatements and prejudices" in the pro-English American press. Viereck portrayed the war as
a battle between German civilization and the "pan-Slavic, half-Asiatic,
and thinly veneered barbarism" of Russia. The French were in it for
revenge, the British for profits and empire. He also denied that the
Fatherland was a tool of German propaganda:

> In fact, the German government has often treated us shabbily.
> The German Empire as such is nothing to us. We are with
> America, right or wrong, at all times. We now propose to set
> America right. . . . [Many] have ridiculed the hyphen. We shall
> make it a virtue.

Indeed, Viereck urged readers to "Celebrate George Washington's Birth-
day by subscribing to *The Fatherland*."[30]

This campaign to cast German-Americans as the true heirs of the
Founders and as preservers of Union was not without valid arguments.
George Washington fought the same foe that Germany now faced. In
fact, wrote Viereck, "just one hundred years ago the British burned
Washington. Today they rule Washington." Notably, it was Germans
who had defended Fort McHenry in Baltimore from British attack under "the rockets' red glare." Moreover, they were commanded by George
Armistead, who was "of German blood." While the British and French
governments had encouraged the Southern Confederacy, it was Prussia
and the German-Americans in the North who had supported the Union.
The states of Maryland, Kentucky, and Missouri were kept out of the
Confederacy only because of unwavering German-American support
for the cause of liberty and union. Editor Rudolf Cronau noted that
the American colonies had waged two "wars of independence" against
"selfish England," the first from 1775 to 1783, and the second from
1812 to 1814. He now called on all American patriots "to wage a *third*

war for independence, and to combat with spiritual weapons the To-ries who, in our midst, make propaganda for King George V with the same loyalty and foul means used by their ancestors in the interests of George III."[31]

England as the "Evil Empire" of its day was a recurrent German-American theme. "This Tartuffe among the nations," declared Dr. Hexamer in late 1914, "has subjugated India, has taken Egypt . . . , has crushed out two South African Republics, has forced opium on China by the mouth of the cannon . . . and has marked her path in history red by the streams of the blood of its victims."[32] The German-American National Alliance sponsored lecture tours by Indian opponents of the British Raj and by Irish rebels against English rule.[33]

In contrast, German-American publicists portrayed their community as consisting of *true* patriots. Hexamer declared that he and other German-Americans were the "real Americans," unlike the pro-British advisors in the White House who were closet Englishmen. He continued: "We know what we owe our new home, the United States, namely, that we protect it from British tyranny." During the American Revolution, it was Peter Muehlenberg, Baron DeKalb, and Baron von Steuben who answered the call of liberty. The 1,500 reinforcements who arrived in Valley Forge in the darkest days of the War for Independence all came "from the soil of fair Germanized Pennsylvania." And it was German-American merchants who raised the $100,000 needed to feed the Continental Army at the same crucial time. Referring as well to Valley Forge, a poem by John L. Stoddard summarized the case against the "Anglophile" in the White House:

> What say you to your nation's chief,
> Too loyal to King George,
> To join his fellow-countrymen
> In storied Valley Forge
> When ardent patriots unveiled
> Von Steuben's statue, where
> The German trained our freezing troops
> And saved them from despair.
>
> Shame on the canting Anglophile
> Who rules by Britain's grace,
> And seeks to keep his sullied post

By cleaving race from race!
Shame on the blood-stained Britonettes
Who toast the King and Tsar
The people yet shall come to see
The creatures that they are.

Great Spirit of Mount Vernon,
With Monticello's sage,
And Franklin, Adams, Hamilton,
Rebuke this servile age!
And you, old time Americans,
Arise from sea to sea,
And once more make our starry flag
The banner of the free.[34]

In their zeal to bear the title of "true patriots," German-American publicists also claimed Abraham Lincoln as their own, arguing that his paternal ancestor, Samuel Lincoln, was actually born a "Linkhorn" and had come from the heavily German Berks County, Pennsylvania.[35]

The year 1916 brought the contest between "Anglophiles" and German America to its climax. In March, the *New York World* ran an exposé of the Alliance. Using documents obtained from German agents through a comic series of errors, the *World* revealed Imperial German efforts to influence American public opinion, as part of "an astounding chapter in the continued story of the German conspiracy against the United States." Arguing that the Alliance worked to "Prussianize" American foreign policy, the *World* called for its abolition.[36]

With the critical presidential election of 1916 looming, Alliance leaders resolved on a risk-laden strategy. President Wilson had already joined Roosevelt in mounting regular attacks on "hyphenated" America.[37] Craving acceptance, German-Americans were stung by Wilson's implication that they were traitors. As a Lutheran pastor from Minnesota wrote: "I have been as good an American as ever any of the Wilsons were. Yea, a better American, because none of my ancestors raised a hand against the Stars and Stripes like Wilson's ancestors. . . . He deliberately insulted us."[38] Another German-American leader mused: "Just as Europe has fallen upon Germany, so America is now falling upon German-Americans, or attacking them; but we have a weapon which we can use to good effect, namely our ballots; and in these days so dark for Germanism, we must use our ballots for our Germanism."[39] Gottfried Kirn, head of the Alliance's Kansas City chapter, warned that "the two and one-half million members of the German-American National Alliance" would soon give "very tangible expression to their feelings about neutrality." The *New York Herald* editorialized that if German-Americans "are insulted, if men in public life turn against what is German and if they scorn and revile it—then German blood flames up, then the 'furor teutonius' appears, then there are German blows."

Dr. Leo Stern of the Wisconsin Alliance, the state chapter of the National German-American Alliance, became an early advocate for a plan to guarantee the nomination of a Republican who shared their strict understanding of neutrality. In Chicago, the Teutonic Sons of America declared Wilson "utterly unfit" to govern a society "composed in the main of people of hyphenated origin." The Chicago chapter of the Alliance endorsed Charles Evans Hughes in late April. A month later, a National German-American Conference convened at Chicago's Kaiserhof Hotel "to give expression to the united opinion of the American citizens of German descent and birth with reference to certain presidential candidates," essentially endorsing Hughes. Hexamer distributed a memo at his own expense that declared that "no self-respecting American of German birth or extraction can vote for President Wilson."[40]

When Hughes won the Republican nomination on June 10, German-Americans congratulated themselves on their success. But they also reaped the "Flag Day" denunciations by Wilson and Roosevelt cited at the beginning of this chapter. Wilson made "anti-hyphenism" and the fact that he " kept us out of war" his major campaign issues. In early September, he warned darkly about "the passions and intrigues of certain active groups and combinations of men amongst us who were born under foreign flags [and] injected the poison of disloyalty into our most critical affairs." He largely succeeded in casting Hughes as the candidate of "the Kaiser" and of extremists of all kinds. When the St. Louis chapter of the Alliance endorsed Hughes and boasted of twenty-thousand members ready to vote as a block, the *St. Louis Post-Dispatch* accused the group of a "vehemently un-American," pro-German conspiracy.[41]

As the November electoral results came in, the failure of the German-American electoral strategy was obvious. Wilson won a resounding victory; he even carried St. Louis. Many "Church Germans," it turned out, remained strictly neutral in the campaign, including German Catholic leaders, the Lutheran Church–Missouri Synod, and the Mennonites. While detailed polling analysis showed that Americans of German birth did vote disproportionately more Republican than the population as a whole, a surprising number of German-American ballots avoided a vote for Wilson by swinging to the Socialist Party candidate, Allen Benson. Ambivalence about Hughes (who never quite repudiated Roosevelt's "anti-hyphen" outbursts) and a fatal misreading by Alliance leaders of their influence within their own community spelled ruin. Not only did Wilson win, but "Prohibition" initiatives triumphed in a number of states, as did women's suffrage. The German-American National Alliance went into "a sudden tailspin." In early 1917, Imperial Germany reinstituted open submarine warfare against Allied freighters, and on February 7, the United States broke diplomatic relations with Germany. Meeting that night, Alliance officers threw in the towel and endorsed the United States's actions. In an Open Letter, Dr. Hexamer wrote: "the German-American National Alliance must, as always, take its stand . . . as a patriotic institution, otherwise it has no right to exist." The U.S. declaration of war came less than two months later.[42]

"Furor Americanus"

The protestations of loyalty by the German-American leaders were not believed. Government officials declared that unlike most other ethnic groups, the German-American cause had "assumed the character of a separatist movement." The 6,500 local societies within the Alliance had become "centers of German propaganda." The German-American newspapers were "more or less under the influence of 'the new German spirit.'" Editor Hermann Hagedorn warned that German-Americans were "prisoners of an illusion," tied to a sentimental view of the old homeland. Germany "sent silver-tongued orators to thrill" the German-American, "she sent ponderous professors to give his beer-dreams a pseudo-intellectual basis; she sent secret agents; she bought newspapers." The *Chicago Tribune* warned that "110,000 German agents" were active in the United States. Dr. Earl Bishop Downer, former physician for the Russian Royal Family, told the same newspaper that "the German of today gets his greatest pleasure in inflicting torture, mental and physical, upon a helpless victim. Tortured, outraged women, blazing homes, murdered men and women, and children—they are the sights that please the eye of the Hun."[43]

What one historian has called the "furor Americanus" followed, with the open suppression and persecution of all things German-American. U.S. Attorney General Thomas Gregory organized 200,000 "volunteer detectives" into the American Protective League. Their task was to provide the Justice Department with information about "suspected aliens and disloyal citizens." The Council of National Defense, designed to speed the assimilation of German-Americans and other hyphenates, was extended to each state. The U.S. Post Office gained authority to censor or shut down German and other foreign-language papers. Meanwhile, the Division of Work among the Foreign Born, of the Committee on Public Information, "mobilized the foreign-language societies and the foreign-language press in the service of the United States," turning those that remained into semiofficial war propaganda arms.[44]

Out in the states, countless vigilante acts directed against German-Americans occurred. In Illinois, there were "nightrider" attacks on Mennonite churches, where skulls and crossbones were painted over the doors. A mob demolished the piano of a German singing society in Eugene, Oregon. Eight men entered the Birmingham, Ohio, study of a German-American pastor and burned his books. In Bishop, Texas, a mob flogged a German Lutheran pastor. The tar-and-feathering of German-speaking clergy was common. Boy Scouts burned German-language papers in Columbus, Ohio, while in Baraboo, Wisconsin, the National Guard torched German books. Pacifist Mennonites and Hutterites were jailed and treated with unusual brutality. German-language classes—called a "distinct menace to Americanism"—disappeared from many school districts; where such classes remained, the number of enrolled students fell sharply. In South Dakota, authorities closed a Mennonite flour mill when a customer reported finding glass chips in the flour. The spirit of the age was ably expressed in *A Disloyal Combination*, a pamphlet linking the Alliance to the brewing industry: "Everything that is pro-German [in this country] must go. The German Press. The teaching of German in the elementary schools. . . . German alliances and the whole German propaganda must be abolished. . . . The brewers and allied liquor trades that back such an alliance should suffer the same penalty." Somewhat surprisingly, given the passions roused, only one confirmed death occurred during the frenzy:

the lynching by four hundred Illinoisans of Robert Praeger, called "an enemy alien" and "German spy" by the *Chicago Tribune*; in fact, he was a nearly blind Socialist Party organizer caught "speaking German" to a woman over a backyard fence. The sixteen persons ultimately charged in the case were acquitted, the jury accepting defense arguments "that the present war situation had developed a new 'unwritten law' which had been invoked by the men who hanged Praeger because he was alleged to be a German spy".[45]

The once mighty Alliance came under public fire as well. In January 1918, Senator William Henry King of Utah introduced a bill to revoke its Congressional Charter. During an April hearing, critics of the Alliance leveled an array of charges: the Alliance was an unofficial arm of "the Junker-dominated Pan-German Alliance"; instead of Americanizing German immigrants, the Alliance "has done much to keep German immigrants German"; it worked "to organize for political action along racial lines"; the Alliance sought to turn America "into a fief of the German Empire"; it had "secret income"; it had "aroused racial antagonism and . . . caused opposition to processes of assimilation"; and it had "developed a rabid and violent opposition to prohibition." The Alliance mounted no real defense, and in July, the King bill cleared Congress on unanimous votes, abrogating the 1907 charter.[46]

More broadly, the associational structure of German America largely disappeared. Thousands of societies folded. The German language swiftly disappeared from Catholic and Lutheran churches. The number of German-language newspapers fell from 554 in 1910 to only 234 by 1920; and total daily circulation in the latter year was only 25 percent of the 1910 level.[47] Historian John Hawgood concludes that German America did not survive 1918: "The war had so enhanced the distance between the German and the American that no hyphen could stretch from the one to the other. . . . German-Americanism was obsolete."[48]

One Hundred Percent Americanism

In its place came a call for "100 percent Americanism," a demand, in John Higham's words, for "an unprecedented degree of national solidarity, loyalty, and social conformity." Among some advocates, the term held a fairly vague meaning. Roosevelt, for example, said that "we must make Americanism and Americanization mean the same thing to the

native born and to the foreign born; to the man and to the woman."
Regarding specifics, though, he offered only somewhat obtuse—if interesting—ideas such as "cooperative ownership and management" of
corporations so "that the tool users may, so far as possible, become the
tool owners."[49]

At a more specific, and nastier, level, Anglo-Saxonism enjoyed a
brief period of political dominance. Since the late 1880s, a string of
books—such as Edward Ross's *The Old World in the New*—had appeared casting the Anglo-Saxons of Old England "as a simple, upright,
freedom-loving race" binding together "Protestantism and Liberty."
William J. Ripley's 1899 tome, *The Races of Europe*, divided the
Continent's peoples into the Teuton, Alpine, and Mediterranean races.
While Germans were a mix of Teuton and Alpine types, he argued that
the English were more purely Teutonic. Madison Grant's *The Passing
of the Great Race*, published in 1916, called the "melting pot" ideal a
folly. The Nordic peoples were the true master race, Grant explained.
Racial self-preservation "clearly demanded" restriction of the "human
flotsam" that characterized too many immigrants.[50]

Cultural anti-hyphenism, a tumbling birthrate among the native-
born, and the new "scientific" Anglo-Saxonism blended together into
a successful push for immigration restriction. The war against Germany, as Higham reports, "destroyed most of what remained of the
old faith in America's capacity to fuse all men into a 'nation of nations.'"[51] A 1917 Immigration Act, passed over Wilson's veto, excluded
adults unable to read some language, mapped out an "Asiatic barred
zone," and denied entry to revolutionaries and anarchists. Concern
over German-American loyalty faded after 1920, only to be replaced
by more racialist concerns. Grant's appeal to preserve "Nordic America"
led directly to the Law of 1921, which limited European immigration
to 3 percent of the foreign-born of each nationality, according to the
1910 census. This slashed overall prewar entry levels by nearly 75 percent, to about 350,000 per annum. The Law of 1924 perfected the ex-
clusion of Asians and moved the census base back to 1890, allotting 85
percent of total immigration to Northwestern Europe and largely shut-
ting off the flow from Southern and Eastern Europe.

The Americanization campaign manifested itself in other ways
as well. The *Chicago Tribune* editorialized in April 1919 that "only an
agile and determined immigrant, possessed of overmastering devotion
to the land of his birth, can hope to escape Americanization by at least

one of the many processes now being prepared for his special benefit."[52] Most Chambers of Commerce boasted Americanization Committees, as did the local chapters of the General Federation of Women's Clubs, the YWCA, and the YMCA. In January 1920, U.S. Attorney General A. Mitchell Palmer launched his infamous raids around the country. Now worried that immigrant communities sheltered Bolsheviks rather than German spies, authorities arrested tens of thousands of suspected communists and radicals for sedition and other crimes of disloyalty. Many were of German and Scandinavian ancestry. A majority of the aliens seized were simply expelled from the country. Meanwhile, the newly reorganized Ku Klux Klan enjoyed an explosive growth in membership, much of it outside the Old South. By 1924, up to four million Americans had joined the secret society's ranks. Behind fear of the immigrant, the Catholic, the Jew, and the Negro lay a "pathetic, if dangerous" effort "to restore a kind of order and morality that had all but disappeared from American life."[53]

The two new amendments to the U.S. Constitution from this era can also be interpreted as having been motivated by anti-hyphenism, in general, and by an effort to dissolve German America, in particular. Where the German-American National Alliance cast all restrictions on the liquor traffic as nativistic encroachments on personal liberty, the ratification of the Eighteenth Amendment on January 29, 1919, meant that German-Americans would "either be compelled to change their habits and adjust themselves to the new environment or else find some beer-soaked, Bacchus-dominated spot in the fatherland and go there," as the *Disloyal Combination* pamphlet put it.[54] The Alliance's fervent opposition to women's suffrage, seen as a threat to the traditional family order, also came to an end in August 1920 with ratification of the Nineteenth Amendment. Anglo-America stood victorious over its Germanic foes, both abroad and at home.

FAMILIES, MOTHERS, AND CHILDREN

Yet at the very time of the defeat symbolized by the Nineteenth Amendment, the familistic inheritance of German America was moving toward acceptance, or victory, on other—and arguably more important—fronts. Among the "Church Germans," leaders had perceived for some time that "their communities and families were under siege from foreign 'American' values," notably extreme individualism and material-

ism. In response, they began in the 1880s to articulate a new "corporatist ideology." With both European roots and a distinct American
accent, this worldview emphasized the vital role of the intermediary
institutions of family, church, and community: those social structures
standing between the individual and the state. Historian Jon Gjerde,
in his important volume *The Minds of the West*, shows how "the flowering of intellectual movements carried from Europe . . . built upon
fears of familial and social decline." In response, these movements
sought to privilege "natural institutions" such as family and community, and to protect them from "artificial" structures such as big corporations and the state.[55]

Gjerde emphasizes that the new corporatist thought "flourished
in German speaking areas" of America, "where romantic notions of
an organic society composed of people enveloped by groups" took root.
Among German Roman Catholics, the influence of the new "Social
Catholicism" was particularly strong in its affirmation of family autonomy and the vital role of small communities of virtue. In 1891, the
German-American Catholic organizations *Central-Verein* and the
Kathiolikentag passed resolutions praising Leo XIII's new encyclical
on the condition of laborers, *Rerum Novarum*. The effort by Bishop
Wilhelm E. von Ketteler to encourage Christian Labor movements and
social reform in Germany received growing praise in German-American periodicals after 1900. Father John Ryan, Irish-American promoter
of the "family wage," found considerable support among German-
Americans. They embraced the idea that fathers, as heads of households, deserved a wage adequate to support a wife and children at home.
At the *Central-Verein's* 1901 Convention, Father Anton Heiter of Buffalo called for the "decisive championing of the cause of religion in
public life according to the principles laid down by Leo XIII." He
stressed the particular need for "the influence of religion . . . in the
relations between labor and capital." German-Americans must now
"enter into the Christian social movement which Leo XIII has so happily inaugurated and to which our Catholic brethren of Germany owe
their great success." When the *Central-Verein* adopted its "Social Program" in 1908, director Frederich P. Kenkel declared: "it becomes imperative that steps be taken to conserve the German [reform] tradition,
sentiment and feeling and to win the young German-American for the
[social] cause for which the *Central-Verein* stands."[56]

German Protestants showed a similar turn toward communitarian thought. Among Lutherans in the Missouri Synod, the intellectual leadership of C. F. W. Walther emphasized the structures that sanctioned the power of the congregation and the family, rather than those of the individual and the state. The family mediated relations between parents and children, husbands and wives, and was "the Foundation not only of the Church but also of the State." Meanwhile, many Dutch and German Calvinists embraced the anti-liberal thought of Abraham Kuyper. This theologian rejected the "artificial" authority founded on individual free will, arguing instead for "a God-willed community, a living human organism" such as was reflected in the religious community or family. He wrote: "The Home! Wonderful creation of God! . . . As for the individual the proceeds of life are from the heart, so for society are the proceeds of life from the Home."[57] As Gjerde concludes:

> In rural Middle West societies, the local community thus was central for [German] Roman Catholics, who followed this corporatist ideology. German Lutherans, under the leadership of Walther, who was also influenced by nineteenth-century German corporatist theory, empowered the congregation and the community so that the individual was connected organically to the group interest. . . . Kuyper maintained that the family was the basic unit of society because it was the only social institution that predated the Fall and had an express mandate from God.[58]

Indeed, internal and external observers had long recognized the special role of the family within the German-American community. "German family life has been held up as a model of peace and happiness," reported George Meyer in 1890. In his 1909 history of the Germans in America, Albert Bernhardt Faust explained: "The German has furnished and continues to furnish an example of simple life and home life. . . . The German is economical and thrifty, and has shown that plain living is conducive to health and progress." Moreover, the "middle class German is fond of home life, and takes his family with him in pursuit of simple pleasures." Jane Addams of Hull House testified to the "strong family affections" found between immigrant German parents and their children and praised their "effort to bring together the old life and the new, a respect for the older cultivation."[59] More boldly, Dr. Hexamer described "the German family" as "the holy place, where love and honor are united, where the children . . . look with respect and also with heartfelt love to their parents, who live for them as a model." Statistics testify to this distinctive home-centeredness: German-Americans were the most likely of all ethnic groups in the United States to own their own homes. The 1910 census showed 26 percent of German-born Americans as homeowners, compared to a mere 5 percent among the native-born.[60]

Individualism, materialism, and feminism stood as enemies of the German-American home. The German *Catholic Tribune* editorialized in 1899 that individualism was "a cold-hearted principle," one tearing "man from man" and proclaiming "selfishness as the mainspring of all human action." The *Luxemburger Gazette* said that individualism inflicted "great wounds . . . if it is not checked in time." In his 1889 booklet, *The Question of Nationality in Its Relation to the Catholic Church in the United States*, Anton Walburg emphasized how the "true Americanism" of the Founders was devoted to the "public good" and the "general welfare." "False Americanism," resting on "infidelity and materialism . . . adores the golden calf and is directed to the accumulation of wealth." He warned: "A republic that is not based upon morality and religion . . . is ripe for an ignoble grave." A 1901 article in the *Catholic Tribune* examining "the disorganization of the family" pointed at "[t]he increase of *crime* against *born and unborn* children," "Godless schools," and the "spirit of pleasure-seeking . . . that draws the parents from the home, [and] separates them from the children, for whom they have no time." It was fear that "the 'German' conception of the home and family was being undermined" by radical American individualism which accounted for the German-American National Alliance's fierce opposition to women's suffrage. The same attitude explained the strong German-American preference for rural life. In an 1887 pamphlet, Nicholas Gonner argued that the Germans preferred farming in order to be close to God, while the Anglo-Americans preferred manufacturing and trade. As Gjerde explains, rural living "not only kept farmers close to nature but also safeguarded religious attitudes and encouraged strong, unified, and large families."[61]

Motherhood was particularly prized by the German-Americans. Albert B. Faust was effusive in his praise of the "domestic type" of German-American woman, and her formative example to the nation as a whole: "[O]ur country [i.e., America] would not be what it is in *vigor, population,* and *the bed-rock civilization* that comes from home training" in her absence. He continued:

> Historically, the emphasis laid upon the household arts, [such] as cooking, sewing, care of the house and children, by so large a formative element of the population from the earliest period of German immigration to the present time, cannot have resulted otherwise than in *impressing the economic advantage of the principle and furnishing an example for imitation.*

In a 1915 speech on the "Great German Ideals," Dr. Hexamer described "that noblest of creatures, the German *hausfrau,* the German mother!" The Alliance president added: "Happy is he who had a German mother, who could pass his childhood in a German home. What depth of feeling, what innate love are embodied in the German home! How sacred is the German family."[62] Others reported that German-American Jewish women also craved training in "domesticity . . . in the arts of housekeeping, cooking, and motherhood." They flocked to the Settlement Houses to absorb—in the words of a contemporary pamphlet called *The Language of America*—an "American idealism expressed in the practice of thrift, cleanliness, the support of a good home, [and] the education of children."[63]

The growing implication was that an unusually strong "maternal instinct" no longer stood as just a distinctive German trait; motherhood was becoming "uniquely American." The hausfrau was making the transition to American mother and homemaker. More broadly, the German-American home was "no longer . . . regarded as a weapon of *Deutschtum* ['German-ness']" but instead seemed to be serving "as an influence in breaking down *Deutschtum*" for the greater goal of familial strength and social reform in America.[64]

THE MATERNALIST CAMPAIGN

Emerging parallel to the German communalist vision of family-centered reform was the Settlement House movement and its direct offshoot, the maternalist campaign. The philosophy of the Settlement House ran counter to attempts to restrict, segregate, disenfranchise, or ghettoize the immigrant. Rather, in the words of historian Gwendolyn Mink, it offered a new vision of citizenship, one largely achieved by recognizing "one motherhood from diversely situated women":

> The manly citizen waged war and engaged in productive labor; the woman citizen raised children and thereby promoted political reproduction. The reformers believed that all women shared the maternalist vocation and that therefore all women controlled the future of the Republic.

As Edith Bremer, German-American executive of the YWCA's International Institute, explained, "to men it may appear that America's great concern is over the immigrants who could be citizens and soldiers. . . . [But] to America the 'immigration problem' is a great 'problem' of homes. . . . When it comes to homes, women and not men become the important factors."[65] McClymer concludes, from a less objective but still useful angle, that "the [maternalist] movement politicized domestic stereotypes of women—transforming images of women as homemakers, wives, and mothers into key components of the 'American Way of Life.'"[66]

Hull House, under the guidance of Jane Addams, stands as the prime source of the maternalist campaign, through both ideas and personnel. Sometimes called "the monasteries of the nineteenth century," Settlement Houses sprang up within impoverished, immigrant, urban neighborhoods, where upper-middle-class women could assist new arrivals in their adjustment to American life. True to her roots in rural Illinois, Addams was guardedly hostile to the new industrial order. She indicted "the ungodly industrial relation" and "the machine," which "dominate[s] the workman and reduce[s] his production into a mechanical distortion."[67] To counter the alienation of workers from their jobs, Addams launched projects such as the Arts and Crafts Society to reintroduce ideals of craftsmanship into the lives of laborers.

As a social conservative in this area, she sought to "preserve and keep whatever of value" the immigrants' peasant life had obtained. Hull House also worked to reassert the authority of parents in the eyes of immigrant children. A central strategy was "to recover for the household arts something of their early sanctity and meaning." Addams founded a labor museum to reveal "the charm of woman's primitive activities"—"the milking, the gardening, the marketing"—which "are such direct expressions of the solicitude and affection at the basis of all human life." The museum featured live displays of spinning, weaving, and food preservation and showed immigrant children something of "the freedom and beauty" of the peasant life and "how hard it must be to exchange it all for a two-room tenement, and to give up a beautiful homespun kerchief for an ugly department store hat." The museum also gave complementary courses in modern housekeeping, showing the historic bonds between tasks done in the peasant household and those now to be done in the urban home.[68]

This reconciliation of old and new extended to culture as well. Addams described how she had encouraged immigrant German women to perform music or read poetry from the old country, and how their children showed "a growing touch of respect" and "a rising enthusiasm for German literature and reminiscence on the part of all the family."[69]

Addams and her associates were also aware of the new currents of corporatist thought coming out of Germany. During one of her lengthy sojourns to Europe in the 1880s, Addams spent the better part of a year living in Germany, where she pondered the social consequences of industrialism and read from the Comtean Positivists.[70] German experiments in social insurance began to draw broader American attention during the 1890s. Young Christian theologians returned to the University of Chicago/Hull House circle from study in Germany, claiming that "the Social Gospel . . . was the natural result of the fusion of piety, science, and the reforming urge," and that German *Wissenschaft*, or science, had "made the 'will to do good' intellectually respectable."[71] The new breed of American sociologists hailed Germany as a "Foreign Experiment Station" in welfare legislation, blowing away "the hazy and preposterous assumptions" of the laissez-faire school of social and economic thought.[72] Shortly after the turn of the century, Hull House associate and University of Chicago sociologist Charles Henderson created and chaired a national commission to study the German model under the auspices of the National Conference of Charities and Corrections. Such schemes were routinely labeled "German plots" by their opponents.[73]

The maternalist campaign took shape through women who worked within or who were inspired by Hull House, among them Julia Lathrop, Florence Kelley, Grace Abbott, Sophonisba Breckinridge, Mary Anderson, Josephine Baker, M.D., and Lillian Wald; but with regard to "Americanization," the key figure was Frances Kellor.

An attorney and former Hull House worker, Kellor became Vice Chair of the National Americanization Committee and an executive officer of the Committee on Immigration of the U.S. Chamber of Commerce in 1916. In 1918, she assumed the post of Director of Americanization Work for the Federal Bureau of Education. In her work, Kellor emphasized that 78 percent of New York City residents in 1910 were either foreign-born or were the children of foreign-born parents. German-Americans there numbered 544,000; from them had come "the pacifist movement" and "a foreign language press circulation that for so long has poisoned the hearts and minds of our foreign born peoples."[74] Kellor trusted that "[s]urely there must be some key to assimilation which will open the doors of racial and American institutions alike, through which both the native and foreign born may pass freely."[75]

In subsequent essays and lectures, she insisted that this "key" was the home. The factory system and military service Americanized the men. Public schools Americanized the children, who became "the interpreter[s] to the family of American life—a bad thing for family morale and discipline." This left "the foreign-born woman and her home" as "the most vulnerable spots in our whole defense as well as in our democracy." The realities of urban American life had crowded the immigrant woman "into tenements, cut her off from American influence, and shown her all the ugliness of low pay, long hours, and overcrowding, exploitation and temptation." In order to renew the family as the basic building block of society among native and foreign-born alike, Americans must begin with her.

> If we start with the family and work upward we get a sound city that will stand the strain of any crisis because its weakest links are strong. Every great strain and burden eventually rests upon the family. . . . Approached from the neighborhood and family and met squarely, the problem of Americanization can be solved adequately.[76]

The resulting maternalist campaign might be fairly labeled pronatalist. To its leaders, the idea of birth control was abhorrent. Instead, the goal was to encourage maternity through better health care for all mothers before, during, and after pregnancy. Jane Addams, Julia Lathrop and Florence Kelley had all seen close relatives—mothers and sisters—die during childbirth, and all were determined to lower the infant and maternal mortality rates. They were also inspired by the immigrant women with whom they worked. The "isolation of the foreign born mother" was a special problem, to be sure; but the maternalists were convinced that these mothers wanted the same high standards of health care as American mothers: "all foreign mothers want their children to keep well." Moreover, there was the curious fact— reported by Josephine Baker—that the "highest baby death rate we have during the first month of life is among the babies of American mothers. Every race group of foreign birth we have in this country shows a better record in this respect than our native born." A higher rate of breastfeeding among the foreign-born was the most likely cause. These factors underscored how "the Americanization program in this country" was directly linked "to the health problems of women and children."[77]

This conclusion rested, in turn, on the understanding of motherhood as a universal trait. The maternalists held that all women had "a common identity as nurturers and a common gift for caring."[78] These characteristics were innate and the consequence of natural differences between the sexes. But now they were threatened. Ellen Richards, the founder of modern home economics, emphasized how industrialization had disrupted the traditional American homestead:

> [T]hat place of busy industry, with occupation for the dozen children, no longer exists. Gone out of it are the industries, gone out of it are ten of the children, gone out of it in large measure is that sense of moral and religious responsibility which was the keystone of the whole.

It was now necessary to build schools of domestic science for girls, to train them to be good mothers and fit wives, "to teach those means of social control which may build yet again a home life which will prove the nursery of good citizens and of efficient men and women with a sense of responsibility to God and man for the use they made of their lives."[79] Before an audience at her alma mater, Vassar College, Julia Lathrop told the young female scholars about the appalling lack of good data and research on the current status of the family. She called on women of the universities to create "a single center of training for research in the problems of the family," in order to give the woman in the home "the status of a profession," and to "elevate into a national system, strong, free, elastic, the cult of the American family."[80] The same emphasis on the mother at home filled the pages of the U.S. Bureau of Naturalization's *Suggested Lesson Topics* for immigrant girls and women. They included "the child," "child welfare," "the mother and the neighborhood," "the mother and the school," and "the mother and the community." Indeed, 148 of 151 topics dealt with domestic and maternal duties. Citizenship for the immigrant woman was to be mediated through her maternal role.[81] As Mink correctly summarizes:

> From women's universal role as natural educators, [the maternalists] derived not only women's crucial role in creating the citizenry but an educational strategy for reforming mothers. Maternalists accordingly eschewed the dominant racial discourse and substituted the promise of assimilation for the ideology of subordination and exclusion.[82]

The counterpart to maintaining the mother in the home, for the maternalists, was securing a family wage for fathers. Here, their interests converged with those of the trade labor unions, who also recognized "the wage base of familial existence." The goal was to combine the maternalists' emphasis on mothercare with the trade union emphasis on the dignity of the home and the self-reliance and responsibility of the male breadwinner. On the one hand, this meant restrictions on the supply of labor. As Alfred Strasser, the German-American President of the Cigar-Makers' International, explained: "We cannot drive the females out of the trades, but we can restrict their daily quota of labor through factory laws."[83] On the other hand, it meant securing higher wages for fathers. Pointing to research showing that as the father's average income doubled, the infant mortality rate was more than halved, Julia Lathrop concluded that "a decent income, self-respectingly [*sic*] earned by the father is the beginning of wisdom, the only fair division of labor between the father and the mother of young children, and the strongest safeguard against a high infant mortality rate."[84] Florence Kelley celebrated the fact that "the American home has hitherto been the most fortunate home of the working class in the civilized world, because . . . the little children in America have had their mothers with them much more than the little children in the other industrial countries."[85]

When a bread-winning husband died or became disabled, the maternalists' solution was mother's pensions, normally provided through local and state governments. Such pensions, they believed, should be large enough to allow the mother to remain at home. As a German-American Jewish delegate to the 1909 White House Conference on the Care of Dependent Children explained: "She has rendered to society a service by becoming a mother, and she continues to render a social service if she devotes herself to her child and brings her child up to good citizenship. Then society is morally bound to help the mother discharge that purpose."[86]

In short, the maternalists held that the universality of motherhood was stronger as a force for social unity than were those ethnic and cultural differences that tended to push toward social division. They defined the family as the true crucible of Americanism, and held up the mother's role along with the family wage as their economic and political program for renewal. The "moral soundness" of the immigrant industrial family was rooted in the family's innate conservatism, which made it "the source and spring of the life of the next economic period."[87] Maternalist educator C. Cora Winchell underscored the natural organization of the family around the infant-mother bond. In "her business of homemaking," each woman contributed to "a clear and well-defined body of principles of right living and right thinking." Indeed, Americanization was largely the task of sharing the values of the American home: "The silent influence of the good housekeeper, surrounded by neighbors from other lands who are eager to learn American ways, is a potent factor in the great work of Americanization."[88] Frances Kellor stressed how "[t]he first principle in race fusion is the opportunity to establish a home base in a country and a genuine love for that home. The home sense in the many peoples that have come to America is inseparable from the sense of the soil itself. . . . Whatever there is of poetry in their lives is associated with the soil, and their worship is inseparable from it." Kellor concluded: "A systematic effort should be made to give [immigrants] a land interest and a home stake and to get them close to the soil."

"[P]aternalistic and patriarchal assumptions about the nature of gender,"[89] the homemaking mother, a social or "family" wage for fathers, maternal pensions, the campaign for infant life or "baby-saving," neighborhood, the central role of home ownership, attachment to the soil: these maternalist themes also serve as a fairly accurate definition of German family ideals. As the first and largest immigrant group passing through the Settlement House environment, it may be that the German-Americans shaped their "friendly visitors" and their "Settlement workers" perhaps as much as they, themselves, were shaped. Meanwhile, the communalist theories spreading among German-American Catholics, Lutherans, and Calvinists gave a philosophical and theological framework to pro-family and baby-saving strategies that went well beyond the practical lessons of Hull House or the old Victorian pieties. Born within German America, this rooted form of communitarianism began to enter American political discourse in the early twentieth century.

POLICY VICTORIES

Between 1912 and 1927, the maternalist campaign claimed a remarkable series of public policy victories, measures that set a pattern for half a century. The maternalists focused on family reconstruction; built on clear distinctions between male and female natures and responsibilities; espoused "broad sympathy for the immigrants;" warned against reckless Americanization; and were consistent opponents of racism.[90] These principles guided all of their programmatic efforts.

Their first policy victory came with the creation of the U.S. Children's Bureau in 1912. The idea had emerged nine years earlier, when Lillian Wald queried Florence Kelley: "If the government can have a department to take such an interest in the cotton crop, why can't it have a bureau to look after the nation's child crop?" In early 1909, President Theodore Roosevelt endorsed the idea, and his successor, William Howard Taft, signed the measure into law three years later. Most of the women's associations, including the conservative National Congress of Mothers, rallied in support. Housed in the Department of Commerce and Labor, the new agency had a miniscule budget and a staff of only fifteen. Yet Julia Lathrop, of Hull House fame, became the Bureau's first director (indeed, the first woman ever to head a federal agency), and she mobilized thousands of volunteers in the Settlement Houses and Women's Clubs to advance the bureau's agenda.[91]

The bureau's principle focus was "baby-saving," to be accomplished through better mothering and family life. Lathrop explained that "the first and simplest duty of women is to safeguard the lives of mothers and babies." This meant raising the status of motherhood and improving the "partnership" between wife and husband so that they were "equally responsible" for the family—"the father for the support of the home, the mother for the wise comfort and peace within it." Toward these ends, the bureau published two trailblazing books: *Prenatal Care* (1913) and *Infant Care* (1914); 1.5 million copies of the latter circulated over the next ten years. Bureau bulletins showed a deep respect for women's work in the home and for "the profession of parenthood." Where most physicians were aloof in their relationships with expectant mothers, the bureau treated them "as colleagues, not subordinates." According to historian Molly Ladd-Taylor, bureau personnel "held a respectful, though somewhat romantic, view of immigrant mothers who seemed to share their cultural values regarding children." Although sometimes engaged in questionable projects (such as the attempt to convince Italian-born mothers to give up spaghetti), the bureau was popular among its clients, operating "more as a distant relative or friend than a government bureaucracy." Lathrop personally answered hundreds of letters sent to her each year from young mothers, an example followed throughout the bureau. Detailed bureau research in Johnstown, New York, underscored—in Lathrop's words—the "coincidence of underpaid fathers" and "overworked and ignorant mothers" as the leading cause of infant mortality. In urging "family wages" for men and full-time mothering for women, the bureau advocated a distinctively "American" conception of family life.[92]

The bureau also adopted an idea pioneered by Josephine Baker in New York in launching Little Mothers Leagues. Girls, particularly from immigrant families, were recruited into these clubs, which taught baby feeding and care. By 1915, fifty-thousand girls in forty-four cities were in Little Mothers Leagues, complete with the paraphernalia of merit badges, club meetings, and the like. As one script for a league skit read:

Child: I belong to the Little Mothers League. They teach us how babies ought to be kept. . . .

Mother: Baby seems to be getting fatter and better every day since I stopped giving it fruit and the other things you told me were not good for the baby.

The bureau also religiously promoted the breastfeeding of infants and discouraged early weaning and the use of infant formula. The maternalists understood that maternal nursing made for healthier babies and also reinforced the parental division of labor. By 1916, Josephine Baker could testify before Congress that "[w]e have induced most of the mothers who come to visit us to nurse their children," markedly reducing infant mortality as a result.[93]

There had been other maternalist victories as well and there were more to come. In 1914, Congress elevated Mothers' Day to a national holiday, to be celebrated each year on the second Sunday of May. Also in 1914, the Smith-Lever Extension Act of 1914 created the nationwide agricultural extension program through the U.S. Department of Agriculture. While men on farms would be given training and assistance in improved farming techniques, specialists would train farm women in home economics and housekeeping skills. The youth component of the program would follow the same division of labor: crops, animal husbandry, and machine maintenance for boys; household arts for girls. The Smith-Hughes Vocational Training Act came in 1917. This measure followed growing maternalist complaints over the failure of public schools to prepare young women for their futures. As Florence Kelley explained in 1914:

> The schools may truthfully be said actively to divert the little girls from homelife. . . . For the schools teach exactly those things which prepare girls to become at the earliest moment *cash children* and *machine tenders*: punctuality, regularity, attention, obedience, and a little reading and writing—excellent things in themselves, but wretched preparation for . . . homemaking a decade later.

Jane Addams concurred that homemaking classes in the schools would assist immigrant girls in connecting "the entire family with American food and household habits." Indeed, the emerging homemaking class might have been considered—in Gwendolyn Mink's words—"as the fulcrum of the maternalists' Americanization strategy." As the first federal involvement in elementary education, the Smith-Hughes Act provided funds for teacher training and salaries in agriculture, the industrial arts, and homemaking. The program rapidly spread across the country.[94]

The baby-saving campaign enjoyed other successes as well. In 1914, the Children's Bureau gave support for a "Baby Week" in Chicago. The idea quickly caught on. The General Federation of Women's Clubs, the National Congress of Mothers, and the bureau cosponsored a National Baby Week in 1916 (March 4–11). Over 4,200 communities took part through lectures, baby-care seminars, and parades. "Best

Mother" contests tested mothers' knowledge and devotion. Orators celebrated motherhood as a sacred vocation and as a vital element of national welfare. As Molly Ladd-Taylor reports, "Like military heroes, mothers with infants in arms paraded down Main Street to the applause of flag waving townspeople." Congress declared 1918 to be "The Year of the Child," and the bureau's campaign to promote good mothering and reduce infant mortality involved an amazing 11 million women, not to mention the weighing and measuring of 6.5 million preschool children.[95]

Meanwhile, as the nation mobilized for war in 1917, Lathrop helped to craft new forms of compensation for soldiers and sailors. Building on "the theory that the family income is profoundly disturbed by the mobilizing of the armed forces" and seeking "to protect infancy and children," the pay system would now have "features entirely novel in the United States." One half of the soldier's pay would go directly to his wife and children, and an extra family allowance was provided: scaled to family size, it was valued at up to $50 per month for four or more children. The plan also featured death and disability benefits for widows and children.[96] As Lathrop told a conference on child welfare:

> The power to maintain a decent family living standard is the primary essential of child welfare. This means a living wage and wholesome working life for the men, a good and skillful mother at home to keep the house and comfort all within it. Society can afford no less and can afford *no exceptions*. This is *a universal need*.[97]

The maternalists' greatest achievement, though, was probably passage of the Sheppard-Towner Act in 1921. Drafted by Julia Lathrop, the measure would expand the "mother- and baby-saving" campaign. Lathrop showed that in 1918 maternal deaths in childbirth numbered 23,000, up from 16,000 two years earlier; 80 percent of expectant mothers still received no prenatal advice or care; the infant mortality rate stood at 100 deaths per 1000 live births—about twice that found in Western European countries. Using the Smith-Lever Act as a model, Sheppard-Towner would provide funds for state-level programs of instruction in maternal and infant hygiene, prenatal child-health clinics, and visiting nurses for pregnant and new mothers. The measure set no income limits on potential clients, although its structure ensured that most help would be focused on rural and working-class women.

The American Medical Association [AMA] fiercely opposed the bill as "German paternalism" and "sob stuff." However, women's organizations ranging from the Women's Trade Union League to the Daughters of the American Revolution actively sought its passage, forming "one of the strongest lobbies that has ever been seen in Washington." When a powerful congressman blocked the measure in a House committee, Florence Kelley appeared before its members and compared Congress to King Herod and his slaughter of the innocents, asking: "Why does Congress wish women and children to die?" The bill was endorsed early on by the Democrat, Socialist, Prohibition, and Farmer-Labor parties, and Republican Presidential Candidate Warren G. Harding gave it his support in an October 1, 1920 "Social Justice Day" speech. After amending the measure to ensure that participation would be strictly voluntary and homes not be invaded, a nervous Congress— soon to face fully enfranchised female voters for the first time—gave the women what they wanted on a 279 to 39 vote in the House and a 63 to 7 vote in the Senate. President Harding signed it into law.[98]

Sheppard-Towner, in Lathrop's view, encouraged "the Americanization of the family." It "is not to get the Government to do things for the family," she explained. "It is to create a family that can do things for itself." In its traditionalist assumptions regarding marriage, fertility, and motherhood, notes Mink, Sheppard-Towner "was also the first national policy to tie cultural and gender role conformity to social welfare."[99] Forty-five of forty-eight states eventually took part in the program (only the AMA-dominated states of Illinois, Massachusetts, and Connecticut did not participate). Funding ranged between $1.4 and $2 million a year. By 1929, Sheppard-Towner workers had held 183,252 prenatal and child health conferences; helped establish 2,978 permanent maternity clinics; visited 3,131,996 homes; and distributed 22,030,489 pieces of literature. Between 1925 and 1929 alone, the program reached 4 million babies and 700,000 expectant mothers. The majority of clients were rural, Lathrop and staff having learned from Children's Bureau correspondence that "white farm women . . . were the main audience for *Infant Care* and *Prenatal Care*." Moreover, fertility remained higher in rural areas, meaning that farms were still "the nursery of the nation."

All evidence points to the grassroots popularity of the Sheppard-Towner work. As one farm woman wrote:

I don't see how we poor mothers could do without them [pre-
natal clinics]. . . . I am the mother of 14 children, and I never
was cared for till I begin going to the goodwill center clinic
[*sic*]. . . . We are so glad the day has come when we have someone to care for our babies when they get sick.

The nation's infant mortality rate did indeed decline, from 76 per thousand in 1921 to 69 by 1928. In fact, deaths by gastrointestinal diseases—
the ones most preventable through education—fell by 45 percent.[100]
Sheppard-Towner educated rural families and saved babies.

"AMERICANIZED" OR "GERMANIZED"?

The repeal of the Sheppard-Towner Act in 1929 brought a temporary
halt to the maternalist campaign. The Act had been renewed for two
years in 1927, but at the price of its automatic termination thereafter.
Between 1928 and 1932, Congress saw fourteen bills introduced to reverse this repeal, but they all failed. Vehement opposition to Sheppard-
Towner came from the American Medical Association and two organizations, Woman Patriots and Sentinels of the Republic, both of which
portrayed Sheppard-Towner as a wedge for socialism. In a limited sense,
they were right, for Sheppard-Towner was the first federal measure to
introduce an "entitlement," without a means test, as an expression of
the nation's shared values, or solidarity. It is a tribute to the vision of
the architects of Sheppard-Towner that this innovation occurred
through a voluntary program to protect motherhood and infant life,
and in a manner that increased family size and strengthened the home
economy.

Moreover, given their goal of encouraging full-time mothering,
the maternalists could claim real success. Not only did infant-and
maternal mortality rates fall steadily because of their work, but the
flow of married women into the labor force remained level. In 1900,
the proportion of married women in the labor force was 5.6 percent,
rising to 10.7 percent by 1910. However, for the next twenty years, that
figure was unchanged. The worldview of the maternalists—that the
policy interests of women and children were largely the same; that
women's first responsibility was to marriage and children; that social
policy should be designed to benefit men as wage earners and women
as wives and mothers—triumphed over the extreme individualism and

egalitarianism of the equity feminists congregated in the National Woman's Party.[101] The maternalists would expand their policy beach-head during the 1930s and remain dominant on domestic issues until 1964-65.

Meanwhile, the furor over Americanization was over by 1929. The Ku Klux Klan's appropriation of the term in the mid-1920s, mounting public disillusionment with the World War experience, weariness with Prohibition, and the end of mass immigration through the acts of 1921 and 1924, discredited the cause and allowed attention to focus on other issues. True German America never did recover, and the great—albeit informal—American experiment in cultural pluralism receded. All the same, Americans of German descent continued to show some peculiar traits. From the 1920s until as late as 1970, they were still more likely to be married than the general population; more likely to have three or more children; more likely to reside in male-headed households; more likely to have some higher education; more likely to be employed; more likely to count farmers in their ranks; and more likely to pass the family farm down through the generations.[102] When the U.S. Census Bureau resumed asking citizens about their ethnicity in 1980, some observers were surprised to learn that "Germans" were 50 million strong. By 1990, they were by far the largest ethnic body in the U.S. at 58 million, and were nearly twice as numerous as those who claimed to be of "English" stock (32.6 million and falling). The map of dominant ethnicity, by county, issued by the bureau showed a great swath of German "blue" across the upper half of the 48 states from New Jersey, Pennsylvania, and New York, through the Ohio River Valley into the great Middle West (particularly Missouri, Iowa, Illinois, and Wisconsin), across the Plains States, ending in eastern Oregon and Washington, with pockets in the Carolinas and Texas. While the nativists of the 1910s and early 1920s had suppressed the more visible cultural attributes of German America, the deeper social and familial traits remained—and helped to people a continent.

This "shadow" German America, it appears, thrived in the policy world constructed by the maternalists. Or perhaps it is just as accurate to say that America was "Germanized" after all—in this case to the special benefit of families, mothers, and babies.

3
"Sanctifying the Traditional Family":
The New Deal and National Solidarity

At the base of American civilization is the concept of the family and the perpetuation of that concept is highly important.

— J. Douglas Brown, 1939

A curious quality of the recent historical treatment of 1930s America has been the uniform loathing shown by feminist scholars toward the New Deal. They do not object simply to some of its parts; they indict and condemn the broad domestic policy of Franklin D. Roosevelt's administration.

The ironies here are significant. To begin with, the New Deal contributed the persona of Eleanor Roosevelt to American mythology, a prominent woman who is usually cited as blazing the trail for women in policymaking roles. Husband Franklin, meanwhile, is commonly hailed as the very model of enlightened progressive liberalism. He also holds the role of chief twentieth-century villain in the American conservative narrative. Nonetheless, contemporary feminist authors find the couple and their New Deal work loathsome.

These judgments rest on barely contained fury. Historian Lois Scharf emphasizes the "victimizing effects" of New Deal actions, the manner in which "female dependency" was "institutionalized in sweeping federal legislation."[1] Mimi Abramovitz deplores the way in which the New Deal "upheld patriarchal social arrangements."[2] Gwendolyn Mink argues that the architects of the New Deal "inscribed . . . gender inequality" in the American welfare state and "codified women's secondary status."[3] Alice Kessler-Harris condemns the New Deal for "locking men and women into rigid attitudes" and for "stifling a generation of feminist thought."[4] Suzanne Mettler fumes that "New Deal policies . . . institutionalized" an array of new discriminations, enshrining them "with political significance."[5] And Winifred Wandersee laments the "damage that must have been done to this generation of women"—a catastrophe so great that it "can never be measured."[6]

These historians are even more troubled by the fact that women in powerful positions—including the sainted Eleanor—were to a considerable extent the architects of the New Deal. Scharf acknowledges this, and laments that in contrast to other periods of reform in American history (e.g., the eras of abolitionism, progressivism, and "the 1960s"), "visible, vocal, and wide-ranging feminism was not a prominent feature of the New Deal era."[7] Mink asserts that leading New Deal women "collaborated with masculine policymakers in closing off [for women] the only two avenues for independence in capitalist America: work and education."[8] Jane Humphries charges that the New Deal women were "cyphers for Roosevelt's policies" and "contributed to the premature deterioration of feminism as a movement and to the subsequent years that American women spent in the wilderness [by this, she means suburban life after World War II]."[9]

These scholars understand that a welfare state requires a sense of national solidarity, or shared normative social values, to succeed. The Swedish political scientist Gösta Esping-Anderson emphasizes in turn how the welfare state serves as an "active force in the ordering of social relations."[10] Indeed, the emerging Swedish welfare state of the 1930s gave highest priority to the social liberty and equality of the individual, especially in matters of gender. In its ideal construct, women and men were to be independent actors, with no bonds beyond those of freely shared affection. Dependency would vanish from human relations; instead, all persons would be equally dependent on the state. This was a welfare state that a feminist could embrace with enthusiasm.[11]

But something very different took shape in the American New Deal. Its intellectual roots lay in the maternalism born in the Settlement Houses of Chicago and New York and bonded to the communitarian welfare ideals centered at the University of Wisconsin. Its principle advocates were a remarkable group of women who rejected equity or liberal feminism as destructive of human bonds. They instead wanted social policy to recognize the centrality of the home and the primary power of the breadwinner/homemaker/child-rich family. Most major New Deal initiatives would build on these assumptions. And the consequences would shape American life and the American identity in profoundly novel and important ways, which would echo into the twenty-first century.

THE TRUE IDEOLOGICAL ORIGINS OF THE NEW DEAL

The American maternalists of the 1920s were firm in their worldview. While accepting the inevitability of an industrial order, they endeavored to diminish its dehumanizing effects. As Frances Perkins, then New York Industrial Commissioner, explained:

> For those who wish . . . to spend their energies and their youth in the solution of one of the greatest problems in the world—namely the adjustment of the mechanistic environment of this modern industrial civilization to the needs of human beings—to them lies open one of the greatest opportunities for human service.[12]

The maternalists justified their work by interpreting society as an extension of the home. Accordingly, they supported the idealized domestic status quo—the bread-winning father, the stay-at-home mother, and children enjoying a true childhood—while attacking the "industrial evils" that threatened to undermine this system. As Florence Kelley explained in a critique of child labor:

> If we valued home life as we hypocritically say that we do, there would not be one of these young girls away from the family home in the dead of night serving [as a phone operator], not because they serve it better than men would do, but because they are cheaper and because the interest of the stockholders and the bondholders of the corporation is of greater importance than the sacrifice of these young girls.[13]

Instead of being prematurely immersed in work, "the fundamental rights of children" must be protected. These included "normal home life, opportunities for education, recreation, vocational preparation for life, and moral, religious, and physical development in harmony with American ideals." Julia Lathrop underscored that these children's rights required "an adequate wage for the father, wholesome and pleasant housing and living conditions, and the abolition of racial discrimination" to succeed. Turning specifically to girls, Kelley added that "the protest cannot be made too strong . . . against sending future mothers and makers of homes out of the schools knowing nothing of what they should know when they shall have homes of their own."[14]

Protecting and encouraging the stay-at-home-mother was the other thrust of the maternalist project. Maternity was the most important of human tasks, a service to the nation, the giving of new life to society. Industrialism, the maternalists held, must not be allowed to intrude. This meant that the mothers of children under age sixteen should not be employed. As the U.S. Children's Bureau explained, "the welfare of the home and family is a woman-sized job in itself."[15] The maternalists argued that the entire economic system needed to be channeled or regulated to protect the integrity of motherhood. Florence Kelley, for example, condemned "the monstrous idea of having a night nursery" for the babies of working mothers, adding: "The mothers of young children cannot be sent away from their home to do such work without the gravest social injury."[16] Priority should also be given to securing adequate wages for fathers to support mothers and children at home. In families where the male breadwinner had died or become disabled, mothers' pensions should be provided by the community. As Mrs. G. Harris Robertson of the Tennessee Congress of Mothers explained: "We cannot afford to let a mother, one who has divided her body by creating other lives for the good of the state, one who has contributed to citizenship, be classed as a pauper. . . . She must be given [the] value received by her nation and stand as one honored."[17]

This respect for the special gifts of women led the maternalists to reject sexual equality as a dangerous abstraction. "The cry Equality, Equality, where Nature has created inequality, is as stupid and deadly as the cry Peace, Peace, where there is no peace," said Florence Kelley.[18] Against the strong opposition of the National Association of Manufacturers and other industrial groups, the maternalists sought special protections for women working in factories, viewing them as actual or potential mothers. As Perkins explained: "The program of industrial legislation for the protection of wage earning women was initiated because of . . . the overwork, exploitation and unhealthy surroundings of the working women who crowded into factories in the latter part of the nineteenth century."[19]

Some contemporary feminist scholars suggest that the maternalists were simply backward or retarded in their social thinking. Linda Gordon, for example, argues that their "unconsciously conservative" views of family life were based on "the *unexamined assumption* that women's full-time domesticity was desirable for all concerned."[20] They imply that these women would have been conventional feminists if given the chance to contemplate their situation further.

This is surely untrue. The maternalists were well aware of the liberal or equity feminist option. Indeed, they literally had it shoved in their faces on a regular basis through the activities of the National Woman's Party (NWP), best known as the architect of the proposed Equal Rights Amendment to the Constitution in 1923. Founded by Alice Paul six years earlier, the NWP opposed all special labor legislation protecting women, arguing that such laws reduced women "to a special class of incompetents requiring such special care as minors and defectives need."[21] They rejected maternalist attention to motherhood and children as sentimentalism that diverted women from the march to full equality. When the maternalist-controlled U.S. Women's Bureau convened the Second Women's Industrial Conference in 1926, the NWP delegates sought to disrupt it. According to Mary Anderson, in the afternoon session of the second day they "got up on the floor and started an uproar by all shouting and speaking at the same time. . . . For fully an hour they . . . rushed up and down the aisles shouting and haranguing and making as much commotion as they could . . . like children having tantrums."[22] Florence Kelley described the NWP delegates as resembling "a pirate band attempting to sink a peaceful boat crew of Quakers."[23] Far from being unaware of equity feminism, then, the maternalists watched the NWP work closely with industrial interests to oppose laws against child labor or to sink measures protecting women from industrial abuse. Maternalist Rose Schneiderman of the Women's Trade Union League reported that "on a number of occasions we charged the Woman's Party with being [financially] supported by the National Association of Manufacturers [NAM], allegations they never denied." Women's Bureau chief Mary Anderson and Settlement House teacher Eleanor Roosevelt, who would become First Lady, shared this belief.[24] Certainly, "the NAM recognized the value of the NWP in defeating labor legislation and endorsed the equal rights amendment in 1923."[25]

The maternalists faced a more subtle ideological opponent as well: the "Hoover technocrats." In 1930, Herbert Hoover created the President's Research Committee on Social Trends, which featured a distinguished list of social scientists. The panel's final report, *Recent Social Trends in the United States*, appeared in early 1933. Much like John Naisbitt's much later and widely touted *Megatrends*, this official report can be read as a brief to abandon the family completely to the industrial process, for reasons of historical inevitability and efficiency.

The committee's chief researcher on the family was William F. Ogburn of the University of Chicago. Well known for his concentration on social functions, he compared the old family system—which stood as "the chief economic institution, the factory of the time . . . the main educational institution"—with the new order where "the factory [has] displaced the family." Modern America saw a falling birthrate and emptying schools as industrialized families were reduced to "the personality function" alone, providing "for the mutual adjustments among husbands, wives, parents, and children and for the adaptation of each member of the family to the outside world." Ogburn showed that all other tasks—baking, sewing, canning, laundering, cooking, health care, child care, care of the elderly, child protection, security, education, amusement, recreation, and even religious activities—had passed or were passing to industrially-organized bodies, be they corporate, governmental, or charitable in nature. Many American homes had already become "merely 'parking places' for parents and children who spend their active hours elsewhere."

But rather than fighting these changes, as the maternalists did, Ogburn essentially urged Americans to go with the trends. He criticized the traditional belief that "women's place is in the home," arguing that "barriers of custom remain and the community is not making the most of this potential supply of able services." He emphasized that "[w]ives, *except* when they work outside the home for pay, contribute proportionately less to the family." The frail nature of the family meant that "schools, nurseries or other agencies" would need to enroll "a *larger* proportion of the very young children in the future" so as "to *conserve childhood* in the midst of rapidly shifting conditions of family life." Only "society" had the new expertise needed to grapple with "developing the personality of *its* children." Ogburn thus implied that even this last family function would necessarily be socialized. Concern should no longer focus on family strength, Ogburn concluded; efforts should instead be directed toward "the individualization of the members of the family."[26]

The apparent rush of social evolution in the direction of atomistic, post-family goals heartened feminists and industrial leaders alike. The former saw the "middle-aged married women" of America as "permanently damaged" by the influences of the traditional home. The American housewife was "a flabby, soft creature of middle age, with no sustained habits of labor and a triumphant incapacity to think straight about any subject," wrote a female academic in 1929. Her home "is notoriously ill-kept, practically negligible as a producing agency, startlingly inefficient as a consuming organization, and seldom worthy of any designation of charm and graciousness." She fed food to her husband that he should not eat and taught her babies "prejudices that will mar their later lives." Better that she move into the labor force, so that experts might rear the children and the "old, materialistic conception of the home" might give way "to one in which the value rests in spiritual assets."[27]

Business leaders also welcomed the remodeling of the family along industrial lines. The "new" family would look outward to the marketplace for its values and human bonds. Industry, rather than family and father, would provide sustenance and meaning. Family autonomy and parental authority would give way to universal adult employment and a consumption-oriented lifestyle guided by advertising, one compatible with feminist ambitions. As one analyst has summarized: "[T]he message of the commodity market dangle[d] before women's eyes that which the feminists among them were already seeing as a possibility: a society in which the patriarchal yoke might be broken."[28]

Against these trends and ideologies, the maternalists chose to stand and fight; to build on the legacy of Jane Addams, Ellen Richards, Julia Lathrop, and Frances Kellor. Who were these women?

The most representative and influential, perhaps, was Frances Perkins, U.S. Secretary of Labor through the whole Roosevelt administration, from 1933 to 1945. According to labor historian Philip Foner, she "was never the radical that conservatives accused her of being."[29] Perkins began her career at the Henry Street Settlement House in New York. In 1910, she became general secretary of the National Consumers League, which focused on harmful industrial conditions and sought protection for child and female workers. A year later, she directly witnessed the legendary Triangle Shirtwaist fire, which saw 146 girls perish in a "sweatshop" the windows and doors of which were locked from the outside. Despite strong opposition from the manufacturers' associations, Governor Al Smith named Perkins to the New York State Industrial Commission in 1919; Governor Roosevelt reappointed her in 1929, and took her to Washington four years later.[30]

Perkins deplored the industrialist "attack" on family life: "I have seen the factory invading and breaking down the home. . . . The poor people have a right to their homes the same as the rich, and we should not be allowed to enslave them to a form of industry which refuses them not only their liberty, but the wage which they ought to have in return for the labor they perform."[31] Perkins steadfastly refused to be dragged into the equity feminist worldview. When asked, as America's first female Cabinet member, to speak to the American Association of University Women on "How Women Achieve in Government," she agreed only if she could change her subject to "Social Responsibility Goes with the Privilege of Education."[32] As the Depression worsened, she denounced the working middle-class woman with an employed husband as a "pin money worker, a menace to society, [and] a selfish short-sighted creature who ought to be ashamed of herself."[33] Meanwhile, she urged policy ideas that would encourage marriage, support large families, and promote population growth.[34]

Perkins worked with a cast of like-minded women. Molly Dewson, advocate of protective labor laws, became a member of the Social Security Board and consultant to the important Federal Advisory Council of 1937 to 1938. Grace Abbott, forceful advocate for the mother-at-home, served as Chief of the Children's Bureau from 1921 to 1934 and then became a member of the Council on Economic Security, which crafted the Social Security Act of 1935. Katharine Lenroot, formerly a research associate at the University of Wisconsin and a strong foe of day care, headed the Children's Bureau from 1934 to 1945. Mary Anderson guided the Labor Department's Women's Bureau from 1933 to 1945. She called day care centers "a stop gap, not a solution to anything;" opposed the Equal Rights Amendment for being "vague" and dangerous; and single-handedly prevented the League of Nations from endorsing it.[35] First Lady Eleanor Roosevelt, a former Settlement House worker and political ally of Frances Perkins, believed "that every girl ought to marry and have a family;" that "the first ten years of a girl's marriage, broadly speaking, should be devoted to the home;" and that mothers with children at home should be discouraged from outside employment.[36]

Finally, Franklin D. Roosevelt himself can be counted a maternalist. As a young lawyer, he worked for the National Consumers League, in which role he defended protective labor legislation in the prominent 1908 case, *Muller v. Oregon* (modern feminist scholars label Roosevelt's characterization, in this case, of women as potential mothers and as significantly different in physical strength from men, as "pathological"). Roosevelt was also closely tied to the Wisconsin School of social reform. Associated with Professor John Commons at the University of Wisconsin, the Wisconsin School sought to use government to protect individuals, families, and communities from predatory "special interests."[37] Roosevelt's maternalist views were well known by his enemies. As the NWP leader Harriet Stanton Blatch reported in 1935, Roosevelt "is not with us and never has been."[38]

Historian Linda Gordon has identified seventy-six women and seventy-six men—a numerical coincidence—who were "national leaders of welfare reform movements from 1890 to 1935." Majorities in both categories were of Protestant, Northern European backgrounds. "Most took their Christianity very seriously and considered their reform work part of a Christian moral vision." Yet a large minority—nine of the women and one-fifth of the men—were Jews of German background. Virtually the whole body looked to social reform ideas taking shape in Europe, "particularly in Germany," for inspiration; and all of them, according to Gordon, adhered to traditional ideas about the family. To her surprise, even the majority of women reformers who were single "*did not* . . . contradict the prevailing premises that children and women needed breadwinner husbands, that children needed full-time mothers, that women should choose between family and career."[39]

Indeed, it is fair to conclude that the concept of the "family wage" stood as the central pillar of the maternalist vision and of the New Deal. At the Children's Bureau, Katharine Lenroot underscored that "the primary essential of child welfare" was "a living wage for the father."[40] At the Women's Bureau, Mary Anderson emphasized that the whole problem of women's wages and working conditions "could be taken care of if the provider for the family got sufficient wages. Then married women would not be obliged to go to work."[41] Speaking for the labor unions, CIO chief John L. Lewis agreed: "Normally, a hus-

band and father should be able to earn enough to support his family
. . . . I am *violently opposed* to a system which by degrading the earnings of adult males, makes it economically necessary for wives and
children to become supplementary wage earners."[42]

The new historians of the New Deal concur. Gordon reports that
"[a]lmost all welfare activists, male and female, endorsed the family-
wage principle and considered that women's employment was a mis-
fortune or a temporary occupation before marriage." Both "tracks" of
the emerging American welfare system—social insurance and means-
tested assistance—"were designed to maintain the family wage system."[43] According to Mink, "The New Deal assumed that men paid
for their families while women raised them." The child's welfare required "a competent domestic mother" and "a living wage for the father."[44] Mettler underscores how New Deal officials, "still adhering to
the family wage ideal," presumed that "policies directed toward male
breadwinners would directly benefit women as well as children."[45]

The companion role to the bread-winning father was the mother-
at-home. Maternalists would use the New Deal to reward the domestic woman and discourage the working mother. They expanded and
nationalized existing state programs that protected mothers and created "new [programs] to deliver social benefits to the wives and wid-
ows of wage-earning men." They "prescribed domesticity to unemployed women in vocational programs that trained [them] for housekeeping and parenting" and they urged "counseling services for mothers tempted to work outside the home." Linking truancy, incorrigibil-
ity, and emotional disorders among children to an at-home-mother's
"absence at her job," the maternalists mounted campaigns to bring
working mothers home. Most modern feminists denounce these
"strenuous [New Deal] efforts to expel married women from the labor
force" as an overt defense of "patriarchy."[46] Only Linda Gordon appears to acknowledge the way a maternalist, circa 2003, would explain
her legacy: "[We] attempted the difficult and perhaps counterhistorical
task of defending the value of women's traditional domestic labor in a
capitalist-industrial context."[47]

FAMILY AND GENDER IN THE NEW DEAL

By March 1933, when the Roosevelt administration took office, one-
third of the labor force was unemployed: 15 million persons. This eco-

nomic collapse was primarily industrial in nature. Since women workers were disproportionately crowded into service sector (e.g., nursing,
domestic work) and white collar (e.g., clerical) posts, and since they
worked for less money (average annual income for men: $1,027; for
women: $525), they actually suffered less job loss in the period be-
tween 1929 and 1933 than did men. Viewed from the household level,
the economic crisis of 1933 was concentrated among once–"bread-winning" men. Meanwhile, marriage and birth rates were tumbling; each
declined by 20 percent during the Hoover years.[48] In this sense, the deep
economic downturn was also a crisis of the family. How did the New
Deal advocates try to restore families and their home economies?[49]

(1) The National Industrial Recovery Act (NIRA). Roosevelt believed
that the nation's business leaders had destroyed the economic system
through reckless speculation and ruthless competition. He questioned
the legality of any firm that continued to exist by paying heads-of-
households less than a living family wage. His NIRA attempted to restore industrial production and employment in the United States
through a series of industry-wide codes that would regulate competition, wages, and working conditions. Specifics included a fixed thirty-
five-hour work week and the banning of overtime. In announcing the
new measures, Roosevelt also declared that the proposed National
Recovery Administration (NRA) codes would "guarantee living wages"
to American workers. "By living wages I mean more than a bare subsistence living—I mean the wages of decent living."[50]

By January 1934, NRA codes covered 90 percent of all industrial
workers, and they raised real income standards substantially. Yet because such codes were restricted to industries engaged in interstate
commerce, over half of working women were excluded from any help
at all. NRA relief projects hired only men; "women were ignored."
And by September 1934, 135 of 233 NIRA codes directly and indirectly
fixed minimum wage rates for women from 6 to 30 percent lower than
those for men doing the same job. NRA officials explained these differentials as the result of "long established custom." It is true that
Frances Perkins, Mary Anderson, and Eleanor Roosevelt opposed the
open discrimination in NRA wage rates. But they and the system cheerfully left in place sex-defined job categories ("men's jobs" and "women's
jobs"), also inscribed in custom, which carried much larger real differentials.[51]

(2) **The Subsistence Homestead Program**. This openly reactionary project, a favorite of Eleanor Roosevelt's, sought to deindustrialize and decentralize American life. It grew directly out of the back-to-the-land movement promoted in the 1920s by Bernarr McFadden of *Liberty* magazine and Ralph Borsodi, an apostle of family self-sufficiency and home production. Before his inauguration, Franklin Roosevelt spoke among aides of his desire to put a million families into subsistence farming. Senator John H. Bankhead of Alabama successfully included a $25 million appropriation for subsistence homesteads in the NIRA measure.[52] During the next eight years, the federal government launched over two hundred projects under the "homesteading" banner. Commonly, the government built homes on three- to ten-acre lots, laid out as a village, which were provided to worthy families for modest rent, with an option to buy.

Leftist critics of the program saw it as an effort "to build up . . . a sheltered peasant group as a rural reactionary bloc to withstand the revolutionary demands of the organized industrial workers."[53] Certainly the hope of subsistence homestead champions was to restore some elements of a pre-industrial, family-centered life. The project reflected a "general disillusionment with laissez-faire capitalism" and an "ardor for conservation" of both human community and nature. Senator Bankhead saw this as a chance for "a new basis for American society, in the restoration of that small yeoman class which has been the backbone of every great civilization." Secretary of Agriculture Henry A. Wallace justified the homesteads by noting that "we are more than economic man." One of the project's staff members, the Quaker activist Clarence E. Pickett, argued that behind "the façade of abundant production," Americans "had forgotten that the hearth where the family gathers and where neighbors are welcomed is at the very heart of human life." The homesteads would decentralize workers in industry, fulfill "yearnings for a home, for a good life for children, [and] 'for community,'" and free the imaginations and intelligence "of men and women who had mostly been treated as cogs in a machine."[54]

Program administrator M. L. Wilson admired the Mormon villages found in Utah—their unity of soil, family, and community. He looked to the homesteads as a way to renew village life nationwide through handicrafts, closer family relations, abundant children, and cooperative work. Every homestead would have a garden, a chicken house, and perhaps a pig or cow "for home consumption and not for commercial sale." The selection of homesteaders would focus on stable and honest married couples, with one or more children. The process especially favored large families. Those who abandoned gardening and other home production acts were weeded out and replaced.[55]

(3) The Early Emergency Work Projects. The first New Deal relief efforts "aimed at [restoring] the male breadwinner as the mainstay of family life in America."[56] A 1936 Gallup poll asked if wives should work if their husbands had jobs. Eighty-two percent of respondents said "No," leading George Gallup to observe that he had finally "discovered an issue on which voters are about as solidly united as on any subject imaginable—including sin and hay fever."[57] Later in the decade, *Saturday Review*'s Norman Cousins captured the popular attitude:

> There are approximately 10,000,000 men out of work in the United States today; there are also 10,000,000 or more women, married and single, who are job holders. Simply *fire the women,* who shouldn't be working anyway, and *hire the men.* Presto! No unemployment. No relief rolls. No depression.[58]

The Federal Emergency Relief Act (FERA) provided, in Katharine Lenroot's words, "for the first time . . . a basis for direct Federal, state, and local co-operation [*sic*] in conserving home life for children."[59] The maternalists urged a modest role for women, provided that they were kept out of the "competitive fields" and the mass projects where men were found. While women constituted about 22 percent of the unemployed, they held only 12 percent of the FERA jobs.[60] Another emergency work project, the Civil Works Administration (CWA), employed 1.6 million persons in 1935, only 147,000 (7 percent) of which were women. Administrator Harry Hopkins meanwhile paid $1 per hour for skilled male labor and 30¢ per hour for "persons on relief and educational projects—largely women."[61] The Civilian Conservation Corps (CCC), at its inception, focused solely on young men and involved 2.5 million of them at its peak in 1936. They worked on outdoor construction and conservation projects in parks and national forests. At the behest of Eleanor Roosevelt, the CCC eventually organized eighty-six camps for 6,400 young women. These included Camp Jane Addams, where instructors stressed domestic training in "cooking, nutrition, and table setting as well as serving [food] and personal hygiene." While the

CCC's young men received $1 per week for their labor, the women were paid only 50¢.[62]

(4) The Works Progress Administration (WPA). The largest of the government work relief programs, the WPA employed over 2.5 million persons by early 1939. Moreover, according to Katharine Lenroot at the Children's Bureau, 4.5 million children under age sixteen were at that time "being provided with maintenance through wages of family breadwinners on Federal works projects."[63]

The WPA had broader goals as well. The New Deal proponents were cognizant that one-third of the nation was either foreign-born or only first-generation American. Alongside the employment of breadwinners, the WPA's emergency education activities openly aimed at nation-building and the creation of solidarity "through Americanization, literacy, and a strong family life." This included an emphasis on "the values of Americanized home life."[64]

WPA regulations limited enrollment to one breadwinner per household. Grace Abbott asserted that the "[e]mployment of mothers with dependent children on WPA is to be deplored as experience shows that . . . the children will be neglected and the mothers' health will break under the double burden of serving as wage-earners and homemakers."[65] Fairly typical WPA regulations from Louisiana held that "a woman with an employable husband is not eligible for referral as the husband is the logical head of the family."[66]

All the same, from 12 to 19 percent of WPA workers were women. Even here, though, the maternalists shaped the program. Over half of WPA women found places in "sewing rooms," where they repaired damaged clothing or sewed new garments from scraps. Critics called the sewing room "a female ditch-digging project." But the sewing rooms were part of a larger plan. The women in WPA—disproportionately of immigrant background—also took instruction in parenting, child behavior, home health, food preparation, and "wholesome adult living." Lessons in "American" family values and maternal skills involved a quarter of all WPA personnel and reached 16 percent of regular enrollees. In addition, the WPA employed 1,700 jobless teachers as home economics instructors, who provided a two-month course in "methods of cooking and serving food, care of the house, care of the children, washing, ironing, and marketing." It employed another 30,000 women in its Housekeeping Aid Project, which offered housekeepers and babysitters to households composed of widowed fathers and their children. In a report on WPA courses directed by the U.S. Office of Education, Doak S. Campbell concluded that the "combined parent and homemaking program is perhaps the *most social* and *democratic* of all of the emergency education activities."[67]

While the WPA did operate daycare centers for enrolled mothers with small children, administrators discouraged any broader use. According to one federal expert, writing in 1943, a woman's desire to work and use daycare for other than emergency reasons might betoken mental unbalance: "If the mother's wish for improved status, economic, or otherwise, seems exaggerated and impossible of fulfillment, the counsellor may help her to relinquish these ambitions."[68]

(5) The National Labor Relations Act. The "Wagner Act" gave a dramatic boost to membership in labor unions, including the overwhelmingly female International Ladies Garment Workers' Union. At the same time, it did nothing to challenge, and in some ways reinforced, underlying gender differentials in labor: "Job categories remained sex-defined. Seniority lists [for men and women] were separate."[69]

(6) The Social Security Act of 1935. Abraham Epstein of Pennsylvania, one of the architects of this crown jewel of the emerging American welfare state, laid out in 1933 his base assumption for calculating "security":

> [It] must be remembered that *the American standard* assumes a normal family of man, wife, and two or three children, with the father fully able to provide for them out of his own income. This standard presupposes no supplementary earnings from either the wife or young children.

Epstein acknowledged that of the 26.2 million married women in 1930, 3.1 million—or 11.7 percent—were employed. However, "[m]ost of the remaining 88 percent were dependent on their husbands for support. The *needs of these families must be considered as paramount.*"[70] Grace Abbott, who served via presidential appointment on the Advisory Council to the Committee on Economic Security, told Congress that "the mother's services are worth more in the home than they are in the outside labor market, and that consequently she should be enabled to stay home and care for the children."[71] Another influential member of the

Advisory Council was Father John Ryan, S.T.D., America's foremost public advocate of a family wage for fathers.[72]

These ideas shaped the 1935 Social Security Act. Two of the maternalists' favorite projects—mothers' pensions at the state level and the expired Sheppard-Towner Act providing prenatal and infant care education—would be federalized and made permanent by the Social Security measure. Moreover, old age pensions funded by contributions to individual accounts, together with death, unemployment, and disability benefits, would cushion the vagaries of the capitalist industrial economy.

Feminist historians see maternalist fingerprints all over Social Security. According to Kessler-Harris, the Act "rested on forms of behavior traditionally associated with white male lifestyles and population" (by this, she means marriage with the mother in the home).[73] Abramovitz argues that the Social Security Act "enforced traditional work and family roles," "began systematically to subsidize the familial unit of reproduction," and structured a "gender bias" into its provisions that "has enforced the economic dependence of women on men . . . and, in general, upheld patriarchal social arrangements."[74]

The National Woman's Party actually welcomed the 1935 Act because it limited old age insurance strictly to workers: no paid labor, no security. Women who married and renounced their careers gave up most government protection as well.[75] But contemporary feminist analysts again underscore how the system actually bypassed most working women. For example, the large majority of female laborers performed tasks *exempted* from the old age insurance program: clerical work; sales; teaching; nursing; domestic service; farm labor; and work for charities. Mettler emphasizes how the system's architects presumed that unemployment insurance had the primary function of "replac[ing] the wages of male breadwinners, who were understood to earn a 'family wage.'"[76] Specifically, according to the contemporary economist and U.S. senator Paul Douglas, this provision excluded part-time workers— mostly female—who "do not need or deserve the same protection as those who are fully dependent upon industry for employment."[77]

Women gained benefits under Social Security primarily through their ability to conceive and bear children, another galling fact for modern feminist analysts. Title V provided $3.8 million to qualifying women for prenatal, maternal, and infant care education. More broadly, the Aid to Dependent Children (ADC) program reinforced women's domesticity. ADC provided financial allowances, through the states, to female-headed families that had lost the male breadwinner through death, desertion, and illegitimacy (a rare occurrence at that time). In her testimony on the ADC provision, Grace Abbott assured Congress that "only nice children" in "nice families" would qualify for support.[78] (In fact, as of 1939, a mere 2 percent of the children accepted by the states into ADC lived with never-married mothers.)[79]

The system clearly gave a preference to welfare motherhood over work. As Abbott told the House Ways and Means Committee: "The whole idea of mothers' pensions is that it should be enough to care for the children adequately, to keep the mother at home and thus to give some security in the home." Or as Frances Perkins explained to a Senate committee: "You take the mother of a large family, she may be able-bodied and all that, but we classify her as unemployable because if she works the children have got to go to an orphan asylum."[80] Another New Deal official, Jane Hoey, described the purposes of ADC as "reconstruct[ing]" homes and "enabl[ing] families now in the dependent class [through loss of breadwinner] to fulfill their own responsibilities to the children and to society."[81]

Feminist scholars are more harsh in their assessments, but are not altogether incorrect. Mink charges that ADC was in fact "an essential defense against wage-earning motherhood," adding: "[i]f social insurance treated the working mother as inconceivable, ADC treated her as incompatible with family welfare." Ann Shola Orloff charges that ADC intentionally undercut feminist ideals and shut off aid to never-married women raising children alone. And Abramovitz asserts that ADC "judged female-headed households harshly," "subjected them to strict control," and financially punished women seen as "out of role."[82]

(7) The Fair Labor Standards Act. This substitute for the NIRA , which was declared unconstitutional in 1935, pleased the National Woman's Party because it established labor protections, maximum hours, and minimum wages without overt reference to gender. Yet contemporary feminist scholars have shown that the Act indirectly exempted nearly half of working women from its coverage (compared to only 20 percent of male workers), left untouched the "customary" division of labor into "men's jobs" and "women's jobs," and implicitly sustained the male "family wage" as the primary measure of labor justice.[83]

(8) Home Ownership Programs. The rise of suburbia and its association with a renewed familism are commonly seen as part of the post–World War II era. In fact, these developments began in the 1930s. During that decade, *90 percent* of new residential construction consisted of single-family dwellings in suburban-type locales, compared to only 60 percent during the 1920s.[84] This shift was attributable to a series of New Deal projects. The Home Owners Loan Act of 1933 provided a novel type of long-term, low-interest loan to homeowners delinquent in their mortgage payments. With Secretary of Labor Frances Perkins as sole stockholder, the Emergency Housing Corporation issued over one million mortgages under this measure by 1936. The National Housing Act of 1934 created the Federal Housing Administration. The FHA quickly "revolutionized" housing finance by regularizing the long-term amortized mortgage, including a low down payment, introducing up-front financial and insurance commitments to developers, and establishing standards that "contributed greatly to more sophisticated builder and tract housing work."[85] According to historian Janet Hutchison, this "focusing on the suburban residence heightened the importance of women's domestic contributions, the home as the woman's proper place, and voluntary, maternalistic reform efforts."[86]

(9) The Social Security Amendments of 1939. The 1936 Democratic platform pledged "the protection of the family and home." Republicans ran for Congress in 1938 criticizing the stinginess of the Social Security Act of 1935, and gained over eighty seats in the House of Representatives. The result was the Social Security Amendments of 1939, perhaps the most important of New Deal innovations, and the one attracting the greatest contemporary feminist scorn.

These amendments "saved" the Social Security system from repeal, were "wildly" popular, and turned the old age pension scheme from an individualistic orientation modeled on private insurance, into social insurance resting on a pay-as-you-go basis, and focused on preservation of the father-headed family.[87] Indeed, according to Orloff, the American welfare state gained its distinctive charter as a family-centered entity here.[88] Mink emphasizes how "the 1939 amendments spelled out the gendered basis of social insurance and spread gender bias throughout the welfare state for the first time."[89] Kessler-Harris argues that the measure "brilliantly convey[ed] a set of messages about how people should live"—notably, that women should marry and should stay married. Men would gain little if wives worked, and women "would have to work mighty hard" to exceed the benefits of staying at home with their children. And, of course, the more children born, the greater the benefit.[90]

The 1939 Amendments were, in part, a consequence of a political embarrassment. Contributions for old age insurance started flowing into the federal coffer in 1936, yet no benefits were to be paid out until 1942. The result was a swelling reserve. In spring 1937, the Senate Finance Committee pressured the Social Security Board to create the Federal Advisory Council (FAC). As Kessler-Harris notes, the panel could have recommended spending the surplus by expanding coverage to the disabled and including occupational groups such as domestics and agricultural workers. Instead, "family protection" became the operative principle.[91]

Of the FAC's twenty-four members, at least six had received their graduate education at the University of Wisconsin. These included chairman J. Douglas Brown, Edwin Witte of the original Committee on Economic Security, chief actuary William Williamson, and chairman of the Social Security Board Arthur Altmeyer. The last—dubbed "Mr. Social Security" by Roosevelt—was particularly influential. Born and reared in small-town Wisconsin, Altmeyer was the descendant of German immigrants who fled their homeland after the failed rebellions of 1848. According to biographer Larry Witt, Altmeyer "inherited . . . liberal progressivism in his genes." Influenced by his German-American background, he took advantage of the FAC to advance a very different approach to security:

> The Council's report, which tracked Altmeyer's agenda almost perfectly . . . fundamentally altered the nature of the program by adding survivors and dependents benefits. . . . This changed Social Security from a program focused on the economic security of the individual worker and made it a program focused on the economic security of the family unit.[92]

The other key group behind the 1939 Amendments was the Settlement House maternalists led by Molly Dewson, who actively served on the parent Social Security Board. To the horror of later feminist analysts, these policymakers "constructed 'men' and 'women' each after particular gendered patterns;" "created the mechanisms that sustain notions of male dignity and female virtue;" "used language that mingled the rights of men with their control over women;" linked "the appearance of equity" for men to "an essentially passive, and even sacrificial, role for women;" gave "issues of masculinity and womanliness . . . paramount importance;" and totally ignored questions of "female security," "justice to women," and the "success and self-reliance" of women.[93]

Specifically, the 1939 Amendments incorporated the familial responsibilities of males into the system of contributory insurance crafted four years earlier. Using common sense and normative values (e.g., J. Douglas Brown: "it is more costly for the single man to live than for the single woman if she is able to avail herself of the home of the [adult] child"), the FAC recommended and Congress approved a series of new benefits. Molly Dewson explained the foundational principle:

> Men who can afford it always consider it their first duty to provide insurance protection for their wives and children. Survivor benefits extend the same kind of protection to families who need it most and can afford it least.[94]

Specifics of the new benefits included:

○ Aged women married for at least five years to eligible men would receive an extra pension equal to 50 percent of their husbands' benefits. Neither work nor prior contributions would be necessary and divorced women were excluded.
○ Widowed mothers with children in the home were removed from ADC, receiving instead a monthly survivors' benefit equal to 75 percent of the pension her husband would have received, so long as she earned no more than $15 per month and did not remarry.
○ Surviving children received a benefit equal to half that which their father would have received.

Overwhelmingly popular, the 1939 Amendments saved and solidified the Social Security system by grafting onto it the core values of the American people. The measure shifted the system from an "individualistic" to a "communitarian" basis. It made the support of marriage, the "family wage," the stay-at-home-mother, and the large family the direct objects of public policy. Deviations from these norms—divorce, illegitimacy, working mothers, deliberate childlessness—faced significant financial disincentives. As Mink has noted, this measure also "assumed that conformity to the maternalists' . . . domestic, conjugal, and behavioral practices would assure [racial minorities] uplift to equality. . . . It assumed, too, that the well-spring of family security and the sign of 'American' family values was the husband."[95]

But more was going on in 1939. Kessler-Harris admits that the gender distinctions "built into the system for men and women tell us less about injustice and inequities than they do about the ways in which men and women conceived the relationship between *national values* and the *role of the state in preserving the family in its traditional form*."[96] Perhaps Molly Dewson explained best the linkage of family, social security, and national solidarity that lay behind the 1939 Amendments:

> [W]hen you begin to help the family to attain some security you are at the same time beginning to erect a National structure for the same purpose. Through the well-being of the family, we create the well-being of The Nation. Through our constructive contributions to the one, we help the other to flourish.[97]

MATERNALISM TRIUMPHANT

As the culmination of three decades of maternalist social reform, the New Deal was the movement's "finest hour." On learning in June 1940 that the new Republican Party platform had endorsed all of the recent Social Security reforms, Frances Perkins declared: "God's Holy Name be praised! No matter who gets elected, we've won."[98] There were other early signs of victory, as well. Despite the disproportionate concentration of unemployment among men, the percentage of women in the labor market changed little during the 1930s. Moreover, by 1934 the marriage and birth rates began climbing again. The domestic or home economy also showed signs of revival. For example, a marked decline in the sale of industrial canned foods occurred alongside a surge in the purchase of home canning supplies. Home gardens flourished. The 1930s saw a revival in home sewing as well as the return of home-based industries: "women took in laundry, ironing, and dressmaking; they baked cakes to sell. . . . Everywhere there were signs in yards advertising household beauty parlors, cleaning and pressing enterprises, grocery stores, and the like." Families began to "de-nuclearize," as the number of three-generation households increased. It appears that the maternalists *were* pushing industrial organization out of the home; that they *had* reversed capitalism's "creative destruction"; that they *were* shoring up traditional family structure and gender roles.[99]

But the maternalists seemed to meet their Waterloo a short time later, when America entered World War II. By early 1942, there was increasingly intense pressure for married women to join the wartime labor force. Maternalists at the Children's and Women's Bureaus fought the idea fiercely. "The first responsibility of women with young children, in war as in peace, is to give suitable care in their own home to their children," opined the Children's Bureau. A later bulletin declared that a "mother's primary duty is to her home and children. . . . This duty is one she cannot lay aside, no matter what the emergency."[100] A Children's Bureau conference on daycare resolved that "Mothers who remain at home to provide care for children are performing an essential patriotic service in the defense program." When the federal government issued an October 1942 directive to recruit all women possible for war work, the document added that mothers of young children should be left alone "until all other sources of labor supply have been exhausted."[101]

Still, the number of female workers during the war years nearly doubled, reaching 19.5 million by 1945. Many of them did have small children. In August 1942, Roosevelt allocated $400,000 in emergency war funds to coordinate childcare programs. Yet, placing the fox in charge of the chicken coop, he also directed the Children's Bureau to approve state plans and oversee the construction of daycare centers with Lanham Act funds. The maternalists at the Bureau sought to ensure that "facilities required for the emergency should not be so permanent in structure that they cannot be changed or discontinued when the temporary need is over."[102]

Indeed, they proved successful here again, turning the wartime surge in the employment of married women into a time-limited event. As military personnel demobilized during 1945 and 1946, the government began to encourage women to abandon paid work and return to domestic responsibilities. Male veterans gained hiring preferences. Child care programs and buildings were dismantled, while "management and unions cooperated in efforts to reinstate traditional divisions of occupational segregation, forcing women to return to clerical and service-sector jobs so that men could regain high-skilled ones." Congress wrote the G.I. Bill, with its generous educational and housing benefits, solely for returning soldiers, sailors, and airmen who were overwhelmingly male. Labor force participation rates among women fell quickly.[103]

With Roosevelt's death in 1945, most of the maternalists still active in federal agencies retired, including Frances Perkins, Mary Anderson, and Katharine Lenroot. Yet they had achieved much. These women had used the opportunity of the New Deal to build barriers against the further industrialization of the home; to construct the emerging American welfare state on family-centered and communitarian bases; to restore prestige to the tasks of homemaking and mothering; to Americanize recent immigrant families through emphasis on a common affection for the home; and to shape the American identity in the image of the traditional family. On social welfare issues, they had vanquished their foes in the National Woman's Party and the National Association of Manufacturers. As Wandersee admits, "[f]eminism . . . suffered a major setback during the interwar years because it refused to recognize the continued importance of family life and family values to most American women."[104] On the immigration front, the maternalists had won out over the Anglo-Saxonists and the cultural pluralists. And these women had created the policy conditions that would undergird the "marriage boom" of the late 1940s, the "baby boom" of the 1950s, and the "happy days" associated with the whole postwar era, from 1945 to 1963. The fatal weaknesses of this restored social order would become apparent only later.

4

Luce, *Life,* and the "New America"

The great significance of Life *is that it includes among its readers all manners and kinds of Americans.*
. . . Life *is for high-brows and low-brows, for women and for men and even for children, for Easterners and Westerners, for "rich" and "poor" in the American sense. This could only happen with pictures . . . . Here is the society bound together in broad and deep consensus yet not a conformist society.*

— Henry Luce, 1956

Few modern nations are natural creations, the expressions of some primeval tribal unity. Rather, divided by regional, religious, racial, and ethnic differences, most nations are ideal constructs, shaped by human intelligence and sustained by shared symbols and learned understandings of history and place.

The American nation has drawn its symbolic shape from the ideas found in documents such as the Declaration of Independence, Washington's Farewell Address, the Gettysburg Address, and Wilson's Fourteen Points. Yet by the middle decades of the twentieth century, a number of influential Americans had reached the conclusion that these symbolic statements of American identity were no longer adequate to the challenges posed by the modern world—and by "modernity." The nation's new global responsibilities and opportunities, they said, demanded a fresh, modified vision of the American experience, one that would mobilize the mass of citizens for sacrifice at home and abroad.

Perhaps the most prominent and most misunderstood of these modern nation-builders was Henry Robinson Luce. Between 1940 and 1964 he guided his publishing empire, and more specifically *Life* magazine, toward two goals: (1) the creation of an American nation sufficiently unified to bear the responsibilities of international power; and

(2) the shoring-up of Western civilization, which involved planting the Western heritage within popular consciousness on this side of the Atlantic. In order to fulfill these goals, family and religious reconstruction were the central tasks.

Indeed, *Life* in this era was a conscious response to Catholic theologian John Courtney Murray's call for "a new act of intellectual affirmation" that would provide Americans with "the basic consensus that we need." Creation of this consensus, Murray had said, would not be the result of public opinion or philosophical brooding by the masses. Rather, it would be "for the wise, who develop the consensus, to give 'instruction' to the generality, in the meaning of its principles as 'matters of necessary observance,' and also in the manner of their application."[1] The public philosophy America needed would be created by an elite; as accepted conviction, it would exist among the people. Luce's assumed task in *Life* magazine was to deliver such accepted conviction to the American public.

The successes and failures of Henry Luce are instructive. They point to the necessity of moral leadership; they underscore the close relationship between familial and religious renewal; they identify the dilemmas posed by the American "pursuit of happiness"; and they offer cautions about the innate weaknesses of a reawakened American nationalism.

"Irredeemable Chaos" or Democratic Order?

Life, as viewed by its contemporary critics, was seldom considered a philosophically rooted tool for nation-building. It was usually dismissed for its crassness, superficiality, and patchwork character: *Life,* felt the literati, was the journal where the average American could feign attention to serious subjects while leering at the legs of a Hollywood starlet. In 1950 Lovell Thompson said *Life* was the equivalent of "going to a large cocktail party where you know no one," a reflection of "the irredeemable chaos" of the modern mind. A decade later, Ernest van den Haag attacked the magazine for its "pseudo-personalizations," which devoured genuine personalities. "Could Jesus go into the desert today to contemplate?" he asked. "Wouldn't he be followed by a crew of *Life* photographers?"[2]

Viewed from another perspective, though, *Life* in the post–World War II era could be seen as a necessary response to the problems posed by a mass, democratic society. As Edward Shils has suggested, the social order that had emerged in the West after World War I was not necessarily the atomized, alienating construct postulated by most sociologists. Rather, it was a mass society primarily because for the first time in human history, a society had incorporated the vast majority of the adult population into its political and cultural processes. A new form of community, one rooted in shared meanings, was still possible; but new tools were needed to instill in the masses loyalty toward the goals set by the elites. Accordingly, the proper function of mass culture became the creation of a heightened "sense of affinity" among the different religions, classes, regions, and ethnic groups of the same country. In this sense, nation-building in a mass democracy depended absolutely on the popular media, rightly directed.[3]

Henry Luce recognized this fundamental change, reinterpreting his editorial role to meet the challenge of the new democratic era. In one respect, this simply meant assuming, on a national scale, the prerogatives of the small-town American newspaper editor. For over a century, such editors had taken on the roles of social critic, educator, and interpreter of events. The editor exercised authority and influence not only at election time or in matters of politics, but also in matters of personal morality and social mores.[4]

Luce also drew on the long tradition in American thought which considered the American experience as unique and providential. From the Puritan quest to create the exemplary Christian commonwealth, through Lincoln's paean to "the almost-chosen people," to Theodore Roosevelt's exhortations on behalf of "a righteous nation," American nationalism had developed within a religious context.

Moreover, Luce had as examples the older, rival "family magazines," which were already filling this role on a limited scale, including *Collier's*, the *Saturday Evening Post, Country Gentleman, Reader's Digest*, and *Ladies' Home Journal*. The editors of these magazines were, for the most part, born and bred in the Middle West. From this background they retained a certain freshness and innocence, a belief in the virtues of frugality, hard work, religious observance, and family values, and a distrust of New York, big business, urbanism, organized labor, and Washington, D.C. Accordingly, these editors had an almost unconscious rapport with their readers, who generally shared their values. Articles in these publications offered a textured portrayal of American life, still spiritually rooted in small towns and farms. The magazines' juxtaposition of essays, art, and fiction—each in some way different but all conforming to this shared vision and to moral standards inherited from agrarian life—reinforced the identity and meaning of America.[5]

In *Life*, however, Henry Luce resolved to do something Promethean in scope. *Life* would not merely reflect and defend values; it would *create* values for the new social, political, and cultural environment that appeared to be emerging in America. Luce was determined to shape a spirit for his age—one that would be compatible with a new era yet still be in service of the good in America's past. Such a vision involved a significant redirection of the magazine. In its origins, *Life* had no apparent ideological pretentions. For Luce the entrepreneur, it was purely a commercial product. During the early 1930s, he had pondered the growing possibilities inherent in the photograph, a new and strangely universal language. Luce instinctively understood the power of the still shot to convey emotion, immediacy, and symbolic meaning in a manner radically different from the printed or spoken word. Research psychologists have since explained the unique impact of the photograph on the symbolic patterns of the brain, and the powerful associations roused by the use of emotion-laden words in conjunction with pictures.[6] Luce also saw the opportunity afforded by newly developed, high-speed photo engraving and printing processes.

Accordingly, in 1936 he decided to introduce a weekly picture magazine, tentatively called *The Showbook of the World*. A master of promotional copy, Luce described his purpose in the magazine's prospectus:

> To see life; to see the world; to eyewitness great events; to watch the faces of the poor and the gestures of the proud; to see strange things—machines, multitudes, shadows in the jungle and on the moon; to see man's work—his paintings, towers and discoveries; to see things thousands of miles away, things hidden behind walls and within rooms . . . ; the women that men love and many children; to see and to take pleasure in seeing; to see and be amazed . . . ; to see and to show, is the mission now undertaken by a new kind of publication.[7]

Fresh, glamorous, and compelling, *Life*—the title was wisely changed—did not seek to explain America. Its sole aim was to show what it saw. With this limited, apolitical purpose, *Life* emerged as the most successful new publication in American history. More than a year passed before the supply of copies came close to satisfying demand. Weekly circulation quickly rose to three million. Time, Inc. and Luce were soon making a considerable amount of money.

Yet with the onset of World War II, Luce grew restless and more philosophical. The first public expression of his new spirit came in his well-known yet frequently misunderstood essay, "The American Century," which appeared in *Life* in mid-1940. Americans were unhappy, Luce argued; the nation was confused, purposeless, drifting. The political deceits of national leaders, he said, derived from deep moral and intellectual confusion, in which "our educators and churchmen and scientists" were deeply implicated. America was already "in" the war. And even as early as 1940, Luce was confident of eventual Allied victory. But the unanswered question was: what are we fighting for? While the American nation had become the most powerful and vital collective entity in the world, Americans proved "unable to accommodate themselves spiritually and practically to that fact."

So far, the twentieth century had been a profound and tragic disappointment, Luce wrote. If it was now to come to life healthy and vigorous, it "must be to a significant degree an American century." Americans were the inheritors of the great principles of Western civilization: justice, truth, and charity. They also had special traits: love of freedom, belief in equality of opportunity, traditions of self-reliance and voluntary cooperation. Luce concluded, "It now becomes our time to be the powerhouse from which these ideals spread throughout the world and do their mysterious work of lifting the life of mankind from the level of the beasts to what the Psalmist called a little lower than the angels." This, Luce declared, was a vision to which Americans could adhere with purpose and high resolve.[8]

Consistent with this new interest, Luce introduced an editorial page to *Life* in 1942. As all *Time-Life* editors understood, this was his page.[9] Priorities within the corporate organization were also rearranged. Luce wrote to a colleague a few years later: "As long as I live, the editorial aims and responsibility of Time, Inc. will take precedence over business considerations."[10]

To some degree, America's active entry into the war following Pearl Harbor diverted energies and attention away from these new purposes. A global war simply provided a photojournalism magazine too much good material. By the mid-1940s however, with peace on the horizon, Luce returned to brooding over the larger questions of national purpose. The results of the war confirmed his belief that the burden of Western civilization had passed to American shoulders; indeed, he would draw a basic equation between Western civilization and the American way of life. As Luce instructed *Life* managing editor Joseph Thorndike in 1947: "If Western Civilization is to be saved, the U.S. must be the principal agent of salvation. . . . And *what* is to be saved? Here I become indeed the barbaric yawper and say, also, in a word, America."[11]

LESS THAN A NATION?

Yet Luce feared that in assuming its new responsibilities, America might lose its distinctive sense of identity and purpose. The "co-mingling of cultures," he acknowledged, seemed to be already occurring: "America is today indeed one of the great—perhaps the only very great—'internationale.'" This was troubling, for Luce believed that living cultures were born and matured in relative isolation. These facts confronted America with great peril: "America can gain the whole world—either by . . . 'assimilation' or by the gravity of power—and lose its soul." In Asia, he noted, there was no real drive to continue Asiatic culture as such. Western civilization, on the other hand, "at least . . . fights to maintain itself." But to maintain a distinctive American identity, there must be no global "culture-by-merger."[12] Instead, Americans must learn that the drama of the Western world culminated in the creation of the United States. They needed to understand their civilization "at the moment of history when the U.S. has become the heir and guardian of the whole body of Western Civilization against the forces of reactionary neo-barbarism."[13]

As Luce saw it, one major handicap to the American global position lay in the fact that, despite its wartime victory, America remained less than a nation. Writing to Reinhold Niebuhr, Luce argued that the United States, "far from having a strong George Washington belief in the rightness of its cause at home and abroad, is actually very uncertain of itself, very divided and confused in its soul." America, he believed, was "a powerful country dissipating its power, tragically, on a false and stultifying defensive."[14] Complicating the situation still further was the specter of the Soviet Union. As early as July 1945, Luce had labeled Russia "the number one problem for America."[15] A huge and powerful nation–state highly assertive of its interests, and a country that served as the center of the politically powerful communist movement, the Soviet Union represented a formidable rival for world influence. Moreover, it was able to play a political and propaganda role within the United States that was unavailable to America within the USSR.

Facing this reality, Luce saw the critical need, as he later put it, "to validate America for its own sake and for its mission in the world."[16] Pursuit of this goal required broad attention to the whole of life. The spirit of the age could not be simply discovered or accepted: it needed to be shaped. As Luce phrased it: "history usually moves *upstream.*"[17] Leadership in the mid-twentieth century meant giving Americans the common identity, values, and confidence that would sustain them in bearing their responsibilities overseas.

Born in China, the son of American Presbyterian missionaries, Luce never developed a tie to any American city or region as "home." Rather, from his first years, Luce saw America as a unified place, a complete entity existing above its particularities. His education at the British School in Chefoo, an institution governed by the British code of "flogging and fagging and toadying," further impressed on him American distinctiveness, with hardly an hour passing in which the Americans in the school "didn't have to run up the flag." Luce later reported that he never went through a period of disillusionment with his homeland. Indeed, everything about America excited and interested him. The United States was a unique nation, brought into being under God's providence, with a singular mission in the world: in short, Americans were a people on a pilgrimage. Yet Luce was also vexed by the imperfections of his country. In his words, America's failures meant that she "was not being as great and good as I knew she could be, as I believed with every nerve and fiber God himself had intended her to be."

It was a reflection of his Calvinist upbringing that Luce believed that good works, along with faith and divine election, bore a relation to personal salvation. He was a God-driven man, an optimist informed by Christian hope. Denying all determinisms, he argued that it was the inspired individual—"his dreams, his indignation, his inventions"— who shaped events. He wrote: "the mutations in human nature that mark the evolution of man must start with one or a few individuals, who in a manner beyond our understanding become possessed of and by the ideal to be proclaimed, the new vision of the eternal *logos*." Accordingly, he set out to make a difference in history; he believed his calling in the post-World War II era was to impress the mark of his vision on human events. As Luce told his Time, Inc. colleagues in 1950: "I have a faithful belief that the America that we work for will win in this time and age, if we do our part. . . . [I]n a sense, *everything does depend on you*." If the editors of *Life*, *Time*, and *Fortune* persevered, he concluded, their lifetime would see "not the peace of God, but certainly the truce of God won by American fortitude, energy, generosity, and ideals."[18]

In 1945, Luce began to try to create a new sense of shared purpose and community for postwar America. The necessary vision, he believed, must be larger than the one reflected in the rural, small-town nostalgia found in *Reader's Digest* or the *Saturday Evening Post*, which he believed to be an image inextricably tied to the Anglo-Saxon, Protestant, farm-oriented, isolationist America of the nineteenth century. The new America must come to terms with the massive wave of immigration from southern and eastern Europe. It must incorporate religious traditions beyond the mainline Protestant faiths, embody the full legacy of Western civilization, and gird itself emotionally for the longterm contest with the Soviet Union.

Luce's central assumption was that this new American civilization would find its locus and social expression in the burgeoning suburbs. In a 1944 *Life* planning memo, he noted that the American scene "must have totally new expression" after the war. Even before the war, Luce continued, American life was undergoing vast changes. The cities were emptying as the auto took people into the countryside. "That trend will certainly accelerate in the postwar period," he concluded, which translated into "a great publishing opportunity" for someone in the mass marketing field.[19]

Luce emphasized the critical role that magazine journalism could play in shaping this emerging new America. "We believe in journalism," he wrote to Thorndike. "[W]e believe it is absolutely essential for the successful passage of the human race through this period of history." Inescapably bound to the fate of democracy, journalism must now "fight its way through to a better and brighter world—or at least perish honorably in the attempt." Believing also in the "on balance good of what we call America," *Life* editors tried to lead Americans though the perils of the age, defending liberty while avoiding anarchy, so that, "with our readers, we can press on to that which is more excellent."[20]

Americans, Luce believed, lacked not only a common worldview but also a shared sense of place. Without a deep emotional attachment to place, he said, civilization was impossible. "We need much more of it in America," Luce concluded in a report to his senior staff. "And then we must seek how this may be compatible with modern conditions of life which tend to cancel dimensions of time and space."[21]

Accordingly, Luce thought the key function of the press was to provide readers with a recognizable picture of their environment. This was especially true for the United States, since "we Americans, more than other peoples, need to know who we are, where we are . . . , pilgrims of what hope."[22] Toward this end, Luce and his executive committee contemplated the introduction of a new magazine, to be called *Measure*, which would feature extended essays. To be edited by Willi Schlamm, *Measure* was to look at America as a civilization. In exploring the choice between right and wrong, the magazine's prospectus explained, it would insist on the right. By presenting a coherent picture of developments in American life, and by featuring the preferences and images of a national, rather than a regional, civilization, *Measure* would "participate in the making of history." Possible articles, according to Schlamm, would include a discussion by one of "the last Mohicans of Determinism" on how to reconcile materialistic dogma with moral values, and a piece on the mounting interest in interdenominational understanding, "what some people already call 'an American Church-in-Progress.'"[23]

Yet *Measure* never saw the light of day in this form. The planned first issue, featuring essays by distinguished contributors such as Niebuhr and Arnold Toynbee, was scrapped for lack of a readily identifiable central focus. Instead, *Life* increasingly became the vehicle for Luce's nation- and civilization-building agenda. As Luce instructed his managing editor, *Life*'s editorial purpose was to interpret American life to citizens "and in interpretation give leadership toward the promotion and defense of what we feel to be good and correction to that which is poor or bad."[24] *Life*'s format, he told an associate, offered a tremendous opportunity: "Life as it is lived in America today is a strange and wonderful tension between the particular little problems of little people (all of us and our families) and the surge of great 'historic forces.'" In one magazine, though, *Life* brought together, in a mutually reinforcing fashion, attention to these little episodes and an intelligent disclosure of the historic forces at work. It showed, through a kind of osmosis, how the small events combined to form the flow of a nation.[25] Moreover, the "special magic of pictures" was that they could make the normal and the good interesting. Accordingly, as a picture magazine, *Life* could both play a profoundly moral role and also contribute to the building of a civilization.[26] The goal in all of this, Luce stated, was to instill a sense of history and destiny in the average American— to show "that 'civilization' isn't just a word—it's a something that 'means you!'"[27]

RELIGIOUS QUESTIONS

In pursuit of his vision, Luce faced three major philosophical problems, each decidedly religious in nature. The first of these might be labeled the "generic" religious question: Could Americans reconcile religious belief with modern liberal democracy? Luce believed that the United States was the "supreme embodiment" of "the Great Liberal Tradition." If even for one generation Americans forgot what it meant to be liberal, he said, then the nation would no longer be itself "but just one more stupid, fear-ridden empire ready to be carted away to the natural-history museum of human failure." Recognizing the great disasters of the twentieth century—World Wars I and II, fascism, communism—Luce took heart that America now led "a last great effort" to establish in the world the liberal principles of political freedom, equal justice, freedom of thought and opinion, and common decency among men. Yet he fretted over the decay of this tradition in the nineteenth century, and traced this failure to the fact that "the struggle for liberty was too often anti-religious and religion was too often anti-liberty." In contrast, Luce saw religion and morality as "fundamental" to liberty, for it was only those citizens who considered themselves accountable to an authority higher than government who could honestly argue for the right to govern themselves.[28]

In the United States, Luce argued, it was Christianity that had to provide the liberal tradition with moral coherence. In his time, at least, there was no other practical alternative. The nation had been born through "the happy concurrence" of strong Christian faith and a distinctive version of the Enlightenment that was anti-clerical but not anti-religious. "[S]urely the only Christian hope for our country," he concluded, "is that there should once again occur, by God's grace, a dynamic tension between strong Christian faith and a society of political freedom." But the internal weaknesses of the culturally dominant Protestant churches in America posed a dilemma. Modern Protestantism, Luce stated, gave "the impression of believing in everything except God." The social Gospel movement had degenerated into idolatrous worship of the "god of sociology." The mainline churches everywhere exhibited "excessive compromise with secularism." Luce speculated in 1946 that, even in this weakened condition, America probably had sufficient moral capital "to see us through for two or three decades of immensely successful effort." But after that interval, the dangers would mount.[29]

He concluded that America must quickly recover its intellectual moorings in the moral law, which he understood as embracing both the Roman Catholic tradition of natural law and the Calvinist emphasis on orders of creation. In a 1951 address at Southern Methodist University, Luce attacked the "materialism, relativism, agnosticism, and . . . cynicism" of the legal tradition represented by Oliver Wendell Holmes. Luce declared, "we ought to believe what is true, . . . that we live in a moral universe, that the laws of this country . . . are invalid and will be in fact inoperative except as they conform to a moral order which is universal in time and space." The secular order conformed to the spiritual order only when citizens accepted—through reason if not through faith—the moral basis of all things. Four years later, in a speech at St. Louis University, Luce praised Walter Lippmann for popularizing the phrase, "the public philosophy," which Luce saw as akin to the moral law.[30] In the same vein, Luce concurred with one of his editors that *Life* could make no greater contribution to the American scene "than to hammer away at the meaning of the word 'moral,' whether we come at it through religion, politics, or any cultural subject."[31]

The second difficulty confronted by Luce could be labeled "the Catholic problem." The publisher's well-known affection for Roman Catholic themes and personalities has usually been attributed to the influence of his wife, Clare Boothe Luce, perhaps the most famous of Catholic converts in America during the 1940s. Indeed, when Joseph Thorndike resigned as managing editor of *Life* in November 1948, he privately confided to his associate and successor, Edward Thompson, that he worried about the Catholic Church taking over the magazine.[32] Yet it seems clear that Luce's public celebration of Catholicism had deeper motivations. He recognized, perhaps better than any of his contemporaries, that a unified America could not be active in the world without the loyalty of its largest single religious denomination. Instead of a Kulturkampf, as had occurred in late nineteenth-century Germany, designed to push Catholicism into the margins of society, Luce sought to bring it into a new democratic synthesis. Moreover, the internal rot affecting mainline Protestantism convinced Luce that his project for the restoration of an American "public philosophy," which rested on the moral law, needed other theological supports. Catholicism, with its deep attachment to natural law doctrine, was the obvious candidate.

These motivations explain Luce's close intellectual attachment to John Courtney Murray, Jesuit theologian and author of *We Hold These Truths: Catholic Reflections on the American Proposition*. Like Luce, Murray devoted his energies during the 1940s and 1950s to the development of a new American public philosophy that would unify America, give Americans a shared identity, and, for the first time, wholly embrace the Catholic community. Murray explained that the old consensus, rooted in Protestant America, had eroded. "[T]here is today," he said, "a need for a new moral act of purpose and a new act of intellectual affirmation, comparable to those which launched the American constitutional commonwealth, that will put us in possession of the public philosophy."

Also like Luce, Murray recognized that his era was witness to a sociocultural revolution focused on the suburbs. Catholic ethnic neighborhoods were clearly disappearing; Murray saw a new suburban layman emerging, one who was casting off ethnic loyalties for the "great ascent" into the American middle class. As a response, Murray encouraged the reformulation of faith practices that had rested on obediential relations to spiritual authority. He believed this would equip suburbanized laymen with a Catholicism strong enough to be "plunged into the modern secularized milieu and confidently left to inner resources of a mature faith that is able to stand *by itself*, supported by the strength of its own deeply experienced reality."

Murray also shared with Luce a desire to differentiate American liberal ideals from continental liberalism. The latter system, rooted in Jacobin precepts, had proved hostile to religious faith, while the former had proved compatible. Moreover, both the Church and American liberalism in the mid-twentieth century were threatened by communism.

With a common enemy, Catholicism and liberal democracy could be drawn together; yet Murray claimed that this "negative consensus" was no firm guide to public policy. He shared Luce's contention that the American consensus must be a version of the natural law. The United States, Murray argued, had been founded within that tradition. It had been Protestantism, "especially its left wing," which had subsequently evolved away from the English natural law framework, leaving the nation adrift. Consequently, the "basic moral laws of human life," sanctioned by both divine authority and the traditions of liberal democracy, would need new affirmation as the foundation of a common American identity.[33]

Murray became a regular contributor to the pages of *Time* and *Life*. In 1951, *Time* labeled him a "cucumber-cool intellectual," "a towering figure among U.S. Catholic scholars," who was "the spearhead of a bold attempt to reconcile traditional Catholic church–state doctrine with U.S. practice." Nine years later, he had graduated to the cover. Murray's contributions to *Life* included the "Catholic article" in *Life*'s 1955 special issue on Christianity, where he laid out the great challenge to Catholicism: "How shall the immense energies resident in the faith of the laity be fully utilized in the work of God's kingdom—which is, importantly, the work of freedom and justice in America and in the world community?"[34]

The Problem of Mammon

The third difficulty Luce faced—perhaps the most personally vexing—was the material problem: how could modern America reconcile great wealth and abundant leisure with moral purpose and spiritual vitality? Here American life confronted its greatest quandaries. "It is not the poverty which is now the great challenge, but the wealth," Luce said in 1946. "Not the weakness, but the power. Not the illiteracy, but the literacy. Not the disease, but the health. Not the back-breaking toil, but the play and the pleasure. Not the squalor, but the lights."[35]

Reflecting his works-oriented Calvinism, Luce saw production and consumption as divine commands that mere humans could not ignore. "The smallness of our national production today is a national disgrace," he argued in 1937, "a wicked disobedience of the ancient injunction to increase and multiply." Americans, he added, must steel themselves for a change of mind toward "the new doctrine of potential abundance."[36]

Yet Luce also fretted about the debilitating impact of material goods and leisure, wondering how Americans could inform with Christian faith and virtue "so vast a prosperity and so great a power."[37]

The central problem facing modern America, Luce concluded, was "how to enjoy what we have" without succumbing to the thrall of mammon.[38] One of the dominant characteristics of Western civilization, he wrote in a planning memorandum, was "the legitimacy of man's fullest enjoyment of life on earth," a proposition symbolized by the distinctively American phrase, "the pursuit of happiness." Such pursuit, Luce added, even represented a kind of duty. In consequence, capitalism had to be maintained, "its defects or obsolescences removed and its merits developed." Moreover, the West could be "saved" only if the "door for enjoyment of the 'good life' in its physical or 'natural' aspects" was kept wide open.[39]

Magazine journalists could play a uniquely creative role here. With the postwar cornucopia of consumer goods, Luce wrote in a May 1945 planning document, America would enter a "super-colossal Adventure into Prosperity." *Fortune,* he said, could make its contribution by turning this adventure "into something which we shall not be ashamed to call Civilization."[40] Yet in facing up to mammon, Luce placed the greater burden on *Life.* Advertising presented the central difficulty. There was "no greater propaganda of materialism than American advertising," he said, no other medium which so inflamed appetites and urged readers to material satisfactions. Was advertising "therefore just plain and unqualified wrong in any serious moral philosophy?" he asked in a confidential letter to the senior *Life* staff. No, he answered, at least not in the judgment of Christian morality, for orthodox theology "does not separate matter and spirit into two different worlds of evil and good."

Christianity, Luce explained, knew the corruption of both body and spirit, and of "the inherent dangers to the life of the spirit in the life of the flesh." From this recognition, faith imposed rules of morality on "the body" in recognition of its role as the "temple of the Holy Spirit." Hence, there was nothing immoral about the production, distribution, and advertising of material goods. The task, Luce said, was to ensure that such things were used for "good" rather than "bad" ends, that the hankering for material goods did not in itself produce evil. The dangers of materialism, he concluded, could "be equated with nothing less than the whole spiritual, political and economic problem of the U.S.—and as such, *Life* must try to make a contribution throughout . . . its editorial pages."

The magazine's Modern Living section, he said, would serve "as the nexus between The Editorial and The Advertising." At a minimum, this section must promote good taste, for "[j]ust as there is a close connection between manners and morals, so there is a close connection between taste and spirit." If all Americans could not be spiritual, at least they could have good taste, "the minimum creed of the decent cynic." Luce was well aware of the "vast incongruity" between the happily abundant life which people might live and the "unhappily abundant life which they do live." *Life's* Modern Living section should therefore describe how a thoughtful, tasteful epicureanism might yield greater enjoyment, and "thereby justify the otherwise unforgiveable materialism of American Advertising."[41]

"THE NEW AMERICA"

Henry Luce's attempt at nation-building, and his creative mixture of editorial and advertising methods directed toward this end, received dramatic visual confirmation in 1947 in a major promotional campaign for *Life* built on the theme, "The New America." Five *Life* photographers were sent by chartered plane across the United States for eight weeks. Using special panoramic cameras, they took 14,000 exposures, which were eventually edited down to 127 sequences. These were put together into a slide-record presentation, using the Picturama process pioneered by Eastman Kodak for the 1939-40 New York World's Fair, and featuring five synchronized projectors, a new fade-in-and-out technique, and a forty-foot screen. Composer Paul Creston contributed a fresh, stirring, musical score.

The presentation's principle theme was that the America of 1947 and the America of the mid-1930s were "almost two different countries, so huge are the changes that have increased our national stature." The components of this New America were:

Demographic Expansion. The script celebrated the return of population growth to America, the surging American birthrate. Since 1940, the U.S. population had grown by ten million, providing new customers with "greater wants and greater buying powers." At county fairs, there were "great new crowds of people being happily taken in by the preposterous exaggeration of the alluring and glittering midway." On "Main Street, we cannot fail to see that there are many more of us, more people in stores, more people with more money." The glitter everywhere proclaimed "how many more Americans there are to enjoy the pleasant things of our national life." There were mushrooming numbers of new suburban grade schools. Over the last forty years, high school attendance had swelled 888 percent. College enrollments were at an all-time high. Everywhere, there was growth.

The New Family. Since 1940, five million new families had formed in America, an increase of nearly 15 percent. Moreover, vast numbers of families were climbing into the middle class. In 1937, only 7 million U.S. families had an annual income over $2,000. Ten years later, the incomes of nearly 28 million families exceeded that figure. In consequence, "we see all around us the pleasant homes of American citizens," and "one of the greatest reasons for our confidence in future prosperity lies in the number of homes that must be built, furnished and equipped." As another "spontaneous expression of our widely shared standard of living," family members were turning avidly toward sports, confirming that "the great size and energy of the New America as a nation and as a market is sharply pointed up."

Economic Growth. World War II, according to the presentation, taught Americans that economic miracles do happen. We had discovered "new muscles and new abilities." Seven million new jobs had been created since 1940, confirming "our tremendous ability to produce." Moreover, the United States now stood "on the threshold of a hall of wonders," with American business poised to "forge ahead and do the job that needs to be done."

Spiritual Reawakening. The New America also had a "significant spiritual quality," manifested "in our devotion to many religions, . . . our love of our country, and respect for our national decency, our love of our children, and our grandchildren, and our faith in the American way of life." These values undergirded "our new-found confidence, our awakening to the new and almost limitless opportunities which lie within our power." The New America had rediscovered the nation's historic "mission of freedom." This freedom was "part of our daily commercial life[,] . . . the bulwark of our success and hopes." Accordingly, power and freedom were, at this moment in history, "American phenomen[a]." The nation stood at "the dawn of its greatness."

Life magazine: At the heart of this New America was *Life*. As a brochure handed out at the Picturama showings explained, the growth of the magazine had paralleled the great growth of the United States. *Life* had met "the ever-broadening interests of the American people—their mounting intelligent curiosity to know more about their own country and the world at large." The nearly 15 million "*Life*-reading families" represented 36 percent of all families in the country. *Life* was clearly "the greatest advertising force in the New America."[42]

There is evidence that *Life*'s "New America" project played a significant role in shaping the manner in which influential Americans understood their nation. Between 1947 and 1948, the Picturama show played before 175,000 persons in sixty cities. The audiences at these invitation-only events were composed of business, community, media, and political leaders. In Hollywood, organizers held four special showings for members of the Academy of Motion Picture Arts and Sciences. In Washington, D.C., two showings in March 1947 reached 65 percent of the members of Congress, a quorum of the Supreme Court, a majority of Cabinet members, Generals Eisenhower and Bradley, Admirals King and Leahy, and the elite of the Ambassadorial corps. Dwight Eisenhower subsequently complimented Luce for seeing in an advertising campaign "the possibility of providing to large numbers of people a better idea of the country in which we are living." Indeed, Eisenhower soon became a one-man promoter of the show. At a September banquet of the American Meat Institute, he used his speech to label the Picturama show "one of the most beautiful things I have ever seen, . . . a thrilling experience to anyone who loves his country."[43]

Other letters and commentaries testified to the show's remarkable impact. U.S. Senator Charles Tobey, Chairman of the Committee on Banking and Currency, said that "The New America" had "the effect of a sermon on my soul. . . . If that picture can be shown throughout the country it will do more to stimulate faith in this country and zeal for greater responsibility and effort on the part of the citizens than anything else that could be done." U.S. Chief Justice Frederick Vinson exclaimed that after seeing the film he was "prouder than ever to be an American." W. Ward Marsh, editor of the *Cleveland Plain Dealer*, also turned to the superlative: "I cannot think of a single other thing, deed, picture, or event which carries more timely, more needed inspiration, more hope for all of us than *Life*'s 'The New America.'" Paul F. Douglass, president of American University, underscored the mind and purpose behind the project:

> [I]t means so much to know that our greatest journalistic force expresses a robust faith in our own economic and spiritual destiny. To speak to millions each week with a confidence which is both deserved and necessary to our achievement is a historic editorial performance and a fountain of the psychological fortitude upon which our hope must rest. To believe in America now is so basic and to portray it so vividly as you are doing *means that we are to have a cohesive faith which can stand the test.*[44]

The Luce-inspired understanding of the New America even carried overseas, as the Army's Civil Affairs division arranged with Time, Inc. for six months of Picturama showings to the citizens of occupied Germany, Austria, Japan, and Korea. As General Robert McClure explained, his division was using the show "to enlighten the people in occupied countries concerning the true facts and advantages of the American way of life."[45]

RENEWING A CIVILIZATION

In one respect, between 1945 and 1964 *Life* merely presented the tangled flow of events and celebrities that marked the period. It ran features on the golden gods of Hollywood, reports on the vitality of small-town America, photo essays on America's war in Korea, and pictures of beach fashions featuring eye-catching female cleavage. Yet within its reams of pages, particularly in special issues and feature stories, Luce's conscious efforts to renew a civilization and build a New America are clear.

The civilization theme found full expression in *Life*'s series on the history of the Western world, which ran between 1947 and 1948. The early episodes on "Renaissance Man" and "The Middle Ages" were, in Luce's words, "remarkably successful in showing to even the casual beholder that there was (is) such a thing as Western civilization that makes it worth 'preserving.'" Luce identified three "superlative values" that characterized the Western ethos: Christianity, freedom, and material advance. The unifying goal of the series was to show "how historic forces and occurrences, under Providence, brought about the USA,"

and how the United States had brought these three values to full con-
summation. As Luce wrote: "today in the U.S., in the midst of all the
most widespread materialistic, pleasure-yielding culture the world has
ever seen, we have both of the great branches of Christianity showing
many evidences of vitality."[46]

Nation-building work surfaced in major essays such as Evelyn
Waugh's "The American Epoch in the Catholic Church." Sent by *Life*
on a four-month tour of Catholic America, Waugh reported in a September 1948 article that "Providence is schooling and strengthening a
people for the historic destiny long borne by Europe." The goal of the
enormous Catholic educational edifice in America, he said, was "to
transform a proletariat into a bourgeoisie, to produce a faithful laity,
qualified to take its part in the general life of the nation; and in this
way they are manifestly successful." There were those in America,
Waugh said, who wanted to create a homogeneous society, where Catholics, Protestants, Jews, and the adherents to all other sects differed only
in the rites they practiced for two hours on a Sunday morning. He labeled this view, "pure make-believe." Yet, Waugh's article concluded
with a strangely incongruous paragraph (possibly added during the
editorial process) stating that "[t]here is a purely American 'way of
life' led by every good American Christian. . . . And that by the Grace
of God is the 'way of life' that will prevail." Photos accompanying the
essay reinforced these themes, showing author Waugh on a romp with
his own small children in England, Catholic girls studying to become
Christian wives and mothers, and portraits of bishops with diverse
ethnic backgrounds.[47]

Luce also worked to define more precisely the social order of the
New America. Population growth, for example, was celebrated in a
1958 cover story titled "KIDS: Built-In Recession Cure; How 4,000,000
a Year Makes Billions in Business."[48] The article trumpeted the fact
that the "number of U.S. small fry is rocketing upward at a phenom-
enal clip, bringing sentimental delight to parents and totally unsenti-
mental pleasure to the nation's economists." Each new citizen, the article said, was a brand-new market for food, shelter, and clothing. Recession may threaten, but there were both "enduring" and "endear-
ing" prospects for prosperity "in the nurseries and on the play grounds."
The number of American families had climbed from 32 million in 1940
to 43 million in 1958, and "[j]ust as impressive has been the return of
the old-fashioned large family." In consequence, 49 million new Ameri-

cans had arrived since 1940, and the first group of these postwar babies was now creating a huge market for teenagers' goods and services. *Life* looked confidently to the decade ahead when these youth would themselves be marrying and forming families. Photos showed a new baby surrounded by the $800 worth of products he would consume in his first year, and featured the ten-child family of Joe and Carol Powers of Port Washington, New York, Americans who "find so much pleasure in growing up together that they never think of themselves the way an economist might, as ten more potential boom-breeding families."

The 1957 special *Life* issue on "The American Woman" presented a strong affirmation of traditional gender roles within the family. Although one article dealt with the problems faced by women in the workplace, the overwhelming thrust of the issue was to affirm the housewife and mother. Especially notable was Margaret Mead's essay on the historic American woman, in which the anthropologist argued that the ideal family in America was one where the wife did not work. The only truly acceptable pattern in American life, she said, was marriage, while the home was still, "as it has been through the ages, women's natural habitat." The editorial in that issue, "Woman, Love, and God," presented the Virgin Mary as symbol of "the love of which Americans stand in most need," and as the model for American women in their sustenance of the home.

The concluding essay was a full-fledged assault on equity feminism. That ideology now seemed "as quaint as linen dusters and high buttoned shoes," wrote author Robert Coughlan, yet it had yielded one fatal consequence, the "career woman." Most working wives, he argued, should return home. "If they are feminine women, with truly feminine attitudes, they will . . . accept their wifely functions with good humor and pleasure." Coughlan saw a hopeful sign in the high birth rate, which suggested that women were "putting a higher premium on motherhood." Beyond that, there was the "astonishing" reappearance of the old fashioned three-to-five-child family in the middle-class suburbs. Even technology, which had once disrupted the home, seemed now to be pulling the family back together. Radio and television had made the home once again the center of recreation. Automated washers gave mothers more time to spend with their children. The dramatic rise in home ownership found father building a barbecue, painting shutters, and pursuing other tasks of symbolic value to his wife. On these suburban foundations, Coughlan concluded, "a new . . . society" was emerging in which "men are men, women are women and quietly, pleasantly, securely confident of which they are."[49]

Life wrestled frequently with the problem of materialism. A 1948 roundtable on the meaning of "the pursuit of happiness" brought together philosopher Sidney Hook; psychologist Erich Fromm; 1948 Mother of the Year, Mrs. Herbert Hines; president of Lever Brothers, Charles Luckman; and "observer," Henry Luce. Preliminary discussions among Jeffersonian scholars, *Life* reported, had demonstrated agreement that Jefferson's intention in coining the phrase pursuit of happiness, had been to give every man the right to interpret for himself the *nature* of happiness. Yet this did not mean moral anarchy. Rather, it was "precisely because man is capable of recognizing the good that he is entitled to pursue happiness in his own way." In grappling with the phrase's significance for contemporary America, the panelists concentrated on the areas of work, leisure, movies, and advertising. Concerning the latter, the panelists agreed that advertising was "a key to the high standard of living" in America, and so was "important to the pursuit of happiness." Beatrice Gould, editor of *Ladies Home Journal*, added that advertising was also "part of the civilization which it both reflects and influences," and so bore a profound moral quality, for good or for ill.[50]

America's religious dimension also drew frequent *Life* attention. A special December 1955 issue on Christianity opened with the observation that as "the Christian era moved toward its 1,956th year, the sights and sounds of an unprecedented revival in religious belief and practice were everywhere in the U.S." Three of every five Americans belonged to some Christian church. In Denver alone, forty-five new churches had been started in only ten months. This growth testified "both to the biggest building boom in church history and to the greatest revolution in ecclesiastical architecture since the Renaissance." Even Harvard University's Divinity School, another article reported, was returning to "the mainstream of church life and devotion." Modern electronics, it noted, were also being used to improve the preaching techniques of seminarians, representing the fusion of past and future.

True, there were sour notes in the issue, such as Paul Tillich's warning that "if Christianity ever dies in America, it will die in the American suburban church." Yet the issue's editorial, "The American Moral Consensus," set the dominant theme. America was not "secular, top to bottom," as charged by some historians. Rather, there was "no wall at all between religion and the American political system." Prayer and religious devotion undergirded the American proposition. Even Tom Paine, "the miscalled atheist," based his argument for the equality of human rights on the fact that "every child born into the world must be considered as deriving its existence from God." In short, the editorial argued that while "anyone can be a good American . . . the ultimate guarantee of his freedom is in America's being a religious nation." The United States was predicated on the Aristotelian belief that politics is a branch of morals, and Washington's declaration that morality is a branch of religion. Accordingly, American constitutionalism was designed to keep the land's laws and institutions in harmony with the natural law, ordained by God. *Life* concluded:

> No doubt most Americans are less religious than they should be. They then owe a vast and continuing debt to the saving remnant in their midst, who do hunger and thirst after righteousness and walk humbly before their God. They do not do this for America's sake; but without them America would be little more than a geographical expression.[51]

BUILDINGS AND BASEBALL

Other Luce initiatives in this era had the same underlying purpose of reinforcing an American identity resting on family and morality. American architecture was a recurring fascination for him: "my favorite mid-century topic," he called it. Back in 1932, Luce had stated that "to influence architecture is to influence life." This was never truer than in the postwar era, when Americans were seized by the challenge of shaping a civilization. Addressing the American Institute of Architects, Luce challenged them to be "the men who, in the fullness of time, made God's country a splendid habitation for God's most fortunate children." American architects had the additional task of reconciling design with the democratic ideal. As Luce declared: "Our welcome shopping centers, our cheerful new schools, our glass-front banks, all emphatically say democracy."[52]

Accordingly, the great suburban housing boom drew Luce's rapt attention and intervention. Time, Inc., acquired the journal *Architec-*

tural Forum: The Magazine of Building in 1935 and quickly moved into a crusading mode. In 1952, Luce created a separate edition of the magazine, *House & Home,* designed for subdivision developers and home contractors.

These publications reflected, in part, Luce's ebullience over the familistic shape of the New America. The Federal Housing Administration (FHA) mortgage insurance program, a 1957 editorial in *Architectural Forum* recorded, had established for the first time a national mortgage market. This capital market had, in turn, created a new private-enterprise industry, changed the whole pattern of cities, and stimulated major changes in "American habits of living." Above all, "the new FHA land" had become "the New Suburbia," a place "occupied by people who looked alike in being young married couples with young children. . . . There was virtually a new class in America—the FHA Class."[53] The inaugural editorial for *House & Home* underscored how the industrial revolution had finally reached the housing industry, a revolution "to which, in other fields, we owe every advance in living standards since colonial times." The editors continued:

> *House & Home* takes its name from the belief that our industry owes the American Family far more than shelter. If the good life is to be the heritage of every American we must build into our houses, from early design to closing finance, all the satisfactions that make a house a home.

There were "deep-seated, age-old, never satisfied desires that make families want houses of their own." Only professionals with a sense of duty could "create for every man a home for the good life."[54]

The Luce publications frequently gave voice to a kind of family-centered populism. Characteristic in this regard was *Architectural Forum*'s discussion of the Levittown developments on Long Island. In 1949, the magazine noted—with sympathetic overstatement—the "eerie similarity" of Levittown's new inhabitants: "The men all look about the same age: there is something military about their stride and their overcoats. The women are pretty. . . . Each set of parents has exactly two offspring in tow, and the offspring are, respectively, exactly 32 and 36 in. high." Chiding modern architects for their fascination with flat roofs, the Levitt brothers marketed the peaked roofs of their houses as "expansion attics" that made it comfortable for families to add "a third party to the standard ratio of two offspring per bungalow." In build-

ing homes for veterans and their young families, the Levitts emphasized certain guiding principles: "the $7,900 for which we sell our house
is a device by which a few thoughts of the progressive architects can be
given to the public"; "we . . . prefer to cut the price to reach a still lower
income group"; and (in explaining the lack of garage in the basic Levitt
home) "until people are decently housed, [we] believe we have no more
right to house autos."[55] A space-ad for *Life* magazine that appeared in
House & Home underscored how housing fit into the larger vision of
Henry Luce: "The Home Today . . . and what is happening to it . . . is
big news to the nation, as the home-building industry approaches
tomorrow's goal—a stable volume of 1,000,000 new homes every year.
And in the course of 13 issues, *half this nation reads* Life."[56]

There was, however, another side to Luce's enthusiasm for the
suburban revolution. To begin with, both *Architectural Forum* and
House & Home showed a studied contempt for earlier housing styles,
from Queen Anne to Victorian to Arts and Crafts to Twentieth-Century Colonial. Such designs were entirely unsuited to "today's ideas of
space, view, and convenience" and needed to be remodeled into "something more genuine."[57] This rejection of the old was complemented by
an undiluted enthusiasm for the modern, international style. With rare
exceptions, the Luce publications featured only modern architects
working in the spirit of Le Corbusier, Gropius, Van der Rohe, Breuer,
and the Bauhaus school.[58] When *Architectural Forum* did carry a long
essay on "the debacle of popular taste" that decried "the raucous ugliness which is taking over the land," it was to denounce the Victorian
architecture on Main Street, the English half-timber and Dutch Colonial homes built in the 1920s, and Mission Oak furniture. By way of
contrast, the magazine praised "development housing," its "crisp contemporary designs" and the "handsome, regional shopping centers"
that typically accompanied it. The author of this piece mocked Americans who, when they saw a modern house, called it "a chicken coop."
What Americans actually needed, she insisted, was education in the
beautiful principles of modern architecture.[59]

Beauty here meant flat roofs, vast expanses of glass, inconspicu-
ous front doors, the absence of porches, large backyard patios, high
fences, and "clean and simple" lines.[60] While most of these designs included large "family rooms," they seem in retrospect strangely alien,
sterile, and lifeless. Arguing that "form follows function," the modern
architects profiled in *House & Home* built an "absolutely private" world

for inward-looking "companionship families" stripped of their productive functions, shut off from neighbors, and focused instead on mutual "personality adjustments."[61] The Luce publications also heaped praise on the huge, multilevel shopping malls designed by Victor Gruen, and on the new federal superhighway program that promised "a much-improved America." In other words, Luce's enthusiasm for the New Suburbia, inspired by genuine affection and concern for the vibrant young families that were its inhabitants, spread to the very design and planning attributes that would, two decades later, sour the suburban dream.

As architecture was to civilization in Luce's plans, so sports was to nation-building: an opportunity for journalistic intervention on behalf of higher goals. As Luce wrote to advertising executive Leo Burnett: "The greatest common denominator of leisure activity and of human conversation among Americans pursuing happiness is—Sport."[62] The problem lay in the segmented, class-bound, and regional nature of most sporting contests. The shared American fascination with sport had no unifying interpretive source.[63]

Luce crafted a response. The first issue of *Sports Illustrated,* dated August 16, 1954, featured the pace-setting essay, "The Golden Age is Now." Breathlessly, the writer hopped from sport to sport, arguing that "this golden age in scores of ways outstrips and outdazzles them all." Rather than a dream world, "the world of sport, booming as it is everywhere, may be keeping another world from blowing its top, literally and figuratively." In the worldwide struggle for freedom, the reporter added, sport "demonstrates everyday its own brand of freedom which makes it possible [for man] to do anything he has enough will to do [as in the example](score: Free Germany 3, Red Hungary 2)."[64] *Sports Illustrated,* Luce concluded, would be "the respected voice of an immense American and democratic public . . . the million leaders in America's glorious quest for happiness." For the first time in its history, America would have "a great sports magazine."[65]

By the late 1950s, Luce seemed to take some satisfaction that his work was showing results. In a remarkable memorandum arguing against a proposed price increase for *Life,* Luce declared:

> The great significance of *Life* is that it includes among its readers all manners and kinds of Americans. . . . *Life* is for high-brows and low-brows, for women and for men and even for

> children, for old and young, for Easterners, and Westerners,
> for "rich" and "poor" in the American sense. This could only
> happen in America—and only in [the] mid-twentieth century.
> It could only happen with pictures. . . . Here is the society
> bound together in broad and deep consensus yet not a con-
> formist society.

Moreover, Luce said, the people of America who read *Life* were also "making progress toward that far greater civilization." In consequence, Time, Inc. did not need a larger profit from the magazine. The stockholders needed to be reminded that in buying Time, Inc. stock, "they become participants in an enterprise which has other purposes besides the maximizing of profits. And by that, I do not mean merely secondary purposes."[66]

A *Life* editorial on the eve of the 1960 Republican Convention gave the same impression of achievement and success for Luce's publishing venture, and for the New America. Dwight Eisenhower had given "the latent unity and goodwill of the American people a chance to recover and grow." His government had helped finance the building industry in its record-setting construction of eight million new family homes. The union had grown by two states. Beyond the direct influence of government, standardized scholastic test scores were rising. Urban skylines were being transformed. American architecture stood as "a new wonder of the world." The birth rate was at a record high. "The American people did all these—and more. They did them under the benign and permissive Eisenhower sun." The Kennedy or Nixon era would be different. Yet it could "scarcely be more sunny or fruitful than these Eisenhower years, in which so many age-old visions of the good life first became real."[67]

By the time he retired in 1964, Luce knew that he had helped to make history with the New America he had helped to shape. Yet at the same time, this vision was already in the early stages of unraveling. The 1960s brought multiple challenges to the varied components of the New America. Key opinion leaders, for example, turned against population growth. As early as 1959, the Departments of State and Defense had concurred that demographic expansion in developing areas threatened global stability. Books such as Lincoln and Alice Day's *Too Many Americans* (1964) made the same Malthusian argument on the domestic plane. Two years later, the U.S. Interior Department issued a volume that labeled overpopulation the "greatest threat to quality living in this country." Similarly, the suburban American family came under new and generally hostile scrutiny, stimulated by Betty Friedan's *The Feminine Mystique* (1962), the seminal work of the new feminism. During this same era, some elements of the old conservationist movement emerged, newly radicalized and sharply critical of continued economic growth. In addition, America's churches entered a period of membership decline and fundamental reorientation. Generally abandoning evangelism as a priority, the mainline Protestant denominations again moved aggressively into social and political action. Stimulated by Vatican II, the American Catholic Church turned reformist and introspective.

In the ensuing cultural conflict, America's general-interest family magazines were counted among the casualties. The demise of *Look*, the *Saturday Evening Post*, and *Life* within a few years of each other has been heavily analyzed. Surely, the competition of newer media, particularly television and special-interest magazines, played a role. So, too, did the related decline in advertising revenue, the rise in postal rates, and the peculiar economics of modern magazine promotion, where more subscribers often translated into greater losses, leading to such bizarre incidents as the *Post*'s announcement to a majority of its readers that their subscriptions had been cancelled by management.

Yet there was a deeper problem with the genre. The editors had lost faith in the values that had animated their magazines. At the *Post*, for example, a new group took charge in late 1961, determined to change the magazine—to root out the old morality of small-town, midwestern America. Instead, the *Post* would speak "in the bubbling staccato of youth, whose language our new young men and women editors dig well." Formality and restraint in artwork were exiled, along with the Norman Rockwell covers. In their place came stark graphics, said to be inspired by record album covers. Longtime editor Ben Hibbs, born in Pretty Prairie, Kansas, resigned that year. As one of the new men who replaced him, and subsequently presided over the *Post*'s collapse, put it:

> By 1960, in the era of Jack Kennedy, Fidel Castro, the civil rights struggle, and rock'n'roll, the viewpoint of Ben Hibbs began to appear somehow irrelevant. The state of Kansas ranks thirty-first in population, and there is no longer any reason—

if there ever was any reason—to think that this bleak prairie
state represents the American spirit.[68]

A similar moral crisis set in at *Life*. As early as 1958, Luce privately began to express doubts about the continued viability of *Life*'s
format. He acknowledged some truth to the charge, heard frequently
from his editors, "that it's harder now to make a big story of the 'normal.'" He could only urge them to show more imagination. "Take pigs,"
he wrote in response. "Pigs are still a big product. And pigs are still
mighty interesting to look at. An essay on a biggish modern Pig Farm
would be a good essay." The very example suggests a faltering vision.

But editorial focus was only a symptom of the real problem. Luce
noted that religion, which "was a more-than-ordinarily high-priority
subject in America in the post-war years," was becoming problematic.
A "huge revival—at least in the sense of church membership" had occurred. Yet he now sensed that the tide of religious interest in America
"may have passed its peak." Statistics continued to be impressive, but
the drive and spirit had slackened. His suggested response was simply
that *Life* "do more. . . . The wave is still high—and man is a religious
animal."[69] Extra effort on the part of *Life* might yet win the day for a
revival of American interest in religion.

Nevertheless, it had always been true that only Luce's driving intellect and direct stewardship of his empire had kept his magazines on
a purposeful moral keel. Shortly after the end of World War II, editorial advisor John Shaw Billings had reported to Luce that "by and large
Time, Inc. researchers, in their personal feelings, are Left-Wingers. . . .
And naturally most of the writers, junior or otherwise, have about the
same political feelings."[70] As the Cold War heated up, such sentiments
undoubtedly faded; yet they never completely went away. In 1958, Luce
wrote on a related theme: "I get the feelings sometimes, harbor the
suspicion sometimes, that *Life* photographers and *Life* editors are more
interested in themselves rather than in *Life*."[71] It was certainly true that
Life's managing editor after 1948, Edward Thompson, shared little of
Luce's enthusiasm for civilizational and nation-building tasks. While
trying to give his editor-in-chief what he wanted, Thompson saw his
primary job as making money for the company and "getting out the
magazine." In exasperation over Thompson's practicality, Luce had
blurted out one day: "Ed, you're just a goddamned technician." It was
a judgment in which Thompson concurred.[72] When Luce retired from

his editorial job, *Life* began to drift, unable to decide who it was trying to reach or what it was trying to accomplish.

In his last years, moreover, Luce himself may have tried to push the American people further than they could go. He redoubled his calls for purpose and sacrifice. In a January 1962 speech in Chicago, Luce again labeled Americans "a pilgrim people," one now summoned to set forth on the greatest pilgrimage of all: "Everything calls us to leave our comfortable habitations which no longer comfort us, and to strike forth on a pilgrimage to a new civilization." Called in 1960 to testify before Senator Henry Jackson's Subcommittee on National Policy Machinery, Luce focused on the demands of the Cold War: "What should our purpose be in the Cold War? Very simple: We must win it, and the sooner the better."[73] In private memos from this period, Luce said that the job of Americans was to see that the world was controlled "by us and like-minded people adapting our 'democratic' pre-suppositions and methods to the circumstances . . . of 'the new age.'" He emphasized that the American people "must be 'nerved' to this task and dangerous adventure. . . . In order to be nerved to this task, people have to 'see it.'" Accordingly, *Life* had acquired "in radically new terms, not yet clear, the . . . assumed mission of nerving America for her task." The "new age," Luce reasoned, combined great material satisfactions with great dangers: "life (*Life*) is to be enjoyed while coping with dangers." Hence, he reiterated his enthusiasm for family fallout shelters, "Not as a retreat—but as an extra assurance to our will and determination to move forward more boldly into the 'struggle for the world.'"[74]

John Chamberlain, one-time editorial writer for *Life* and later a columnist for *National Review,* saw in such sentiments what he called Luce's "Gnostic heresy"—the belief that heaven could be created on earth through human will. In his 1940 response to Luce's "American Century" essay, Chamberlain had warned that the United States could never succeed as a world power because of its internal divisions and strong isolationist streak. Uncle Sam would someday desert his trusting friends, he wrote, "the moment that his internal troubles become more important to more Americans than the world situation." With the fall of Saigon thirty-five years later, Chamberlain's prophecy was fulfilled.[75]

A more fundamental criticism of Luce's ambitions came from the antimodernist Richard Weaver, a professor of rhetoric at the University of Chicago. In his *Ideas Have Consequences,* Weaver described the awful problem facing elites in a society where the true "primordial" philosophical consensus had dissolved. For practical men, "those in charge of states, of institutions, of businesses," the task became "to persuade to communal activity people who no longer have the same ideas about the most fundamental things." He noted that "the vested interests" of the twentieth century, for various motives, sought to maintain traditional values or set new values in their place. Accordingly, they had constructed a wonderful machine, the "Great Stereopticon," which projected "selected pictures of life in the hope that what is seen will be imitated." Moreover, these "metaphysicians of publicity," had absorbed the idea that the goal of life was "happiness through comfort." Weaver believed that the true consequence, though, was a "sickly metaphysical dream" too weak to sustain anything more burdensome than wealth and abundance.[76]

Luce would not have wholly disagreed with Weaver. Indeed, in a 1949 memo he commended the book to his editors as a powerful challenge to the whole of modernity. Luce was fully aware of the fragility of the New America's strength unless it was undergirded by genuine religious revival. Not the suburbs, nor the Baby Boom, nor material prosperity would be sustained unless rooted in authentic spiritual soil. As Luce had written in 1946, America's inherited moral capital could carry the nation for two or three decades. Success beyond that timeframe required either a theologically and spiritually reinvigorated mainline Protestantism or, more likely, a newly self-confident, avowedly culture-shaping Roman Catholicism. Neither emerged in his time.

5

Cold War and the "American Style"

*[The] success of the whole doctrine and strategy developed in this paper
. . . depends on the capacity of the U.S. to sustain a performance at
home which reaches deeply into our domestic arrangements and which
requires widespread understanding and assumption of responsibility
and sacrifice for public purposes by our people.*

—"Basic National Security Policy," 1962

he tension between cultural pluralism and national unity became
an acute problem in the mid-twentieth century for the architects
of American national security policy.

While it was relatively isolated from great-power politics in the
hundred years after 1815, the American republic had little compelling
need to impress a common identity onto the dozens of immigrant communities scattered throughout the country. The existence of a free,
largely unregulated economy; the decentralized nature of the era's print
media; the emptiness of a vast frontier; the overshadowing of national
politics by state and local concerns; and the maintenance of only a
tiny peacetime army further diminished both the necessity for and the
means of achieving national integration. Beneath an Anglo-Saxon ve-
neer, and notwithstanding the "Americanization" efforts of the Settlement House and public school movements, the great wave of immigration after 1840 created a multilingual, culturally diverse society. The
minimum measure of American unity that did exist arose from the
primacy of the English language; a common (if not universal) European cultural heritage; and popular reverence for those ideals—freedom, democracy, social equality, respect for law, individual rights, and
the self-directed pursuit of happiness and virtue—that animated the

nation's founding documents and were reflected in analyses such as Tocqueville's *Democracy in America.*

America's entry into the Great War and its postwar flirtation with international responsibility put new strains on the nation's domestic arrangements. "European questions" of national identity became critical American questions as well. "It is not how people will live in the future," German sociologist Max Weber wrote in 1895, "which stirs us when we think about the conditions lying beyond our own graves, but rather who they shall be. Neither peace nor the pursuit of happiness but the eternal struggles for the preservation and development of our national identity are the goals we have to bestow to our children."[1] Wilsonian internationalism, a fresh extension of the American adventure, emerged briefly to answer this challenge, but it quickly faded as a motivating creed. Instead, the American nation began to grope for an identity that went beyond ideal constructs; one involving a common conception of "the good life" and giving shape to the norms of individual behavior in the family, marketplace, and place of worship. Enormous cultural, political, and legal pressures were directed toward the Americanization of existing immigrant communities. The campaign to throttle "hyphenated" America, the "Red Scare" of 1920, and restrictions on immigration from southern and eastern Europe all reflected a national search, however crude, for a common identity.

In the 1940s, the United States' full assumption of great-power status and global responsibility again raised questions about the nation's identity, values, and purposes—and about the meaning of the phrase, "the American way of life." But in contrast to the 1920s, American scholars and intellectuals took the lead in confronting these problems. Significantly, the three persons most responsible for the intellectual shape of postwar U.S. national security policy—George Kennan, John Foster Dulles, and Walt Rostow—were each drawn into the new debate on national character. The "challenge of communism" emerged as the common foil for their efforts to identify and analyze the American identity.

Remarkably, U.S. society appeared to generate a clear value consensus in these years, one resting primarily on a strengthened model of the American family. Pessimism among scholars over the shape and direction of the American character gave way by the late 1950s to optimism. This image of a solidifying, uniform social identity critically influenced the national security decisions made during the Kennedy and early Johnson administrations.

Yet the newly achieved identity consensus celebrated by most American intellectuals proved to be more fragile than they had anticipated. It began crumbling in the mid-1960s and collapsed altogether during the early 1970s, the victim of ideological challenge and an unprecedented normative revolution. Its loss left a vacuum at the core of American national security policy, and contributed markedly to that policy's disarray.

GLOBAL RESPONSIBILITY AND THE NATIONAL CHARACTER

The late 1940s and 1950s, according to one commentator, was a time of "national self-analysis" when scholars and amateurs alike dissected American character "as though we were a newly discovered tribe of aborigines."[2] Noted anthropologist Clyde Kluckhohn expressed typical uncertainties in a widely published 1950 essay, in which he declared that "the United States needs a good five-cent ideology far more than it needs a good five-cent cigar." The overwhelming majority of Americans, he believed, rejected communism. "But they long for a creed less partisan, less vague, and less anachronistic than that of most of their political oratory." Even those Americans who had never entered a church, Kluckhohn maintained, agreed "that common values are urgently necessary to a healthy society." The search for such a "pan-human value code," he insisted, was the great task before the social sciences.[3]

Yet the first major sociological study of postwar American identity turned national self-analysis in a negative direction. In his 1950 book, *The Lonely Crowd*, David Riesman (with the assistance of Nathan Glazer) presented a deceptively simple thesis, arguing that the "inner-directed" individual, who linked Greek-style rationality to Judeo-Christian visions of morality, was passing away as the ideal American type. Increasingly dominant in postindustrial America, Riesman argued, was the "other-directed" man. Whereas "inner-directed" individuals responded to a fixed, internalized moral code set by the extended family, "other-directed" men looked to their peers and to shifts in fashion for guidance in ordering their lives. "Other-directed" families, Riesman added, no longer formed a closely knit unit based on a hierarchy of values to be passed on to their children. Instead, parents were now virtually helpless before the influence of school systems and "the real or imaginary approving group" that shaped their offspring's attitudes. The decline in America's birthrate during the interwar period and the resulting "gerontocracy" that blocked upward social mobility symbolized "a profound change in values—a change so deep that, in all probability, it has to be rooted in character structure." Family ineffectiveness, demographic decline, and moral faddishness were, according to Riesman, the hallmarks of the American way in the postwar era.[4]

The Lonely Crowd proved to be a national sensation. Widely quoted and popularized, sales surged beyond the half-million mark after the release of a paperback edition in 1954. A flood of books and articles on the American character followed, many of which voiced the same sense of relative stagnation. Representative was William Whyte's *Organization Man*, which emphasized the decline of the "Protestant Ethic" as an internalized social control and its replacement by tools of conformity within the corporate organizational structure.[5]

This absorption with American character and identity became intertwined with the debate over national security policy. Writing in 1949 for *Foreign Affairs*, Geroid T. Robinson claimed that, in the face of "a simultaneous domestic and foreign crisis" brought on by world communism, America's "principle weakness" was not economic or military, "but ideological." The United States faced the crisis of 1949 with "the ideological equipment of 1775." Piecemeal answers, Robinson argued, would not inspire men and women to make sacrifices on behalf of their nation. Only "a total conception of the good life," one with "some valid connection with their experience and some valid promise of a realization in the future," could mobilize Americans to meet the communist challenge. There was an "urgent need," he insisted, for philosophic reconstruction both "to say what America now is" and "to suggest what America might become." Significantly, Robinson rested his hopes for such a universalized vision of "Americans" on the "family farm" and "the individual household"—the sole surviving centers of the "independent and self-directing individual."[6]

In a lecture given the same year, theologian Reinhold Niebuhr stated that Americans stood "before the enemy in the first line of battle" with ideological weapons "frequently as irrelevant as were the spears of the knights, when gunpowder challenged their reign." In working out his response to this American predicament, Niebuhr stressed the critical importance of communities of family and of faith in broadening and enriching the idealized American identity. The "most genuine community," he declared in a 1951 lecture, was "established below and above the level of conscious moral idealism. Below that level we find the strong forces of . . . sex and kinship, common language and geographically determined togetherness, operative. Above that level of idealism, the most effective force of community is religious humility." Such resources were "of greater importance in our nation today than abstract constitutional schemes," Niebuhr explained, because they appealed more directly to "the urgencies and anxieties which nations, less favored than we, experience."[7]

Somewhat later, J. Robert Oppenheimer acknowledged the same problem but offered a very different response. "[B]y matching ourselves against a remote and unloved antagonist," he wrote, "we have come upon a problem of the greatest gravity for the life of our people." The communist challenge had raised basic questions about the contemporary American character and had given rise to "a rather deep, refractory, and quite unprecedented cultural crisis." As a liberal skeptic with regard to values, however, Oppenheimer believed that this land of "diversity" and "true pluralism" could never yield any unifying theory of what human life was about. "There is no consensus as to the nature of reality or the part we are to play in it," Oppenheimer concluded, "no theory of the good life, and not much theory of the role of government in promoting it." Compared to the more communitarian European peoples, Americans were individualistic nomads. Oppenheimer believed that only a common faith in pragmatic science, "the community of the concrete undertaking," could provide a sense of common American purpose.[8] Writing for *Partisan Review*, historian Arthur Schlesinger Jr. reached essentially the same conclusion. He noted, in words echoing Horace Kallen, "[t]he only answer to mass culture. . . lies in the affirmation of America, not as a uniform society, but as a various and pluralistic society made up of many groups with diverse interests."[9]

The principal theoretician within the State Department during the late 1940s, George F. Kennan, was, at first, more sanguine than Oppenheimer or Schlesinger about America's ability to achieve unity. In fact, he openly welcomed the communist threat as a stimulant to the development of a firmer definition of the American character. "The issue of Soviet-American relations," he concluded in his famous 1947 "X" article for *Foreign Affairs*, "is in essence a test of the overall worth

of the United States as a nation among nations." The "thoughtful observer of Russian-American relations," he added, would indeed "experience a certain gratitude to a Providence which, by providing the American people with this implacable challenge, has made their entire security as a nation dependent on their pulling themselves together and
accepting the responsibilities of moral and political leadership that
history plainly intended them to bear."[10]

DULLES, THE MORAL LAW, AND THE CHALLENGE OF COMMUNISM

Wall Street lawyer John Foster Dulles developed during the 1940s a
similar belief in the need for a reinvigorated American character and
sense of purpose. Echoing Niebuhr, Dulles came to insist that the
American identity have a moral and religious foundation. The intellectual path he followed to this conclusion is instructive.

Dulles's service as part of the U.S. delegation to the Versailles
Peace Conference in 1919 had stirred in him a strong sense of Wilsonian
idealism. "[I]n Woodrow Wilson," Dulles stated in 1941, "we had leadership which was calm, wise and powerful and which would utilize
victory to make transition to a better world order." Dulles's attendance
at the 1937 Oxford Conference on Church and State made an equally
strong impression on him. "Up to that time I confess I had kept such
Christianity as I had in a separate compartment from the activities of
international affairs in which I was engaged," he later wrote. "At the
Oxford Conference . . . I began to see that the problems separating the
human race into hostile warring factions could only be solved in the
atmosphere of something broader than nationalism and narrow patriotism." In consequence, Dulles pledged the remaining years of his
life to "more effectively serve the cause of international peace" and to
seek out "the fellowship of Christians," believing as he did that results
could best be achieved "by the cooperative action of those who possess
the spiritual qualities Christ taught."[11]

In early 1941, Dulles was named chairman of the Commission to
Study the Bases of a Just and Durable Peace, a project of the Federal
Council of Churches. In his early remarks, Dulles stressed the need for
a rallying public purpose, one which would transcend parochial American interests. "Our great national weakness today is not physical, but
spiritual," he declared in May. "We lack a constructive purpose which

is inspiring and contagious. We appear to be purely on the defensive and to be supporting the status quo of a national sovereignty system which has become vitally defective." In his September 1941 response to Franklin D. Roosevelt's and Winston Churchill's Atlantic Declaration, Dulles criticized the document for falling "short of the conceptions of President Wilson" and "short of the conceptions expressed by the great ecumenical conferences of recent years." The true imperative, Dulles charged, was to plan "fearlessly" for "a new world order." He called for the eradication from the American national consciousness of "that immoral principle of national irresponsibility which the sovereignty system now sanctifies;" and, "[a]s a beginning of world government," he called for the organization of "an international federation for peace."[12]

Few would recognize this Dulles by the late 1950s. Significantly, consideration of the postwar role of the Soviet Union drew no attention from him or the Commission until 1946. It was only in May of that year that Dulles admitted "that our Commission has been derelict in not facing up to the Russian problem." He blamed himself for this and pledged to do better, claiming that "I [now] have a clear understanding of the fundamentals, at least, of Soviet foreign policy."[13] His emerging new vision combined recognition of the unprecedented dangers of communism with an unsettling awareness of America's moral and social weaknesses. The net result was to give Dulles a heightened sense of American identity and ideological purpose.

In an address to the Presbyterian General Assembly, also in May 1946, Dulles focused on America's uniqueness and fragility. The proponents of human freedom, he stated, had never been more than a tiny minority. Today, the prestige of freedom was tarnished and the confidence of its proponents waning. Twenty-five years of war and depression had revealed serious infirmities in Western society. World leadership seemed to be passing to the Soviets.[14]

In the face of these worrying developments, Dulles urged the reconstitution of the "great American experiment" in liberty. It was a task, he added, that placed primary responsibility on the churches. "For the truth is that a society of freedom *cannot* persist, and probably *ought not* to persist, except as a religious society." Individual liberty, he insisted, must be tempered by self-control. Indeed, it was "dangerous to give freedom to people who do not feel under a moral compulsion to exercise self-restraint and self-sacrifice. . . . An atheistic society is inherently a dictatorial society." While he recognized that Americans daily witnessed against their professed faith, Dulles believed that "the moral law"—usually defined by him as the Ten Commandments, supplemented by Christ's Great Commandment—still found resonance in the United States. He concluded that "[t]he future of the world depends, above all, on whether we Americans demonstrate that a people who, by the grace of God are free, are also a people who, through acceptance of divine commandment, are people [sic] of self-restraint, self-discipline and self-sacrifice."

Elsewhere, Dulles stressed historian Arnold Toynbee's argument that change is inexorable and that societies *demand* challenges in order to remain vigorous and creative. "A sense of mission is . . . needed if a society is to become and remain free," Dulles stated. "A people without a dynamic faith are constantly on the defensive and that is a losing posture." Communism, he hinted repeatedly, provided the Christian West with just such a challenge.[15]

Yet Dulles's vision of a global American mission—a necessity for responding to the communist challenge and animated by Christian principles— ran into logical and practical difficulties when faced with the pluralism of American society. In a 1950 address to a Jewish group in Cleveland, for example, Dulles found himself stressing "the strength of diversity" and "the right to be different and independent." While still calling for "a free people of dynamic faith," he termed it "dangerous business to mix politics and religion" and cited "the unwisdom of invoking religion as a means of advancing political ends."[16]

Dulles was not entirely happy with this formulation, though. Less than two years later, he declared that "diversity alone is not enough. It must be contained within a framework of unity." Interestingly, the communist challenge again provided an out. "In time of external peril," he declared, "it is necessary for a nation to maximize what unifies, so that differences become minimized. That is why our nation today stands in need of unifying forces, for never before has our peril been so great." Dulles believed that the proper way to achieve unity was to "emphasize values that we hold in common." The irreducible minimum, Dulles stated, was "love of God and love of country." These must be the nation's "great dependence," keeping "differences within tolerable bounds."[17]

Dwight Eisenhower shared his Secretary of State's perception of the communist danger and the demands it placed on America. "Russia is definitely out to communize the world," Eisenhower wrote in his diary in 1947. Six years later, in 1953, he affirmed that "the great struggle of our time is an ideological one." Again, in1957 in his inaugural address, Eisenhower focused primarily on the sinister "designs" and "dark . . . purpose" of international communism, which he believed sought "to seal forever the fate of those it has enslaved." In a 1958 speech at the U.S. Naval Academy, Eisenhower stressed that "the threat imposed by militant and aggressive atheism" demanded "the strengthening of all phases of our moral and spiritual foundations" in order to enhance "the national security of our nation." He added: "The stronger we become spiritually, the safer our civilization."[18]

Indeed, the 1950s found Americans again groping semi-consciously and imperfectly for the domestic unity deemed necessary to a world power locked in struggle with an ideological foe. The expanded activities—even the name—of the House Committee on Un-American Activities, the loyalty oaths, the security checks, the new emphasis on the paraphernalia of civil religion (these were the years during which "In God We Trust" was added to the currency and "under God" inserted into the pledge of allegiance), and the founding of the National Council of Churches of Christ in 1948 under the influence of lay leaders such as J. Howard Pew, were all manifestations of a nation that, called to global responsibility, was seeking a common identity, moral legitimacy, and ideological purpose.

FAMILY, FAITH, AND NATIONAL SECURITY

In fact, by 1960 a remarkable degree of cohesion in values had been achieved. Church membership and attendance, for example, had risen dramatically. The demographic evidence also suggests striking success in achieving a common value base focused on "the traditional American family." Familial norms that, when measured statistically, had been deteriorating since the turn of the century showed dramatic and wholly unexpected turnabouts. The divorce rate, for example, peaked in 1946 and then began a sustained decline that lasted through the 1950s. The marriage rate rose. The average age of persons entering first marriages declined to historically low levels: age 20 for women, 22 for men. Most dramatically, the American birthrate soared above Depression-era lows. Whereas one-third of women in their prime childbearing years during the 1930s remained childless, only 11 percent did so in the 1950s. Among married, college-educated, white women in their most fertile years, the average number of children born rose to 2.7 during the 1950s, compared to 1.4 for the same demographic in the 1930s. Even the remarried showed higher fertility.

A coherent, internally consistent value system that focused on family life, civic duty, and economic growth also took hold during these years. The popular media, from *Life* magazine to television's family-oriented situation comedies, helped define and undergird a uniform image of the American family. From the late 1940s into the early 1960s, most Americans came to share a common view of what they wanted for themselves, their families, and their country. Symbols of normalcy and respectability—a stable family life, home ownership, a rising standard of living, a good education for one's children, position in the community—were strongly reinforced. On the basis of polling data from the 1950s, social analyst Daniel Yankelovich concluded that "these [common] symbols gave Americans a sense of self-esteem and identity, a feeling of effectiveness and a conviction that their private goals and behavior also contributed to the well-being of others."[19]

Self-denial for the sake of obligations to family, faith, community, and nation also emerged as an American ideal. Instrumental activism, or the "inner-directed" personality, seemed to be reborn. This linkage of "family" and "national" sentiments—"the intensity of sentiment about the 'American home'"—was interpreted by Harvard scholar Talcott Parsons as America's way of preserving community within the turbulence of the industrialized nation–state.[20]

Parsons, in fact, became a key figure during this time, leading the American intellectual community away from Riesman's negative portrait of a demographically and spiritually stagnant America and toward a positive, even a celebratory, assessment of American identity and character. Perhaps the most influential sociologist of his generation, Parsons argued that the stakes were high. The Cold War, he noted, was at once a national security problem requiring political solutions, and a domestic problem challenging the legitimacy and very meaning of "the American way." He suggested that America's social organization, while ideally suited to the working of a free economy, was ill-prepared for the burdens of world leadership. The nation's class structure, for example, was fluid, rooted primarily in occupational roles. Its economy was decentralized and still hostile to government guidance. Its elite class was relatively weak and ill-defined. Sectional conflicts

lingered, and large immigrant populations had still to be fully assimi-
lated.

In consequence, Parsons insisted, "a major problem" facing the
United States was how to "motivat[e] large sectors of the population
*to the level of national effort required to sustain a position of world
leadership* in a very unstable and rapidly changing situation." He attributed manifestations of isolationism and McCarthyism, in part, to
the strains that resulted from this challenge. Mobilization to meet the
external danger of communism, Parsons wrote elsewhere, brought "an
enormous increase in pressure to subordinate private interests to the
public interest." The situation demanded "a stringent display of loyalty going to lengths far beyond our tradition of individual liberty."[21]

Such pressures toward domestic conformity, Parsons believed,
merged with independent social trends into a coherent value scheme
grounded in the norms and nuances of daily family life. Where Riesman,
looking at data ending in the mid-1940s, had linked the prevailing low
birthrate to basic and generally negative character changes among
Americans, Parsons viewed recent demographic developments with
optimism. By the mid-1950s, he noted, the proportion of the population married and living with their spouses was at the highest level in
American history. The ownership of single-family dwellings was also
at an all-time high. The birthrate was climbing. The American nuclear
family, he concluded, had successfully reorganized itself around two
primary tasks: the socialization of children and the psychological "tension management" of adults. Even gender-roles within the family had
adapted themselves in a positive way: "managerial" matters were increasingly concentrated in the "wife-mother" role, while the "husband-
father" tended to hold a "fiduciary—'chairman of the board'—type
of role" and performed extrafamilial functions.[22]

Beyond this instrumental restructuring—or "upgrading"—of the
family, Parsons affirmed that there was "a single and relatively well-
integrated and fully institutionalized system of values in American
society . . . that at this most general level . . . has not undergone a
fundamental change in recent times." Its roots, he insisted, were and
remained religious. Parsons denied that America had been secularized.
True, the United States maintained a multitude of churches and sects
and there was no established church. Nonetheless, "values derived from
common religious orientations are still institutionalized. . . . Thus pluralism . . . does not imply that there is no institutionalization of reli-

gious orientations at the norm and the value levels." Rather, Parsons concluded, one found "'higher' levels of generality in the religious requirements of *normal* societal membership." Thus conceived, American society retained "a moral mission" rooted in the fabric of family and religious life, toward which the individual was "conceived to be an instrumentality."[23]

Dulles had argued that faith in God and a private life resting on the moral law should be the prerequisites of normal American identity. For him, though, necessity and reality remained distinct. In his most reflective moments, Dulles remained a pessimist. Parsons, though, employing a scientific database, went beyond Dulles and affirmed that faith and family *were* the American identity. For Parsons, the gap between necessity and reality in Cold War America had been closed.

Large numbers of sociologists backed Parson's optimistic assessment. In 1958, for example, two researchers argued that existing trends toward bureaucratic management and economic security would further "lower the rate of divorce and separation" and "raise again the criteria of competence and the gifts of homemaking to renewed importance in the choice of a marriage partner." Clyde Kluckhohn became convinced that the oft-criticized conformity characterizing the decade sprang "from [a] deliberate and somewhat reflective choice" that recognized "the implacable necessities of gigantic organization." Similarly, the return to religion showed an "increasing recognition of the need for explicit and shared values." Speaking for an "older" generation, Dennis W. Brogan expressed wonder, pleasure, and "irritated bewilderment" over the "indecently large families" covering the American landscape in the 1950s. "A big family in modern society," he wrote, "is seldom a good material investment. Is it not then important that so many young Americans are making this materially unwise decision?" Sociologist Seymour Martin Lipset stressed the historical continuity of American identity. He noted that the United States now had one of the highest rates of population growth in the West, a trend which, given the Riesman thesis, "presumably should presage a return to [Puritan-style] inner-direction." Lipset denied that there had been any radical change in American values between 1920 and 1960. "Only a profound social revolution," he noted, "one that destroys the mainstays of the preceding order—habitual social relations, socializing agencies, and ideas of right and wrong—can produce sudden major changes in values and social character."[24]

Indeed, some scholars argued that the American family model had taken on global importance. In his influential book, *World Revolution and Family Patterns*, William J. Goode declared that the "conjugal family," linked to an ideology first shaped by Western Protestant asceticism and to the principles of laissez-faire economics and political liberty, was the emerging family norm among virtually all developing peoples.[25]

Not through the zeal of Christian missionaries, and not because of any pressure from the West, but solely because of underlying social and economic forces, this modern family structure stood at the fore of the true, capitalist world revolution.

ROSTOW AND "THE AMERICAN STYLE"

Another key figure in the 1950s debate over American identity was Walt Whitman Rostow, then professor of economic history at the Massachusetts Institute of Technology. Starting in 1955, he directed a "fundamental re-examination" of American society and institutions for M.I.T.'s Center for International Studies, a project funded by the Carnegie Corporation. As Rostow's colleague Max Millikan subsequently reported, the project participants were continually forced to the conclusion that "a more imaginative and constructive international performance by the United States" was inhibited not so much by outside, intransigent forces as by "our values," "the American image of the world we live in," and "our historically determined national style."[26]

In his indomitable manner, Rostow set out to remove these obstacles to American performance. His presentation at a 1957 M.I.T. conference on "The American Style" stands as an extraordinary historical statement.[27] In it, Rostow rejected the Riesman thesis, terming it "a kind of defeatism." In particular, he denied Riesman's contention that men "lose their social freedom and their individual autonomy in seeking to become like each other." The true American style, Rostow insisted, was not as Riesman had described it but rather was rooted in the mores of Protestant Britain. It had emerged in the late seventeenth century and, although constantly evolving through cumulative experiment, its broad outlines had not substantially changed. Americans had fashioned national unity and a kind of conformity out of Protestant values and the dreams of the eighteenth-century Enlightenment. Such "shared values" and "participation in the special adventure of America" served as "more than a substitute for conventional patriotism."

From the time of its origin, moreover, the American nation had had a sense of "transcendent ideological destiny." American diplomacy in the nineteenth century, Rostow believed, was successful in large part because it was undergirded by a feeling of moral legitimacy, "a sense that it was right to expand on this continent the American system and way of life." While somewhat chastened by events in recent decades, Americans had "by no means wholly lost a sense of mission, based on confidence and pride in the success of a unique moral, political, economic, and social experiment." In the minds of Americans and throughout the world, the American nation retained a sense of ideological purpose and destiny.

Significantly, Rostow stressed the social stability and unchanging value system that now grounded the American adventure. America, he stated, had maintained "a set of social conventions which exact a high degree of conformity." Innovations in the nation's culture and values took the form "of relatively minor, piecemeal adaptations of a stable basic structure." In contrast to the aristocratic Old World, Americans' "masters" included "a narrower but perhaps more intense family" and "a tendency overtly to conform to the will and manners of the political and social majority." Private social communities—families, churches, and voluntary associations—worked "to ramify and to weave a highly individualistic and mobile population into a firm social fabric" exhibiting "a widening area of common values."

Moreover, the principal long-term trends affecting American society represented a solidification of these developments. The "average American," Rostow noted, was increasingly a resident of a suburb. The "white collar experience of the office" was more typical than the factory or farm experience. With the end of mass immigration, the coming of the industrial revolution to the South, and geographic mobility, there had been "a marked increase in the social homogeneity of the American population." The pressures of the Cold War, he noted, had imparted "a strand of garrison life to the society as a whole," yet had also "converged with many of the trends built into our domestic dynamics," including suburbanization, bureaucratization, the trend toward homogenization, and the development and application of the social sciences. Under the strain of the Cold War, Rostow insisted,

Americans had "retained the old link between nationhood and ideal values."

Other recent shifts, Rostow added, also reinforced the historic American identity and contemporary social stability. Higher incomes allowed the option "of increased leisure, earlier marriages, and more children." The insecurities of the postwar world appeared to have increased Americans' "concern with values which transcend the vicissitudes of a life span—notably family and religion." Both the "welfare state" and the "garrison state" mentalities were "reflected in phenomena as palpable as the birthrate [increase]." With the exception of the desegregation issue, high levels of employment and increased American physical and social homogeneity had resulted in a marked softening of traditional areas of conflict. For Rostow, in sum, the social stability, return to religion, and reinvigorated family life evidenced during the 1950s led to a stirring affirmation of the essential strength and vitality of the American identity and character.

But voices of doubt, even of despair, remained. George Kennan, for example, seemed shaken by McCarthyism. Domestic anticommunism, he noted, left "the impression that we no longer believe in ourselves and . . . are prepared to sacrifice the traditional values of our civilization to our fears." Consequently, he questioned the wisdom of existing U.S. policy, doubting the merits of both anticommunism as a determining ideology and American culture as an international model. "In no area of our foreign policy," he stated during his 1954 lectures at Princeton University, "will we be well served . . . by an approach directed strictly to countering the Soviet threat as a straight military problem." America's "best traditions," which he had summoned in 1947 to counter the Soviet challenge, also now appeared to be less useful. Based on specific national and religious traditions, they did not "necessarily have validity for people everywhere." In fact, Kennan suggested, the American identity should be submerged into a cosmopolitan internationalism. "(T)he development of our society," he explained, "will not be a healthy one unless it envisages and works toward the ultimate merging of its social and political identity with those of at least certain other nations."[28]

In another context, Philip E. Jacob, in his 1957 study of the values found among college students, discovered most of them to be "gloriously contented" and "cheerfully expect[ing] to conform" to contemporary business society. Yet, he added, there was a "ghostly quality" to this conformity, for "the undergirding of the Puritan heritage" on which many of the value assumptions of American society rested was conspicuously absent. "Perhaps these students are the forerunners of a major cultural and ethical revolution," Jacob suggested, "the unconscious ushers of an essentially secular . . . self-oriented . . . society." Essayist Caroline Bird argued that youth were turning to religion as a form of personality adjustment, foregoing experimental sexual relationships, and committing themselves to "lasting marriages" rooted in the belief "that the proper end of love is a child." Yet she was still uneasy. "There is a chance," she offered, "that while the young seem tame, uncommitted, they may be invisibly moving in a direction so radical that we cannot as yet conceive it."[29]

Predictably, David Riesman also dissented from the Parsons-Rostow vision. In his published commentary on Rostow's 1957 paper, Riesman found suburban Americans—whom Rostow celebrated—to be bland. Compared to the self-made men facing personal hardships who had built this country, the new suburban generation was "society-made" and society-dependent, lacking "not only the anxiety which often haunts but also the sense of accomplishment which sometimes enriches the self-made." Rostow had escaped the parochialism of academe, Riesman suggested, only to succumb in his enthusiasm "to the very much larger parish of the United States of America."[30]

In a subsequent essay, coauthored with Nathan Glazer, Riesman responded more completely to his critics and offered warnings of America's vulnerability to internal collapse. Riesman and Glazer acknowledged that the baby boom of the 1950s—reflecting as it did "a decisive change . . . in the value placed in the middle class on having more children as against the value placed on saving or consumer goods"—had obviated the demographic component of their thesis. Yet, they insisted, their broad argument remained sound. The Cold War's psychological pressures might have delayed the full blossoming of the "other-directed" personality. "Many upper-middle-class people," Riesman and Glazer wrote, "who in the 1940s were proponents of 'life adjustment' in school, would today, after Korea and Sputnik, be found in the ranks of those demanding discipline and 'hardness.'" Other Americans, they added, "have no better utopia than a mad return to the epoch of Theodore Roosevelt . . . as if it were possible to make a whole nation inner-directed again by internalizing the arms race under the label of 'national purpose.'" Moreover, while "relics of parochialism" might persist, conscious efforts to restore a unique historical legacy by appeals to traditionalism actually symbolized the end of that legacy's normative quality and its transformation into ideology. The institutions created by the Protestant Ethic still found recruits who possessed the old-time religion. "But we know historically that institutions, like nations and whole social strata, can look very imposing at the very moment when they are about to decline."[31]

In sum, Riesman and Glazer suggested that the recreated America of the 1950s celebrated by their critics was—if superficially impressive—internally a house of cards. In contrast to a hundred or even fifty years earlier, it had now become impossible for "thoughtful Western men" to take their own cultures and beliefs as absolutes; "in fact, the current wave of talk about 'the American Way of Life' is a propagandist's vain defensiveness against this very discovery." Cracks in the American identity, the authors concluded, were already appearing at the elite colleges, seen in the new vogue of Beat music, "non-showy sex," and lingering over espresso. "The Beats symbolize for a great many people the passive rejection of instrumental activism."

However, Rostow chose—either through moral courage or through hubris—to ignore these signs of fragmentation. The struggle against world communism, he believed, would be determined over the next two or three decades. As the primary anticommunist power, the United States needed an identity much like the one he had delineated. "[A] widely shared sense of where we are in the world and a sense of participation in what we seek to do as a community to save ourselves is essential," Rostow told those attending his conference on "The American Style." With the evident demographic strength and strong family norms characterizing the 1950s to support him, Rostow was able confidently to dismiss the Riesman prognosis and transform his understanding of necessity into his view of reality. As he told the same audience, "[t]he public and private sectors of our lives cannot be clearly separated." Rostow's vision rested on the apparent vitality of the latter sector to endure the strains and sacrifices that the war against communism would entail.[32]

KENNEDY, SOCIAL STABILITY, AND THE COLD WAR

When the members of the new Kennedy administration moved into Washington in early 1961, they carried with them a portentous combination of assumptions. On the one hand, they presumed the solidarity of American society and the continuation of the growth-oriented economic and demographic trends of the 1950s. For example, an August 1961 memorandum sent to the White House by the Assistant Secretary of Health, Education, and Welfare, Wilbur J. Cohen, projected an increase in annual births from 4.2 million in 1960 to 5 million by 1970, and the continued expansion of the young component of the population.[33] In the social arena, as in the economic, the continued success of the American experiment was considered a given. The tasks remaining were for the purpose of fine-tuning—whether through the use of Keynesian devices to stimulate further economic growth or through the development of programs to help lagging population groups.

On the other hand, the Kennedy administration was still haunted by an inability to identify an overarching American purpose. "The United States needs a Grand Objective," wrote one Kennedy aide in September 1961. "[W]e behave as if . . . our real objective is to sit by our pools contemplating the spare tires around our middles. . . . The key consideration is not that the Grand Objective be exactly right, it is that we have one and that we start moving toward it." This secular liberal wish for some form of "instrumental" challenge seemed finally to be fulfilled with John Kennedy's 1961 pledge to place an American on the moon before the end of the decade. As Kennedy explained in an address at Rice University, such a goal would "serve to organize and measure the best of our energies and abilities." National unity and identity, devoid of moral overtones or divisive religiosity, might be attained through technical achievement.[34]

A second theme evident in the 1950s debate over national identity took root within the national security apparatus. Not surprisingly, its principal exponent was Walt Rostow, serving first as Kennedy's Deputy National Security Advisor (1961), then as chairman of the State Department's Policy Council (1961–1966), and finally as Lyndon Johnson's National Security Advisor (1966–1969). Rostow retained his commitment to a teleological policy orientation rooted in the nation's solid "domestic arrangements." "[T]he whole objective of our military and foreign policy," he explained at a convention of the League of Women Voters in May 1962, "is to protect the kind of society we are and wish to become." Communism had risen up as America's great adversary, intent on shaping "the life of this planet in ways hostile to every fundamental value incorporated in our national purpose." Much would be demanded of American citizens, for foreign and domestic policies were tightly intertwined. But Rostow placed his hope in the "poise and confidence" of his society, stressing that it had proven "vastly more resourceful and flexible in weaving together public and private interests than our textbooks would suggest."[35]

Rostow's attitudes helped shape Kennedy administration policy. Indeed, policymakers' assumptions about America's domestic identity and strength were most clearly revealed during 1961. That year witnessed the bureaucratic wrangling over production of a presidential letter and booklet outlining what action citizens should take to prepare for nuclear attack. The Kennedy administration actually proposed mailing these materials directly to every household in the country. As such, this project represented the first effort by the federal government to reach every American home directly with one unified, written message. With an anticipated mailing of 60 million copies, the book would be, in one aide's words, "the most widely distributed piece of literature in man's history outside of the Bible."[36]

The project grew out of John Kennedy's July 25 public statement that "in the coming months I hope to let every citizen know what steps he can take without delay to protect his family in case of attack." In fact, the idea of sending a letter or booklet to every home seems to have come from Kennedy himself.[37] Drafted by the staff of the Defense Department's Office of Civil Defense, with contracted editorial assistance from the editors of *Time* and *Life*, the booklet purported to provide essential information on nuclear war and civil defense. Significantly, its authors followed the Parsons line of the late 1950s by assuming that their audience of sixty million households was almost uniformly composed of suburban, middle-class families. The draft introduction, bearing Kennedy's name, called on Americans to "turn with courage and vigor to prepare your family and your community to better your chances to live." In pictures and text, the booklet featured family teams of husbands, wives, and children, in their single-family dwellings, working together to prepare their homes for a nuclear blast by improvising shelters in basements, piling dirt around window wells, sharing shelter life, storing supplies in their boats, working with neighbors to build a community fallout shelter (which could double as an "after school hangout" for "gregarious teenagers . . . where they can relax with sodas and play the jukebox"), and so on. On one page, "a skillful and handy homeowner" constructs a home fallout shelter. On another, a wife efficiently shuts Venetian blinds, removes quick-burning material, and closes the chimney flue in response to the appropriate warning signals.

It is important to recognize that the document assumed that the underlying fabric of American society was so solid as to be capable of handling the strains imposed by civil defense. The rhetoric, for example, was not calculated to soothe. "If there is a nuclear attack on the United States," Kennedy's draft introduction intoned, "no one can be sure that he will be spared." The draft continued:

> But neither can anyone be sure that his home or neighborhood will suffer a direct hit. . . . By protecting yourself and your family, you will be strengthening your country and its allies. The American response to danger is not to turn away but to deal with it by doing the practical things within our reach. The American response is not fear but action.

Similarly, the document referred to the American frontier tradition and the dangers settlers faced in

> lonely cabins and stockades of New England forests and western plains where pioneers lived under the constant threat of Indian attack. If we are to maintain or rebuild the kind of nation they dreamed of—a vigorous dynamic society championing ideals of individual liberty throughout the world—each of us must be willing not merely to die for his country, but to live for it.

More directly, the booklet projected a wholesale transformation of American life in a garrison-style direction, action deemed necessary to meet the civil defense challenge. Page one boldly declared: "Your government intends to see that effective civil defense becomes an integral part of American life." The book suggested that "every citizen who looks squarely at the kind of world we must live in will do what he can to see that civil defense reaches his family and his community." Prudent defense measures, it added later, required "some adjustments in the intimate fabric of our political and private lives." The validity of such sentiments aside, the authors of the document clearly held a strong vision of what "Americans" were and a sense that the nation's social fabric—of families, neighborhoods, and communities—was healthy and strong.[38]

The booklet generated a potent opposition. Some critiques were rooted in partisanship. Ambassador to India John Kenneth Galbraith, asked by Kennedy to review the draft, responded with consternation over the booklet's implicit political sociology. "The present pamphlet is a design for saving Republicans and sacrificing Democrats," he wrote to Kennedy. "I think it particularly injudicious, in fact it is absolutely incredible, to have a picture of a family with a cabin cruiser saving itself by going out to sea. Very few members of the UAW can go with them."[39]

A more measured voice of protest, rooted in Riesmanesque pessimism, emerged in the person of National Security Council staff member Marcus Raskin. Although he himself believed that the chances of thermonuclear war breaking out during the 1960s were very high (he suggested 50-50 odds), Raskin had opposed from the beginning the direction of civil defense planning. His reasons for doing so are enlightening. On the one hand, he feared the dangers to liberty that civil defense posed. In a May 1961 memorandum to National Security Advisor McGeorge Bundy, Raskin asked whether "we are building a world which is safe for democracy—or one only finitely safe even for a garrison state." In July, he objected to a Civil Defense Office report listing the strengthening of "our national will" as one contribution of a fallout shelter program to national defense. This suggested to him "the enforcement of a consensus and the forbearance of moral criticism" and the creation of a permanent "war psychology" that could alter the nature of a free society. In a subsequent memo, Raskin accused the government of "promoting Prussianism" by offering a program that was "shallow, confused, and contradictory." On the other hand, Raskin doubted that American society was strong enough to bear the civil defense burden. He suggested, for example, that such planning risked increasing the "decadence of our values, ideals and true purposes as a free society."[40]

Raskin's reaction to the proposed civil defense booklet was similarly grounded. He noted the draft's faulty scientific assumptions, incorrect information, implicit yet unofficial policy decisions, and absurd language (a criticism with merit; one section heading actually read: "A Nuclear Attack Can Kill You but Its Dangers Can Be Avoided"). Significantly, he also stressed his belief that the booklet's message might "radically change a free society" and "deteriorate [*sic*] an already weakened national moral fiber." Even in the wake of a limited nuclear exchange, Raskin foresaw widespread social breakdown, characterized by "the all encompassing factor of death, bereavement with everyone [*sic*], hostility against authority, sickness, personal treachery and local dictatorship." Where some policymakers saw social cohesion and strength, Raskin saw social deterioration and weakness, and he concluded that effective civil defense in such a milieu would be impossible.[41]

In the end, a classic bureaucratic compromise was reached. The White House abandoned plans to mail a copy of the booklet to every household. But twenty-five million copies were printed and distributed through post offices and federal, state, and local civil defense offices.

"To Sustain a Performance at Home"

Walt Rostow, meanwhile, continued to press for the more-or-less official adoption of his vision of national identity and purpose within the national security structure. Though until 1966 he had held only second-level positions, Rostow nonetheless emerged as the individual most successful in developing the overall strategic concepts for the Kennedy and Johnson administrations. His influence on policy direction was clarified in the 1962 drafting of an annual document titled "Basic National Security Policy (BNSP)." Such exercises had begun during the Eisenhower years and had resulted in generally uninspired compilations of official doctrine and policy. At 284 pages, however, the 1962 document was significantly longer than its predecessors, and it presented a much more complex and consistent ideological framework. As supervisor of the project, Rostow filled the document with his unmistakable language and intellectual constructs. Although never formally approved by Kennedy, it was widely circulated within the government and according to historian John Lewis Gaddis, it stands, along with Kennedy's public pronouncements, "as the most comprehensive guide to what the administration thought it was trying to do in world affairs."[42]

The explicit ideological context of the 1962 BNSP paper was Rostow's view that humanity was involved in a fundamental "contest between competing conceptions of how . . . a new world order can be constructed to replace the one which existed before 1914 and which has been shattered by a half century of war and revolution." The American goal must be to deter communism and shape world events toward the emergence of an "evolving community of free nations," a development that would be "congenial to our abiding national values and purposes." Such a goal, the BNSP draft maintained, proceeded "directly from values and commitments deeply embedded in our national style and domestic arrangements."

The document emphasized (in words undoubtedly Rostow's) that the "success of the whole doctrine and strategy developed in this paper . . . depends on the capacity of the U.S. *to sustain a performance at home which reaches deeply into our domestic arrangements* and which requires widespread understanding and assumption of responsibility and sacrifice for public purposes by our people." America would only fail, the document suggested, if "we do not adequately articulate our goals and do not move positively and effectively toward their realization at home and in the international community." All of America's security and foreign policies required, "for their effective execution, a firm base at home." "We must generate a national perspective," it concluded, "such that we confront the 1960s with a posture of national poise and confidence," overcoming the "understandable difficulties within a pluralistic society" and dissipating "the corrosive conception that our policy is defensive, negative and reactive." Implicitly, Rostow reaffirmed his confidence that America's domestic life was solid enough to support this national security agenda.[43]

Indeed, a strong sense of social peace and tranquility within the United States, and a belief in human ability to guide positive social evolution through the tools of the natural and social sciences, carried over during the Kennedy years into deliberations on the Vietnam situation. Much like those Kennedy-era economists who assumed that the problems of production and sustained growth had been solved by modern Keynesian economics, analysts of the Vietnam situation assumed that social science could be used to adequately understand a society and build a nation. Building on arguments articulated in Rostow's 1959 "noncommunist" manifesto, *The Stages of Growth*, the Kennedy strategists believed that through social science they could alter the internal arrangements of foreign nations so that they were able to withstand the pressures of modernization without falling to the "disease of Communism." In September 1961, Rand Corporation executive George Tanham suggested to Rostow the creation of a ten-year development plan for Vietnam "whereby the country is gradually made secure and prosperous." The "plan of action" for Vietnam drafted by an interagency task force in May 1961 included a series of nation-building objectives that emphasized the development of "political and economic conditions which will create a solid and widespread support among the key political groups and the general population for a Vietnam which has the will to resist Communist encroachment." Rostow himself criticized Vietnam's "lack of a program of positive national goals and purposes" and urged the creation of a long-run development program "reflecting the positive ambitions of the Vietnamese people." It should include, he added, "a coherent military, political, economic plan designed to win the war in Vietnam." That country, Rostow later stressed, was "a test of our durability; our understanding of the political process in a new, young country; a test of our creative capacity."[44]

Faith in America's ability to sustain a long-term, counter-guerrilla effort was also strong. McGeorge Bundy, in a February 1965 memorandum to President Lyndon Johnson, described the situation in Vietnam as "deteriorating" and "grim." He nonetheless urged, with Defense Secretary Robert McNamara's backing, a massive increase in the American commitment. "At its very best the struggle in Vietnam will be long," Bundy said. Yet it was "our own belief that the people of the United States have the necessary will to accept and to execute a policy that rests upon the reality that there is no short cut to success in South Vietnam." As late as September 1966, Rostow was confident that nation-building in South Vietnam was moving well and that "Hanoi cannot count on a political cave-in of U.S. public opinion which would destroy the foundations of the President's policy toward Vietnam."[45]

Most importantly, both the Kennedy and Johnson administrations stressed the indivisibility of domestic and foreign policies, a unity rooted in a sense of common national identity. The "new economics" of the Kennedy administration, for example, presumed that the economy would benefit from increased government spending on defense and social programs. As economist Paul Samuelson wrote in an early 1961 pre-inaugural task force report, "any stepping up of these programs that is deemed desirable for its own sake can only help rather than hinder the health of our economy in the period immediately ahead." More euphorically, Walter Heller declared in 1966 that "prosperity and rapid growth . . . put at [President Johnson's] disposal, as nothing else can, the resources needed *to achieve great societies at home and grand designs abroad.*"[46]

Indeed, proposed new government social programs and racial integration efforts were viewed as intimately linked to national security needs. In October 1961, presidential aide Henry Owen noted the interlocking nature "of civil rights and foreign reputation;" "of the moral energy of life and our will and ability to defend it;" "of understanding and sacrifice: how can our men in Southeast Asia do their job if the rest of us don't care?" and "of what we are with what others may choose to be. If we are selfish, narrow and blind—or weak, ineffective and soft—they will turn elsewhere." In a January 1963 memorandum, presidential advisor Arthur Schlesinger Jr. stressed that "domestic policy should not be treated as a separate subject. It should be presented as a means of strengthening the national foundation for sustained international effort." Similarly, a July 1967 memorandum from Rostow to Lyndon Johnson explained the "parallels" between the administration's domestic and foreign policies. He wrote:

> [W]e cannot play our part in the world scene unless we do so from a base of order and progress at home. . . . And equally, we cannot build order and progress at home in a world where U.S. withdrawal from its responsibilities result [*sic*] in an international environment of chaos and violence. . . . [T]herefore, we must—and we can—find the energy, talent and resources to work for order and progress at home and abroad.[47]

SOCIAL UPHEAVAL AND INTERNATIONAL DISARRAY

Yet the hint of desperation found in Rostow's words was rooted in a growing pessimism over both foreign and domestic developments. For by mid-1966, a sense of unease was already settling in among the architects of American national security policy, as the society they thought they knew seemed to be unraveling. In retrospect, an underlying shift in American values was occurring, one with significant social, political, and foreign consequences. The "single and relatively well-integrated and fully institutionalized system of values in American society," which rested on the mutually reinforcing attitudes toward family, morality, and work that Parsons had identified during the 1950s, was beginning to crumble.

There were many challenges to Americans' social and moral cohesion. Not surprisingly, the first evidence of value disintegration came
from African Americans, a group all but ignored by Parsons in his implicit celebration of Americanism and one usually cited by Rostow as
the single exception to his otherwise optimistic assessments. Warnings
concerning the "ghostly quality" of the conformity of the 1950s also
proved portentous, particularly Philip Jacobs's suggestion that seem-
ingly contented students might prove to be "the unconscious ushers"
of a new, secular, "self-oriented" society. The perceived hollowness of
suburban living, particularly as it affected the attitudes and goals of
women, also gave impetus to radical change.

Curiously, beginning in the mid-1960s, the federal government itself became an active force encouraging the abandonment of the "Parsons family model" as a guide. Neo-Malthusian theories about the
danger of America's "excessively" high birthrate, for example, began
winning official sanction. In 1965, Lyndon Johnson convened a White
House Conference on International Cooperation that included a panel
on population. This panel suggested, as one speaker put it, that "population stabilization" was "a necessary means to the enhancement and
enrichment of human life." Two years later, Congress allocated $50
million for population and family planning work by the Department
of Health, Education, and Welfare, marking the first entry of the federal government into those intimate human spheres. In 1968 Johnson
appointed a President's Committee on Population and Family Planning, which urged an enhanced government presence in the area of
population control. In an unprecedented July 18, 1969, "Message to
Congress on Population," President Richard Nixon called on all Americans to recognize and respond to "the population crisis" facing the
United States and the world. Subsequently Congress established a Commission on Population Growth and the American Future to "formu-
late policy" dealing with "the pervasive impact of population growth
on every facet of American life." The Commission's 1972 report declared that the United States should "welcome and plan for stabilized
population" through a comprehensive program of fertility control and
population and sex education that would counter the normative "three-
child family". Large families and population growth—viewed in the
late 1950s as signs of robust national health and as the domestic foundation of a vigorous foreign policy—had become virtual social pathologies and the targets of state activism by the early 1970s.

Demographic trends affecting the family had undergirded both Riesman's abject pessimism and Parsons's and Rostow's subsequent optimism concerning America's identity. It is important to note that all such indicators showed changes in direction beginning in the early 1960s, changes that for five years accelerated slowly and then rapidly between 1968 and 1980.

These demographic changes marked, to borrow Lipset's words, "a profound social revolution;" one destroying "the mainstays of the preceding order—habitual social relations, socializing agencies and ideas of right and wrong." For example, the American fertility rate—Riesman's original key indicator—plunged from a peak of 122.7 births per 1000 women ages 15–44 in 1957 to 66.7 in 1975, reflecting a rapid retreat from childbearing. America's divorce rate, after declining during the 1950s, rose 150 percent between 1960 and 1975. The number of divorced persons per 1000 married persons climbed from 35 in 1960 to 100 by 1980. Among African American women, the increase was from 78 to 257. The number of children annually affected by divorce nearly tripled in the same time span. Meanwhile, the United States' out-of-wedlock-birth ratio (illegitimate births per 1000 live births) rose three-fold over the course of the 1960s and 1970s. By 1980, one million teenagers were becoming pregnant annually. The incidence of human abortion increased from an estimated 100,000 illegal abortions each year during the late 1950s to 615,000 in 1973 (the first year when the procedure was legal in every state) to nearly 1.5 million in 1980.

Such massive statistical swings reflected underlying and equally extraordinary shifts in values. Simply put, the family-centered conformity of the 1950s had faded; accentuated pluralism became the new imperative. In the late 1950s, polling data indicated that 80 percent of Americans criticized as "neurotic" or "immoral" those men or women who consciously rejected the idea of marriage. Two decades later, only 25 percent did. As late as 1967, 85 percent of Americans with college-aged children still judged premarital sex to be morally wrong; in 1979, only 37 percent did. In the latter year, 75 percent professed to believe that it was acceptable to be single and bear children, a dramatic turnaround from the time when extramarital pregnancy was considered a scandal. Concerning children, 75 percent of Americans agreed in 1980 that "parents should be free to live their own lives even if it means spending less time with their children."[48]

Given the linkage of work and family that traditionally supported the fading "inner-directed" American ethic, it is not surprising that cultural norms affecting labor showed equally dramatic shifts. Where 34 percent of Americans placed work "at the center" of their lives in 1970, only 13 percent did so eight years later. The average number of working hours per week fell from 38.6 per person in 1960 to 35.4 in 1980. According to the Monthly Labor Report, Americans were instead increasingly engaged in "personal care," sleep, "active leisure," and television-watching. Two-thirds of Americans reported that they spent "a great deal of time" contemplating their own lives. The number of men in their prime working years who voluntarily dropped out of the labor force nearly doubled in the two decades after the 1950s, reaching 22 percent.[49]

In sum, the Puritan ethic of "instrumental activism," while arguably showing renewed vigor during the 1950s, was deteriorating twenty years later. Not coincidentally, faith in government collapsed over the same time span, and was replaced by widespread cynicism. In the late 1950s, 72 percent of Americans believed that the government was "run for the benefit of all." Twenty years later, 65 percent affirmed that it was run for the benefit of "a few big interests." A startling 81 percent of Americans professed in 1980 that their society no longer had "rules," since those who complied with the ones that had heretofore existed were left empty-handed while those who flaunted them were rewarded. The disease of social anomie had spread widely and deeply.[50]

The strengthened family orientation and solidifying value consensus of the United States during the 1950s had demonstrably influenced policymakers' understanding of American identity, purpose, and strength, and had correspondingly affected their judgments and actions. Hence, the apparent crumbling of that consensus, accompanied by signs of social turmoil and decay, should have altered policymakers' background assumptions and, ultimately, affected their actions. While such connections are difficult to isolate, there are incidents suggesting that this is what happened.

RACIAL UNREST AND NARROWING THE IDEOLOGICAL GAP

The first domestic shock with significant foreign policy implications came from that festering divide in American society: race. Trouble began brewing in May 1963 when Alabama Governor George Wallace made clear his intention to defy federal court orders mandating the admittance of two black students to the University of Alabama. Between June 6 and June 11, civil disorder broke out in Alabama, and—following the shooting death of civil rights leader Medgar Evers—spread to Mississippi, North Carolina, Ohio, and Maryland. The crisis culminated in Kennedy's June 11 dispatch of federalized National Guardsmen to the University of Alabama campus to ensure the enforcement of federal law.

During those very same few days, American national security policy underwent a basic emotional and structural shift away from a Cold War, anticommunist posture and toward what would come to be called détente. The defining public moment marking this shift was the commencement address on "peace" given by John Kennedy at American University on June 10, 1963. Evidence suggests that the content of this speech was not wholly unrelated to the racial unrest the nation was suffering.

The idea for a presidential speech on "a peace race" rather than "an arms race" had actually originated in a letter from *Saturday Review* editor Norman Cousins to Kennedy. Cousins's argument was tactical, not ideological. He noted that Nikita Khrushchev, following his November 1962 retreat during the Cuban missile crisis, was under increasing pressure from the Chinese and would react either by denouncing the United States as an imperialistic warmonger or by pointing with pride to the growing success of a policy of peaceful coexistence. Cousins argued that, whichever course Khrushchev chose, it would be to the United States' advantage to be "on record" for its peaceful intentions. In addition, Kennedy had been contemplating since early 1963 ways to revive talks on the proposed nuclear test–ban treaty. More or less by process of elimination, the American University speech was selected by speechwriter Theodore Sorensen as the best forum for these themes.[51]

The drafting of the speech, though, did not begin until June 6, by which time the civil rights crisis was at full boil. Over the next few days the themes of domestic disorder, national failure, confused purpose, and the inadequacy of anticommunism as a determinant of foreign policy became thoroughly intertwined. Sorensen himself was drafting several civil rights speeches and statements while working on the American University address. In addition, the suggestions he received for these projects from other people dwelt on America's inadequacies, even on a crisis of American nationhood. Norman Cousins again played a role. Suggesting to Sorensen that the U.S. government was "committed to the cause of freedom," Cousins added that "we must not confine our attention to the struggle for freedom outside the United States. The struggle for freedom goes on inside America. This nation will not be fully free until all its citizens are fully free." He also urged that "we put all misunderstanding on one side and proceed as quickly as possible to put an end to nuclear tests." Attorney General Robert Kennedy forwarded his own draft comments to the White House, in which he described America as being in "a time of profound national unrest," which he termed "the result of a slow and malignant disease" in the tissue of U.S. society. Recent racial riots and bloodshed had not only "damaged our standing as a free nation in the eyes of the world," it had also "damaged our own national conscience, our very ability to take pride in calling ourselves Americans." Something was "wrong" with America, "in the full sense of that word;" something was "wrong North, South, East and West in our country."[52]

Sorensen's own first draft of John Kennedy's June 11 televised speech on the civil rights crisis drew heavily from both Cousins's and Robert Kennedy's suggestions. It linked the Alabama situation to the United States's commitment "to a world-wide struggle to protect and promote the rights of all who wish to be free." But, the draft added rhetorically, do we say to the world and to ourselves "that this is the land of the free, except for Negroes. . . ?" American inconsistency on the issue of freedom had fanned the "fires of frustration and discord" in every major city. The nation faced "a moral crisis." Sorensen even suggested that a "social revolution is at hand."[53]

It was within this domestic context that Sorensen wrote the June 10 American University speech. Its content quickly moved beyond Cousins's original suggestion. In his second draft, Sorensen cited the need for Soviet leaders to adopt a "more enlightened attitude." He then added: "But I also believe that we must re-examine our own attitude—as individuals and as a nation—for our attitude is as essential as theirs." In particular, the draft called for reexamining American postures toward peace, the Soviet Union, "the course of the Cold War," and "freedom and peace here at home."

"[E]nmities between nations—and conflicts of ideology—do not last forever," Sorensen wrote. Americans must not believe their own propaganda; they ought not "see only a distorted and desperate view of the other side" nor view conflict as inevitable and accommodation as impossible. "No government or social system is so evil that its people must be considered to be lacking in virtue." Both the United States and the USSR had "a mutually deep interest in a just and genuine peace and in an end to the arms race." If the two systems could not settle their differences, "at least we can help make this world safe for diversity." Concerning attitudes about the Cold War, the Sorensen draft stressed that Americans "are not engaged in a game, seeking to pile up points. We are not here distributing blame or pointing the finger of judgment. We must deal with the world as it is, and not as it might have been." And regarding domestic disorder in America, the draft stressed that "[we] must all, in our daily lives, live up to our faith that peace and freedom walk hand in hand. In too many of our cities today, unfortunately, the peace is not secure because freedom is incomplete." With generally minor changes, this draft served as John Kennedy's final text.[54]

The speech marked a basic shift in the tone and, implicitly, in the substance of American policy toward the Soviet Union. Henceforth, anticommunism—specifically the use of "foul language against communism," in which Khrushchev repeatedly accused Dulles of indulging—would be muted in the interests of peace and mutual tolerance. In general, ideology would be downplayed as an operative factor in foreign policy, and would be replaced by efforts at functional cooperation. The Soviet leadership, at least, viewed the speech that way. One Russian emissary termed the address "historic." The USSR deliberately silenced the jammers aimed at Voice of America frequencies to allow a Russian translation of the speech to be broadcast unhindered in the Moscow area. Nikita Khrushchev himself labeled the address as "a step forward in a realistic appraisal of the international situation," to be welcomed as in line with "the Leninist principle of the peaceful coexistence between states with differing social systems."[55] As CBS News suggested in a June 16, 1963 broadcast, President Kennedy's efforts the week before "to narrow the emotional gap between Negro and White" appeared to be linked to his effort "to narrow the ideological gap between East and West" through an "appeal for an end to the Cold War."[56]

Disintegrating Values and Vietnam

Early in 1963, Arthur Schlesinger Jr. had stressed the mutual reinforcement of a vigorous social foundation and an effective international presence. "In order to fulfill our objectives in foreign policy," he wrote, "we need, above all, a strong and vital domestic base." America could win the "long-run contest only by building the long-run strength of our nation."[57] Such a connection was implicit in the work of both Kennedy and Johnson during the period between 1963 and 1965, which sought to bring African Americans into the social mainstream, to "raise" them up to the middle-class norms of white America. Such efforts, however, began running afoul of the crumbling social arrangements governing family life and sexuality by mid-decade. The imperatives of foreign policy and the reality of a disintegrating value consensus collided in the publication of the *Moynihan Report*.[58]

During 1965, Daniel P. Moynihan, then serving as Assistant Secretary of Labor for Policy Planning and Research, guided the preparation of an internal government report, *The Negro Family: The Case for National Action*. It was to serve as a guide for the "post–civil rights" phase of the "Negro problem." Distilling three decades of sociological, economic, and psychological research on African Americans, the report represented in many respects a summary of pro-family progressive liberalism, persuasively linking America's common family values and national character to mutual guilt and shared responsibility. Appropriately, the report assumed a common American identity rooted in the traditional family of a bread-winning father, a stay-at-home-mother, and a robust group of children.

In the document, Moynihan termed the family "the basic social unit of American life." He argued that the mass media and the development of suburbia had, in recent decades, "created an image of the American family as a highly standard phenomenon." Out of a pluralistic background, Americans were now "producing a recognizable family system." White families evidenced a high and increasing level of stability. In contrast, the family structure of "lower class Negroes" was "approaching complete breakdown," evidenced in such "pathologies" as divorce, desertion, female-headed families, working mothers, and illegitimacy. "Negro children without fathers," Moynihan concluded, "flounder and fail." The source of this social disorder, he argued, was the heritage of slavery and racial discrimination. Consequently, it was incumbent on all Americans to shape and support federal programs that would enhance "the stability and resources of the Negro American family." The implied solution was to turn African-American men into successful husbands, fathers, and breadwinners.

In a June 1965 address at Howard University, Lyndon Johnson made these same arguments the basis for his proposed domestic reform program. "The family is the cornerstone of our society," Johnson intoned. "Unless we work to strengthen the [Negro] family—to create conditions under which most parents will stay together—all the rest . . . will not be enough to cut completely the circle of despair and deprivation."

As presidential counselor and speechwriter Harry McPherson noted, the emphasis on the presence of fathers and the maintenance of an intact family "[w]as a Catholic middle-class view of Moynihan's; it's a Protestant middle-class view of mine."[59] Yet Johnson's message and the *Moynihan Report* itself were soon embroiled in controversy. Attacks did not come, as expected, from the political Right, but rather from certain social scientists, minority activists, and reawakened equity feminists who—for different reasons—rejected middle-class family values as guides to policy formation. For example, sociologist Frank Riessman, writing for *Dissent* magazine, denied that the female-headed family was abnormal. "The Negro" had responded to oppressive conditions by "many powerful coping endeavors." "One of the most significant forms of his adaptation," Riessman argued, "has been the extended, female-based family." Similarly, Robert Staples argued that "[d]ivorce, illegitimacy, and female-headed households are not necessarily dysfunctional except in the context of Western, middle-class, white values." Anthropologist Ray Birdwhistell made even more sweeping charges, claiming to debunk "the sentimental myth" of the American family. Men, women, and children trapped in their suburban homes, he declared, had become "cage dependent," while marriage counselors, psychiatrists, and social workers who considered this model "healthy" had become "zoo-keepers" supporting a dangerous disease.[60]

Thus, whereas Moynihan, using arguments grounded in the maternalism of the interwar years, had surveyed black America and identified social pathologies needing correction, this growing segment of the sociological profession saw in the same data a welcome "new pluralism" in social relations. Strangely, a government prepared in mid-1965 to mobilize national resources to bring African Americans up to middle-class family norms simultaneously found itself backing these new theories, which denied both the need for, and the existence of, social standards. Moynihan was muzzled. The Johnson administration's "War on Poverty" programs began funding a plethora of organizations openly hostile to "white, middle-class" patterns of behavior. Somewhat later, Forum 14 of the 1970 White House Conference on Children and Youth came to celebrate a "pluralistic society of varying family forms and a multiplicity of cultures." Defining the family with almost nihilistic breadth as "a group of individuals in interaction," the Forum 14 report described optional forms ranging from nuclear families to "single parent," "communal," "group marriage," and "homosexual" varieties. Decrying American conformity, the report's authors—a cross-section of the nation's most prominent and well-connected sociologists—welcomed contemporary efforts "to destroy the cultural myth of a 'right' or 'best' way to behave, believe, work or play."[61]

By the early 1970s, such views on the American family—at least judging from the standard professional and governmental publications—could be accurately labeled the new orthodoxy of the social sciences. In sharp contrast to the 1950s, the most vocal family theorists in and out of government came to deny that there was—or that there should be—any single set of unifying social standards in American society.

The new confusion over America's domestic arrangements was complemented by a waxing sense of despair about Vietnam. Quiet panic spread among key policy makers as both Vietnamese and American societies seemed to spin out of control. "I see no reasonable way to bring the war to an end soon," Robert McNamara concluded in October 1966. Enemy morale had not been broken. The Vietcong had adopted a "waiting out" strategy aimed at "attriting [sic] our national will." Pacification had "if anything gone backward." Only "extraordinary imagination and effort" could turn that program around. During his visit to the war zone that same year, presidential emissary John Roche, a staunch anticommunist, commented that the American effort in Vietnam "resembled the Holy Roman Empire going off to war" with countless confusing and overlapping feudalities and an "incredible input of Americans and American stuff just piling into this little country and literally tearing its social fabric." As the Tet Offensive rolled over South Vietnam in early 1968, Lyndon Johnson concluded that "it appears to be the judgment of our enemies that we are sufficiently weak and uncertain at home."[62]

DISILLUSIONMENT AND STUDENT UNREST

At the core of this sense of disorder was growing confusion over war aims, leading to an inversion of the original linkage between domestic and national security policy. The de-emphasis of anticommunism and the Cold War, informal policies since Kennedy's American University speech, had quickly spread to analyses of the Vietnam conflict. By early 1965, the predominant concern, in Under-Secretary of Defense John McNaughton's words, was simply "to avoid a humiliating defeat." The first draft of his influential July 1965 memorandum on "analysis and options for South Vietnam" cited as the purposes of the American commitment: 70 percent, to preserve national honor as a guarantor of treaties; 20 percent, to keep the territory out of hostile, expansive hands; and 10 percent, to "answer a call from a friend." Except for a back-handed reference to the communist "wars of liberation" theory, resisting the spread of communist ideology was not mentioned. Two weeks later, Johnson announced to the National Security Council that escalation in Vietnam would proceed quietly. "We will neither brag about what we are doing or [*sic*] thunder at the Chinese Communists and the Russians." An early March 1968 internal memo termed the U.S. objective to be "an honorable peace that will leave the people of South Vietnam free to fashion their own political and economic institutions without fear of terror and intimidation from the North." Aggression and communism were neatly compartmentalized, in the interests of diversity and peace.[63]

By 1968, the confusion was all encompassing. Harry McPherson, one member of the growing circle of administration "doves," noted that the United States had "no desire whatever to take a foot of North Vietnam, nor to change their government." Militant anticommunism was antique; vague sentimentality had taken its place. All "we wanted to do," McPherson related in early 1969, was to "love these little brown brothers that we were killing!" In consequence, he said, the war "was like a semi-erection for the American people; . . . completely unsatisfactory." Significantly, McPherson even hinted that the major motivation behind Johnson's steady escalation of the war was the need to move Great Society legislation through Congress; this was a total reversal of the earlier approach, which considered social reform a means of providing strength for America's international policy. "The real question," McPherson explained, "is as to whether you would have been able to get a domestic legislative program—a liberal program—through if you had let South Vietnam go down the drain."[64] Seen this way, the Vietnam War was a de facto political vehicle for building a new kind of American welfare state.

The only administration figures who retained a clear sense of the war's purpose by 1968 were hard-line, ideological anticommunists such as Rostow and Roche. In the face of adverse developments, Rostow kept turning the argument back to communism. Almost alone in the White House at that point, he labeled the Tet Offensive a part of a "widespread, desperate and dangerous Communist effort along the whole front in Asia to divert us from Vietnam, upset the progress made in Vietnam, and discourage and split the American people." Rostow urged the President to call "for unity and responsibility in the face of this Communist challenge."[65]

Yet the "peace" group, including Clark Clifford and McPherson, pointed to "growing disaffection" over the war, which was accompanied by "growing unrest in the cities because of the belief that we are neglecting domestic problems." This unrest threatened to provoke "a domestic crisis of unprecedented proportions." Such arguments brought Johnson onto the doves' side in late March 1968. He scrapped plans for the deployment of 206,000 additional U.S. troops to Vietnam and a call-up of the reserves. The United States would instead adopt a "winding down policy" aimed at a negotiated withdrawal from the country. Johnson also announced at this time his decision not to seek reelection. "[O]ur country is in great and serious danger," he explained to his cabinet on April 3. "[W]e have an explosive situation in Vietnam and the Middle East that could go up at any moment. . . . We have . . . troubles that could be very deadly here at home, right here in this Nation's Capital."[66]

"Great societies at home" and "grand designs abroad" died together.

Growing levels of antiwar activity in America and student activism worldwide added further to the anxiety and confusion of the administration as it confronted the society it sought to govern. Johnson asked the Central Intelligence Agency to investigate the international, potentially communist-affiliated connections of U.S. peace groups. The agency reported back in November 1967 that such contacts were limited. Moreover, while many antiwar leaders had close communist associations, "they do not appear to be under Communist direction." The movement was complex; its most striking feature was "its diversity."[67]

A much more detailed CIA report on student unrest in the United States and abroad, sent to the President in September 1968, represented applied sociology in its most dismissive mode. Unrest could be traced to the explosion of the student population, a growing cynicism "with respect to the relevance of social institutions and to the apparent gap between promise and performance," and certain other readily explainable—and sometimes justifiable—factors.[68]

However, a similar report developed by the State Department's special Student Unrest Study Group in late 1968 reached a more ominous conclusion. The emergence of nihilistic attitudes associated with the New Left, it said, were "indicative of a historical turning point in national attitudes." It continued:

> We are unable to understand the full ramifications of this intuition, but we suggest that a major contributing factor is the relative absence of broadly accepted national concerns that would foster a stronger "nationalism" or "patriotism", in their traditional sense. . . . Perhaps it was the prosperity of the sixties, the seeming recent decline in the Soviet threat, and disillusionment with their country's national purposes that have contributed most to this situation.[69]

Embroiled in a war that had lost its purpose and exhibiting the strains of a society losing its cohesion, the American nation stumbled out of the post–World War II era.

THE AFTERMATH

Richard Nixon and Henry Kissinger ushered in a new approach to national security policy. It reflected, in part, a perceived transformation in the nature of the communist challenge and the alleged emergence of new policy issues "transcending" geography and ideology. Yet it also rested on the belief that American disunity and exhaustion necessitated retreat. The "American domestic consensus" had been "strained by 25 years of global responsibility," stated Nixon's second report to the Congress on foreign policy. America's unique postwar burden had also come to an end. It was time to move "into new avenues of peace, and to realize the creative possibilities of a Pluralistic world."[70]

In contrast to the preceding twenty years, anticommunism would consciously be abandoned as a principle of American foreign policy. The ideologies of the Cold War were considered the irrelevant baggage of another period. "Today, the 'isms' have lost their vitality," Nixon's first report to Congress declared. "[I]ndeed, the restlessness of youth on both sides of the dividing line testifies to the need for a new idealism and deeper purposes." National Security Advisor Kissinger stated in December 1969 that "we have no permanent enemies. . . . [W]e will judge other countries, including Communist Countries . . . on the basis of their actions and not on the basis of their domestic ideology."[71]

Realism and geopolitics now became the prime determinants of international relations. "Our objective," Kissinger wrote in his memoirs, "was to purge our foreign policy of all sentimentality." The geopolitical interests of countries with widely varying ideologies, Kissinger argued, could in certain instances be congruent. The bipolar model of the world, which had guided American thinking since World War II, needed to be replaced by a multipolar vision. In this newly pluralistic world, America would work with any system, even Marxism–Leninism, so long as it shared the American interest in preserving the status quo.[72]

There would be aberrations under Nixon and Ford that would point to older models of action, such as the effort to destabilize Allende in Chile or to back pro-Western forces in Angola. Kissinger, moreover, sometimes sensed gaps in the new order of things. In the past, he stated, Americans' "conviction of our uniqueness contributed to our unity, gave focus to our priorities, and sustained our confidence in ourselves." Yet, he continued, the world was now more complex; our "broad margin of survival" and our "margin of safety" had shrunk considerably. We could "no longer expect that moral judgments expressed in absolute terms" would command broad acceptance. As Nixon told Chou-En-Lai in Peking in 1972, the world had "changed" since the Dulles era. In place of "the constant crises and high arms budgets of the Cold War," Kissinger concluded, stood détente: a means of regulating a competitive relationship during the nuclear age.[73]

The new American strategy, however, produced results that undermined the Nixon–Kissinger reconstruction effort. The "opening to China" and the cozier relationship with the Soviet Union, for example, developed during the same time period that American soldiers were still fighting communists throughout Southeast Asia. Indeed, these approaches to the two communist giants were motivated, in large part, by hope that they could help extricate the United States from the Vietnam quagmire. But such episodes left many of the Nixon administration's other diplomatic moves—such as the Allende affair—devoid of moral coherence. Détente also obscured the Soviet Union's massive military build-up, which had begun after the Russians' humiliation in the Cuban missile crisis. American public opinion, already battered by the Vietnam conflict, was lulled by talk of a new era of peace. A strong antimilitary bias emerged in Congress. Between 1969 and 1975, the defense budget was slashed while non-defense spending soared. Where expenditures for national defense accounted for 40.8 percent of the federal budget in FY 1970, they had fallen to 24.3 percent by FY 1977. Saigon fell in spring 1975, marking a failure for détente and for U.S. influence in the region. In retrospect, the Nixon–Kissinger policy had to fail, for it offered no consistent, compelling vision of national identity and purpose.

Grasping the Problem

Jimmy Carter understood this weakness of the Nixon-Kissinger approach to some extent, and moved to reinsert a moral element into American foreign policy. In doing so, however, he insisted on following his predecessors in rejecting anticommunism as a guide to policy. In his famous phrase uttered at the University of Notre Dame in May 1977, the United States was finally free of "the inordinate fear of Communism." Instead, a new commitment to "human rights" stood as "a fundamental tenet of our foreign policy." America was the "most diverse" nation the world had ever seen, Carter explained. "No common mystique of blood or soil unites us. What draws us together, perhaps more than anything else, is a belief in human freedom." While rooted in moral principles, "which never change," his administration's foreign policy reflected "a larger view of global change" that would allow the United States to help shape a new world.[74]

Under the "human rights" umbrella, the Carter administration came to emphasize a mélange of issues: the release of political prisoners; moral earnestness; openness; decentralization; the pursuit of détente without linkage to other matters; withdrawal from Korea; support for black liberation movements in Africa; and acquiescence to the apparent rise of Eurocommunism. Yet, lacking any dominant theorist (in fact, exhibiting what one historian calls "a curious resistance to systematic thought"), by 1980 the Carter administration was floundering over crises in Afghanistan, Poland, and Iran—crises that its amorphous theories of "human rights" and détente could neither explain nor guide to an effective resolution.[75]

In addition, the Carter administration proved incapable of articulating a comprehensive vision of "the good life." It did not recover the vision of family preservation held by the maternalists and the New Dealers, nor did it craft a substantive new interpretation of the American social order. Carter's popular 1976 campaign declaration, "The American family is in trouble," exhibited this confusion; new federal efforts to shore up America's decaying family structure fell afoul of the rising feminist- and homosexual-rights wings of the Democratic Party. By 1978, his planned "White House Conference on The American Family" became one "on Families," plural. Instead of focusing on the problems of divorce and illegitimacy, Carter's personal concerns, the conference celebrated "the realities of today's families, their diversity and pluralism" and "the emergence of a pluralism in family ways."[76]

Diversity abroad, pluralism at home. The words reflected the loss of a shared American identity.

6
From Maternalism to Reaganism and Beyond

It is the power of the family that holds the Nation together, that gives America her conscience, and that serves as the cradle of our country's soul.

— Ronald Reagan, 1988

On February 8, 1964, the American political order experienced a seismic shift. It was a day of high drama. The occasion was the debate taking place in the U.S. House of Representatives over the Civil Rights Act of 1964. In order to rush this unusual and controversial measure through, the chamber had turned itself into the Committee of the Whole. The language of the bill on that Saturday morning—as first drafted in the Lyndon Johnson White House—aimed at ending discrimination "on the basis of race, color, religion, or national origin" in the areas of voting, public accommodations and education, federally assisted programs, and private employment. Reading between the lines, it was clear that the latter provision, Title VII, would renew an old maternalist goal from the interwar years: to remove those job barriers that prevented African-American men from being good fathers, husbands, and breadwinners. Advocates used an argument that would surface again one year later in the Moynihan Report: if the traditional family home was the basis of American civilization, then full citizenship for African Americans required shoring up the economic side of their faltering family system. Disproportionately characterized by matriarchy, female-headed households, and illegitimacy, the need was for the African-American family to be reconfigured on the prevailing breadwinner/homemaker model found among whites. If this could be done, racial equality would result.

Yet the white segregationists in the House chamber, their backs to the wall, had resolved on a desperate and portentous strategy. Seeking a "killer" amendment, these "Dixiecrats" sought a change in the language of Title VII that would reveal the danger, even absurdity, of the concept of "equality." They also may have dimly seen that if their strategy failed, they might at least refocus the future civil rights enforcement apparatus away from concern for the well-being of African American males (about 5 percent of the population) toward attention to the economic status of white females (45 percent of the population), thereby compromising the Act's real purpose.

Congressman Howard Smith of Virginia rose and, with a broad smile, proposed that the word "sex" be added to the list of prohibited discriminations in employment under Title VII.[1] To the laughter of his colleagues, he reported on a letter he had received from a woman protesting the excess number of American females, when compared to the count of American men, revealed by the 1960 Census. Smith read:

> Just why the Creator would set up such an imbalance of spinsters, shutting off the "right" of every female to have a husband of her own is, of course, known only to nature. But I am sure you will agree that this is a grave injustice to womankind and something the Congress and President Johnson should take immediate steps to correct.

After making his little joke, though, Smith moved to other, real issues: "Now, I am very serious about this amendment," he told his colleagues. "I think we all recognize . . . that all throughout industry women are discriminated against in that . . . they do not get as high compensation for their work as do the majority [sic] sex." To bring the matter closer to his fellow politicians' hearts, he added: "I just want to remind you here that in this election year it is pretty near half of the voters in this country that are affected, so you had better sit up and take notice."

As the debate continued, his Dixiecrat colleagues added their sometimes whimsical support. J. Russell Tuten of Georgia said that as "a man, which places me in the minority and makes me a second class citizen—and the fact that I am white and from the South—I look forward to claiming my rights under this legislation." Joe Pool of Texas argued that the amendment would "safeguard American women from such inequities with regard to their civil rights as are now threatened in the pending civil rights bill." L. Mendel Rivers of South Carolina praised the proposed change for "making it possible for the white Christian woman to receive the same consideration for employment as the colored woman." Albert Watson, also of South Carolina, urged adoption of the amendment "to prove to everyone that we believe in equal rights for all people, and especially for the ladies of our Nation."

It appears that the heirs of the maternalist vision, and of the New Deal policies that solidly embedded it in the law, understood viscerally that their legacy was threatened. Pro-family progressivism mounted its last stand.

Emanuel Cellar, chairman of the House Judiciary Committee, Democrat from New York, and floor leader for the Civil Rights bill, rose to challenge Mr. Smith. Notably, he argued for the natural *inequality* of woman and man:

> You know, the French have a phrase for it when they speak of women and men . . . "vive la difference." I think the French are right. Imagine the upheaval that would result from the adoption of blanket language requiring total equality. Would male citizens be justified in insisting that women share with them the burdens of compulsory military service? What would become of traditional family relationships? What about alimony? . . . Would fathers rank equally with mothers in the right of custody to children? . . . This is the entering wedge, an amendment of this sort.

He noted that the Women's Bureau of the U.S. Department of Labor (long a maternalist stronghold) opposed the amendment, because sex discrimination involved "problems significantly different" from race and other factors covered by the bill's language. Protective legislation for working women would also be threatened, he warned. Edith Green, a Democrat from Oregon, decried Smith's proposed amendment as an attempt to "jeopardize" the primary purpose of the Civil Rights Act: "For every discrimination that has been made against a woman in this country there has been 10 times as much discrimination against the Negro. . . . Whether we want to admit it or not, the main purpose of this legislation today is to try to end the discrimination . . . against Negroes." Moreover, she insisted that there were real "biological differences" between men and women that should be taken into account "in regard to employment."

A true son of New Deal maternalism, Congressman James Roosevelt, a Democrat from California and the son of Franklin and Eleanor, rose in support of Cellar and Green. He urged that the issue of "sex" discrimination be deferred until Congress had a chance to consider fully the report of President John Kennedy's Commission on the Status of Women, chaired by his late mother. He noted, as well, that the American Association of University Women opposed adding "sex" to Title VII.

But the equity feminists hibernating in Congress, having spent forty years in the political wilderness, sensed on that day their extraordinary, if peculiar, opportunity. Congresswoman Martha Griffiths, a Democrat from Michigan, urged support for Mr. Smith's amendment so that white women would not be left "down at the bottom" of the employment list "with no rights at all." She rejected the concerns about protective legislation for women, noting that most of it "has really been to protect men's rights in [gaining] better paying jobs." More importantly, she raised the ideological stakes by noting that "the Swedish sociologist" Gunnar Myrdal, "in his great work, 'The American Dilemma,' . . . pointed out . . . that white women and Negroes occupy relatively the same position in American society." Absolute gender equality, Swedish style, was her implied solution. Congresswoman Katharine St. George, a Republican from New York, followed at the podium, suggesting that foes of the "sex" amendment continued to see women as "chattels." Hearkening back to the great feminist push for the vote a half-century before, she added: "We have fought . . . a long way ever since the beginning of this century. Why should women be denied equality of opportunity? Why should women be denied equal pay for equal work?" Republican Congresswoman Catherine May from Washington cited the deep concerns of The National Woman's Party over the effect of an unamended Title VII on "the white, native-born American woman of Christian religion." Pointing to the failure of Congress to approve the NWP's Equal Rights Amendment, Representative May stressed that the Smith initiative was "the one possibility we may have of getting effective action."

Much to Mr. Smith's surprise, this unexpected coalition of equity feminists and Dixiecrat segregationists carried the day, by a vote of 168 to 133: discrimination in employment on the basis of "sex" would henceforth be a federal crime. Two days later, the House approved the Civil Rights Act, as amended. The measure went on to the Senate, where Hubert Humphrey pushed the measure through, throttling a Southern filibuster. Senate Minority Leader Everett Dirksen briefly questioned the addition of the word, "sex," to Title VII, but the language was left in. Senate debate focused instead almost exclusively on the issue of race.

MATERNALISM DECONSTRUCTED

In July, the Civil Rights Act of 1964, as amended, became law. For several years, however, the full implications of the "sex" amendment were unclear. Since no hearings on the idea had been held, Congress' intent was foggy, at best. But in 1967, President Johnson issued Executive Order 11375, which prohibited federal contractors from discrimination in employment on the basis of sex, and mandated "affirmative," "result-oriented" measures toward this end. Over the next four years, according to one friendly analyst, the Equal Employment Opportunities Commission (EEOC) "converted Title VII into a magna carta for female workers, grafting to it a set of rules and regulations that certainly could not have passed Congress in 1964, and perhaps not a decade later, either."[2] Among these actions was the EEOC's directive that all state labor laws crafted by the maternalists to give special protection to women be stricken from the books, under the reasoning that these measures had "ceased to be relevant to our technology or to the expanding role of the female worker in our economy."[3]

Most significantly, perhaps, the EEOC also eliminated sex-specific hiring, seniority, and promotion practices. These forms of job segregation by gender had long served as the primary buttresses to America's informal family wage system, guiding men toward the higher paid positions and women toward the lower. But now the economic foundation of the family began to shift in basic ways. The flow of married women into the labor force accelerated. Consequently, it became more difficult to sustain the "traditional American family" on one income. As female wages rose, male breadwinners working full time experienced a 28 percent decline in real wages between 1970 and 1990. The median income of married couple families in which the wife did not participate in the labor force was $34,956 in 1973 and $30,218 in 1993 (using constant 1993 dollars), a 14 percent decline.

A final legal blow to the family wage system came in March 1975, when the U.S. Supreme Court struck down the restriction of survivors' benefits under Social Security to widowed mothers; widowed fathers would now be eligible as well. This ruling, delivered in *Weinburger* v. *Wiesenfeld*, openly rejected two longstanding assumptions about family life: "that male workers' earnings are vital to the support of their families, while the earnings of female wage-earners [*sic*] do not significantly contribute to their families' support" and that "women as a group would choose to forego work to care for children while men would not." The Fifth Amendment to the Constitution, the High Court said, did not allow the government to make such assumptions about gender differences.[4]

But beyond the impact of these specific legislative and judicial defeats, why did the maternalist project ultimately fail? To begin with, these family advocates had put too much faith in the power of the state. Whereas conservative opponents of the New Deal erred in their near-mystical faith in the ability of corporate America to police itself, the maternalists were blind to the fragility of their hold on the federal government. A bureaucratic structure peopled with the maternalists' members and disciples could ensure that a governmental system built to undergird the traditional family would do just that. Even well into the 1970s, the Social Security Administration fought federal court challenges "every step" of the way in its defense of the traditional assumptions regarding male and female roles that were embedded in the American welfare state.[5] Yet this very example reveals the problem: an ideological shift within the courts, or a political change within the executive branch, could quickly turn "a good system" into a bad one, with predictably negative effects. More broadly, the concentration of power in centralized authority inevitably weakened local communities and institutions. Julia Lathrop's characterization of the 1921 Sheppard-Towner Act—that the act's purpose was "not to get the Government to do things for the family . . . [but] to create a family that can do things for itself"—was solid public relations, but it obscured the reality that thousands of federally-funded visiting nurses were infiltrating the countryside and, by their very presence, displacing home-grown solutions to various problems.

Second, the maternalist concept of the traditional family, rooted in the experiences of late-nineteenth and early-twentieth-century America, was subtly undermined after 1945. The initial focus on the natural wonder of the maternal-infant bond, the virtues of domestic production, the dignity of male labor, and the struggle for the autonomous home was commercialized and "suburbanized." As manipulated and trivialized by Madison Avenue, the image of the "housewife" became a caricature, a woman dancing with her vacuum cleaner and pursuing "the whiter than white" toilet bowl. Many suburbs, moreover, constituted incomplete and ultimately inadequate communities, in which poor development design made the creation of household-to-household bonds very difficult. The "companionate" family model, described by Talcott Parsons as resting on the socialization of children and the psychological "tension management" of adults, also proved to be a frail foundation for the "New America" in the suburbs. Enthusiasts for this family model believed that emotion alone could sustain a home life that separated men's labor from family living and left women in their houses as professional childcare workers and home managers. As it turned out, love was not enough to hold the suburban family of the 1950s together as a sustainable icon. Once this became clear, the moral legitimacy of the "suburban American family" was exposed to ideological assault.

Third, the architects of the maternalist policy structure were retiring or dying off by the mid-1940s, and they failed to nurture a third generation of leaders to protect their handiwork. It is a tribute to the power of their ideas that a mind as nimble as Daniel Moynihan's continued to argue from their worldview in 1965. In his report on *The Negro Family*, Moynihan held that "the Negro community has been forced into a *matriarchal* structure which . . . seriously retards the progress of the group." Yet, whereas the maternalists had grounded their defense of the breadwinner/homemaker family in both nature and history, Moynihan could find for it no genuine philosophical justification: "There is, presumably, no special reason why a society in which males are dominant in family relationships is to be preferred to a matriarchal arrangement." American society simply "presumes male leadership in private and public affairs."[6] Here was a sociopolitical system on its last legs.

Finally, maternalism failed because its rival—the equity feminism of the National Woman's Party—was much closer to the spirit of the era's dominant institutions: centralizing government and great corporations. Relative to the state, Carole Pateman has convincingly argued that women's growing dependence on government was a logical corollary of feminist goals—better to be dependent on Uncle Sam than on a real man—and a stimulus to reconfigured state entitlements as substitutes for lost home production.[7] Frances Fox Piven has stressed the "large and important relationship" of women as direct employees of the welfare state, noting that over 70 percent of government social welfare jobs were held by women.[8] The great corporations, for their part, benefited from an expanded labor pool, which held down wages and rid them of the "family wage" concept they found so noxious. They also gained from shrunken household economies, which meant that more of what families consumed would be purchased commodities, rather than homemade goods. Thus, whereas maternalist goals sometimes swam against the tides of corporate power and bureaucratic centralization, equity feminism consistently floated happily along.

A Perverse "New America"

The broad result can be visualized through a simple "family wage" ratio:

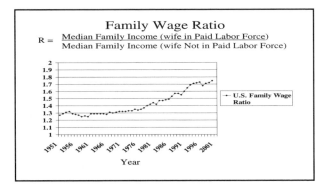

This ratio is sensitive to a variety of aggregated factors: the impact of job segregation by gender on household income; the relative degree of career commitment by men and women; the effects of protective legislation; the influence of seniority; and the relative use of part-time work. In a "family wage" economy, which focuses on the economic status of the male breadwinner, this ratio would tend toward (but never reach) 1:0. In an economy of pure gender equality, this ratio would tend toward 2:0, with men and women approaching full gender equality in all aspects of life.

Figure 6.1 shows the results for the period from 1951 to 2000.[9] From 1951 to 1974, the ratio is relatively stable, varying between 1:25 and 1:33, and reaching the lower figure in 1958 and 1960. Between 1975 and 1982, in the wake of maternalism's rout, the ratio begins a slow increase, reaching 1:42. Thereafter, the ratio rises sharply throughout the 1980s, apparently stabilizing at just below 1:75 by the turn of the century. It is safe to conclude that a fairly strong and stable family wage system, codified in custom and law, and clearly operational in the 1950s and 1960s, has now all but disappeared.[10]

What has this meant for America? At the demographic level, the end of the family wage regime coincided with an implosion of the "traditional family," as this way of life lost much of its economic logic. Nobel Laureate Gary Becker has shown that notable economic gains associated with marriage come from a division of labor in the home, as when a housewife focuses on domestic tasks and a husband on outside labor.[11] As American men and women became more alike in economic function after 1970, the financial advantage of the joint (married) household faded, and the marriage rate began to fall. Partly for the same reason, the divorce rate rose by 150 percent. With women shifting their priorities away from home toward outside work, the marital birthrate tumbled sharply as well, particularly during the early 1970s. Meanwhile, the number, rate, and ratio of out-of-wedlock births climbed steadily. African-American fathers faded further into insignificance: one in four African-American children in 1964 had no father at home. By the 1980s, the same ratio was two out of three. Another "New America"—a perverse mirror image of Henry Luce's vision— had emerged.

There were other consequences, as well. First, the central assumption behind the American welfare state had been discarded by a reckless government, with scarcely any thought of the consequences. The premise of a family wage was the foundation on which the benefit systems of Old Age Insurance, Survivors Insurance, Unemployment Insurance, and Aid to Families with Dependent Children (AFDC) rested. As bread-winning father/homemaking mother families became a minority among households, deep contradictions in the Social Security system rose to the surface.[12] By what logic did a dependent wife gain a pension, but not a dependent husband ? Why should any "homemaker" deserve a benefit? How could AFDC payments to divorced, abandoned, or never-married mothers-at-home be justified if a majority of married mothers were now working? "Motherhood" had lost its sanctified aura, and so had Social Security. As constructed by the maternalists and the New Dealers, the system had served social and moral purposes: the protection of maternity and young children; the restoration of authority to fathers; the renewal of families; the unification of the nation. But after the fall of the family wage regime, Social Security became merely an insurance policy, and not a very good policy at that. Welfare reform aimed at putting AFDC mothers to work (and their children in daycare centers) became one logical response; so did the search for alternatives to a retirement insurance plan with anemic financial results.

Second, a great political realignment occurred with the demise of the family wage. From the late-nineteenth century until 1964 (with the prominent exception of the Theodore Roosevelt years), the Democratic Party was, broadly speaking, the "party of the family." It tended to favor the small business, the family farm, and the protection of motherhood, children, and workers' homes from "the depredations of capital." Labor unions allied with the Democrats stood for the family wage ideal, as did the maternalists who built the American welfare state. Roman Catholics—with their communitarian values centered on family, social justice, and the family wage—also found a congenial home in the Democratic Party. When the family wage order was challenged during the 1964 Civil Rights debate, *only* Democrats rose in its defense. In contrast, the pre-1964 Republican Party tended to be the party of equity feminism and the industrial order. Republicans consistently opposed restraints on children's and women's labor as violations of the freedom of contract. They dismissed the family wage as another meddling socialist dream. It was Republican politicians who first introduced the Equal Rights Amendment in Congress in 1923, at the behest of the National Woman's Party. In 1940, the Republican Party became the first major party to endorse the ERA in its national platform. It was a Republican administration that supported the 1955 Conference on the Effective Use of Womanpower, which urged women to defer marriage and to enter scientific and technical careers. And it was Republicans who first openly embraced the deadly gods of neo-Malthusianism and population control during the 1950s.

Between 1964 and 1980, in a process still poorly documented and analyzed, all this changed. The failure of the Civil Rights Act of 1964 to bring racial peace; the demise of the Dixiecrat wing of the Democratic Party; the ordeal of the Vietnam War; the cultural and sexual revolutions launched in the mid-1960s; the *Roe* v. *Wade* decision of 1973 legalizing abortion; and equity feminism's triumph over its nemesis, the family wage—all these brought fundamental coalition change. Equity feminists left the GOP and moved into the Democratic Party, where they soon became a dominant faction. Social conservatives, meanwhile, migrated into the Republican Party. Pro-life, pro-family, and pro–Social Security (e.g., as defined by the system of 1939), these voters were the "Reagan Democrats" who turned American politics upside down in 1980.

The third consequence was that the "traditional family" of breadwinning father/homemaking mother and their happy brood of children disappeared as an American icon at the very moment when Congress reopened the doors of immigration. The great controversy in the early-twentieth century over assimilation into America had been resolved, in part, by the immigration restriction laws of 1921 and 1924 and, in part, by the policy victories of the maternalists, which rested on the assumption of a common family order rooted in a shared human nature. Both racialist Anglo-Saxonism and the moral neutrality of cultural pluralism were superseded by the vision of America as a peculiarly family-centered land. American unity *and* identity were formed around the hearth, the home, and the "sanctified" traditional family; they bound immigrant and native-born alike. Later expressions of this idea—such as Henry Luce's "New America" campaign and Walt Rostow's promotion of the "American Style"—remained faithful, at their core, to this familism.

Still beset by guilt over American racism, Congress approved the Immigration Reform Act of 1965. The old limits and preferences enshrined in 1924 were tossed out, and the number of immigrants entering America began to climb, from about 200,000 a year in the early 1960s to 530,000 by 1980 and 1,536,000 by 1990. For the whole period, 1970 to 2000, 21 million legal immigrants entered the United States, along with perhaps another 5 million illegal immigrants. The typical backgrounds of immigrants also changed. Europeans were few in number; the great majority of these new Americans came from Latin

America and from Asia. Religious diversity also grew. For the first time, Muslim, Buddhist, and Hindu immigrants arrived in large numbers. Yet they all came to a nation that now had little idea of what "Americanization" meant, a nation in the throes of a moral and social revolution.

THE REAGAN RESTORATION

The Ronald Reagan administration, however, tried to reverse recent trends, and to usher in a restoration of "the mores and customs of the past," binding anticommunism to a defense of the family. Overt hostility to Marxism–Leninism returned as a powerful metaphor in foreign policy and as a basis for national self-definition, as it had been during the 1950s and early 1960s. No longer burdened by the demands of equity feminists, the GOP jettisoned its support of the Equal Rights Amendment. Instead, the Republican party drew in the Reagan Democrats by becoming the party opposed to abortion and in favor of the family.

As Walt Rostow had predicted, the 1980s was the decade when the great contest between communism and liberal democracy came to a head. Communist morality, President Reagan stated in his first news conference, rested on the goal of promoting "world revolution and a one world Socialist or Communist state." Soviet leaders reserved "unto themselves the right to commit any crime, to lie, to cheat, in order to attain" that goal.[13] In his May 1981 address at the University of Notre Dame, Reagan asserted that the West "won't contain Communism, it will transcend Communism. It won't bother to . . . denounce it, it will dismiss [communism] as some bizarre chapter in human history whose last pages are even now being written."[14] Before the United Kingdom's House of Commons in June 1982, Reagan declared that "the march of freedom and democracy . . . will leave Marxism–Leninism on the ash heap of history as it has left other tyrannies which stifle the freedom and muzzle the self-expression of the people." He underscored how it was "totalitarian forces in the world who seek subversion and conflict around the globe to further their barbarous assault on the human spirit." Using language not heard since the days of Dulles and Rostow, Reagan pointed to antinuclear demonstrators in the West, and asked: "Must freedom wither in a quiet, deadening accommodation with totalitarian evil?" He summoned Americans "to the global campaign for democracy now gathering force," to tell "the world that a new age is not only possible but probable." Turning to the issue of national identity, Reagan asked: "'What kind of people do we think we are?' . . . Let us answer, 'Free people, worthy of freedom and determined not only to remain so but to help others gain their freedom as well.'"[15]

On the domestic side, Reagan sought verbally to resurrect the American identity built on religious morality and shared family life. It was "time for the world to know our intellectual and spiritual values are rooted in the source of all strength," he stated in the same Notre Dame speech, "a belief in a Supreme Being, and a law higher than our own."[16] In time of crisis and challenge, Reagan said elsewhere, families kept "safe our cultural heritage and reinforce[d] our spiritual values." He added: "it is time to recommit ourselves to the concept of the family—a concept that must withstand the trends of lifestyle and legislation."[17]

Reagan was surely aware of the new turmoil within the American social order. He noted in 1984 that throughout American history, "we've relied on the family as the principle institution for transmitting values." But the American family had now become "very different from what it was. Many families are headed by a single parent. Families are smaller, not only with fewer children but with fewer generations living together."[18] From 1986 until the end of his presidency, Reagan gave mounting attention to strengthening the nation's family system. "The family provides children with a haven of love and concern," he told the Student Congress on Evangelism. "For parents, it provides a sense of purpose and meaning in life. When the family is strong, the Nation is strong. When the family is weak, the Nation itself is weak."[19] Speaking in Chicago, Reagan added:

> [T]he family is the bedrock of our nation, but it is also the engine that gives our country life. . . . It's for our families that we work and labor, so that we can join together around the dinner table, bring our children up the right way, care for our parents, and reach out to those less fortunate. It is the power of the family that holds the Nation together, that gives America her conscience, and that serves as the cradle of our country's soul.[20]

Reagan also hinted that the family could again serve as a force for assimilation and national unity in a time of massive immigration. "We have all been enriched by the contributions of Hispanics in every walk of American life," he told an audience in the White House Rose Garden. Characteristic of Hispanic culture "most of all," he continued, was "the *casa*, the almost mystical center of daily life, where grandparents and parents and children and grandchildren all come together in the *familia*." The President quoted poet Octavio Paz: "In Hispanic morals, the true protagonist is the family." He then added: "But I fear that too often, in the mad rush of modern American life, some people have not learned the great lesson of our Hispanic heritage: the lesson of family and home and church and community."[21] Like the German-Americans of an earlier time, Reagan implied, Hispanics were now teaching other Americans lessons about morality and unity centered on the home.

The most coherent effort by the Reagan administration to resurrect a traditionalist family policy was the sixty-six-page report developed by a twenty-two-person interagency the Working Group on the Family, chaired by Undersecretary of Education Gary Bauer. Titled *The Family: Preserving America's Future*, and released in November 1986, the document blasted the "abrasive experiments of two liberal decades" such as day care, population control, no-fault divorce, sex education, and values clarification in the schools. In their place, the report affirmed "home truths":

> Intact families are good. Families who choose to have children are making a desirable decision. Mothers and fathers who then decide to spend a good deal of time raising those children themselves rather than leaving it to others are demonstrably doing a good thing for those children. . . . Public policy and the culture in general must support and reaffirm these decisions.[22]

Compared to the family vision of the maternalists and the New Dealers, however, the Reagan policy contained two significant differences. While giving indirect praise to full-time mothers at home (e.g., "unlike Sweden . . . the mothers of America have managed to avoid becoming just so many more cogs in the wheels of commerce"), the Bauer Report directly emphasized the virtues of working mothers ("*They are nothing short of heroic*") and urged caution that policy "be sensitive to the perception of favoring one type of family arrangement over another (e.g., two-parent families with dual earners versus families with a single earner)."[23] Moreover, where the maternalists had seen capitalism as at odds with the family, the Bauer Report positively linked the defense of traditional family values to "the essence of democratic capitalism." Although noting that "some contend that the consumer ethic of capitalism undermines family values, it is more true that neither the modern family nor the free enterprise system would long survive without the other." The report continued: "*Families which teach that effort results in gain prepare skilled and energetic workers who are the engine for democratic capitalism.* . . . Without employees, investors, and entrepreneurs nurtured in families and instilled with the work ethic, democratic capitalism fails."[24]

Some critics have interpreted the Bauer Report as twisting family life and family policy into instrumental goods in service to capitalist ideology.[25] But it is probably more accurate to say that the report reflected the never-ending attempt by conservative writers and policymakers to provide some coherence to the new, historically odd, and uncertain Reagan coalition of "free-market capitalism" and "traditional values;" in other words, that it was an effort to convince business-oriented Republicans that they needed "the family" for more than just votes.[26]

The difficulty of this coalition building was underscored by President Reagan's Executive Order 12606, signed on September 2, 1987. A direct consequence of the Bauer Report, this order required federal agencies to develop "family impact statements" when crafting and implementing regulations and policies. Specific criteria included: "Does this action by government strengthen or erode the stability of the family and, particularly, the marital commitment?"; "Does this action strengthen or erode the authority and rights of parents in the education, nurture, and supervision of their children?"; and "Does this action help the family perform its functions, or does it substitute governmental activity for the function?" These were excellent questions. However, in deference to coalition politics, the Executive Order avoided any language that would threaten the interests of big business. Moreover, it was intentionally vague about defining the *type* of family that was to be strengthened. Key issues for the maternalists, such as gender roles within marriage, the desirability of the stay-at-home mother, and the necessity of a family wage were simply ignored. Partly as a consequence, the Executive Order had little real effect. President Bill Clinton finally rescinded it on April 21, 1997.

OLD DEBATES REBORN

The 1990s actually saw old debates regarding the American identity take on new life. Regarding immigration, restrictionists despairing of America's assimilation process squared off again against the advocates of cultural pluralism. The former group underscored that, in Chilton Williamson's words, "[i]mmigration is a failure, because assimilation, contrary to national myth, never really occurred."[27] Any full accommodation of cultures is impossible to attain, they argued. Immigrants held onto their old ways and continued to resent the "old American stock." The unique American values instilled in the nation at its founding were not compatible with the ideals that many immigrants brought with them. According to Williamson, the "most significant contribution" of Germans such as Carl Schurz had been to "infect" American life "with notions of Prussian bureaucracy and Prussian centralization."[28] Journalist Peter Brimelow held a more positive view of the American experience with immigrants: assimilation worked between 1850 and 1920 because immigrants were told they had to "Americanize." "Now they are told that they should retain and reinforce their diversity." Today, he concluded, there is no "American Idea," only "diversity."[29] The liberal historian Arthur Schlesinger Jr. summoned up Theodore Roosevelt's fear of America becoming "a tangle of squabbling nationalities, an intricate knot of German-Americans, Irish-Americans, English-Americans, French-Americans, Scandinavian-Americans, or Italian-Americans, each preserving its separate identity." Schlesinger wryly commented that seventy-five years later, "we must add a few more nationalities to T. R.'s brew." He saw the contemporary "attack on the common American identity" as "the culmination of the cult of ethnicity," and espoused an assimilation process that would guide immigrants to embrace the English language, existing institutions, "and the political ideals that hold the nation together."[30]

Recovering the voice of Herbert Kallen, multiculturalists of the 1990s, such as Bill Ong Hing, claimed that America was "already a multiracial, multicultural country whose culture is constantly evolving." They urged an understanding of cultural pluralism, "which respects diverse views and cultures, which is constantly attentive to race relations, and which shares a core set of values." Such values tended toward the instrumental, the economic, and the political, such as "respect for laws, the democratic political and economic system, equal opportunity and human rights." Above all, "diversity must be the basis for an 'American' identity,"[31] including, most certainly, diversity in lifestyles. For as another multiculturalist, Nathan Glazer, explained: "one can see little reason why the process should stop short of gays and lesbians." He reasoned that since late-twentieth-century multiculturalism "already extends beyond race and ethnic differences to include women's studies," the "cultures" of varied "life-style" groups should be embraced as well. Glazer argued that "history moves toward ever greater equality, recognizing equality in new spheres, from the civil, to the political, to the economic, to the cultural." With regard to gender, he noted that Americans had already "tried to make good the inequality in all these respects of the female sex. If progress is the spread of equality and liberty, *one does not see how any good argument* can be made against gay and lesbian claims."[32]

Meanwhile, the debate over "family values" polarized as well. The equity feminists, heirs to the NWP, pushed for the apotheosis of their post-family order. The twin principles of industrialism and individualism stood triumphant, they declared. According to Jody Heymann, "the revolutionary movement of men and women into the industrial and post-industrial labor force has transformed the United States."[33] Nonetheless, the process remained incomplete: "The struggle for the creation of new and more varied lifestyle options is far from over," reported two prominent professors of management. Women must more fully enter the corporate world, they argued, for they were more skilled at handling ambiguity, building networks, and doing simultaneous tasks, all necessary for "success in the brave new world of twenty-first century careers." Men, meanwhile, should be retrained to spend more time in elder and child care, for "in contrast with mothers . . . it is *less* career involvement for a father that increases his psychological availability to his children." They urged that all children attend "innovative summer camps"—indoctrination centers that would open children's minds by "challenging the traditional gender roles."[34]

For these advocates, family policy meant adjusting laws and benefits to an order where "the wage-employment system is universally understood as desirable for all adults, men and women, mothers and fathers alike."[35] Specifics included: "affordable day care" subsidized by corporations and government; paid family leaves; greatly expanded early childhood education; more after-school programs for children; state-provided elder care; universal health insurance; and "repeated increases" in the minimum wage. Such steps would help bring about the full industrialization of human life, organized under the gaze of a great corporate state.

Meanwhile, pro-family advocates worked to save the family as at least a partially autonomous social institution. But in deference to political realities, they usually did so in ways that threatened neither important corporate interests nor the new orthodoxy of gender equity. Measures promoted by pro-family advocates during the 1980s and 1990s included:

o Tax reforms that would expand the value of the personal exemption, create an additional child tax credit, and repair the "marriage penalty" in the federal income tax by restoring the policy of the 1948–1969 period known as "income splitting";
o Social Security reforms that would create true "personal accounts" that might serve as a family patrimony;
o The extension of child care subsidies by making the existing "dependent care tax credit" for day care available to stay-at-home parents tending their own children;
o The promotion of "educational choice" through tuition tax credits, vouchers, "charter schools," and related schemes to increase parental influence over schooling; and
o The pursuit of strategies to increase the prospects for work-at-home, including zoning reforms and a loosening of the Fair Labor Standards Act.[36]

The results of this advocacy included some policy victories, particularly through the tax reforms of 1996 and 2001 and under the "school choice" banner. In terms of social data, it appears that the marital birthrate rose by 5 percent between 1996 and 2000, a positive shift not seen since the mid-1950s. The flow of married women with small children into the labor force also may have halted, and even slightly reversed.

Yet in truth, these were only tiny shifts on the great scale of social change evidenced since the mid-1960s, and they may not have survived the recession of 2001–2002. Certainly, there was no evidence of a restoration of the family wage regime. Other measures of social life—the rapidly growing number of "unmarried partner households" (e.g., both heterosexual cohabitation and gay and lesbian couples), the continued growth in out-of-wedlock births, and a still declining marriage rate—did not alter their course. Judged more soberly, the thirty-five-year-old retreat from marriage and children probably continued, much to the delight and encouragement of the "post-family" pluralists. And there was certainly no reason to believe that the "traditional family" still served in any real way as a compelling, successful assimilation device.

"American" Beliefs

Perhaps it does not matter. For one thing, the American national security apparatus proved capable of projecting considerable power overseas after 1990, despite the lack of a unifying set of social values at home. Military victories in the Gulf War, Kosovo, and Afghanistan showed the remarkable effectiveness and dramatic superiority of American arms over those of their foes. Moreover, the collapse of the USSR in the period between1989and 1991, caused by some combination of American resolve and internal Soviet weaknesses, eliminated the only real Great Power rival that America had. In retrospect, it seems that George Kennan, Talcott Parsons, Henry Luce, and Walt Rostow all worried over nothing.

Perhaps the strictly instrumental values of equality and economic and cultural liberty are all that are really needed to hold this vast nation and its varied people together. The views of an immigration restrictionist such as Arthur Schlesinger Jr. and a cultural pluralist such as Bill Ong Hing are actually almost indistinguishable when it comes to core social values: they differ only in the degree of pressure to be exerted on immigrants to adopt these values. In his recent book *American Beliefs*, John Harmon McElroy even pulls together a fairly compelling "list of American cultural beliefs" that emphasizes individualism and avoids at least direct mention of controversial lifestyle issues. His list includes "primary beliefs," such as "everyone must work" and "persons must benefit from their work"; "immigrant beliefs," such as "improvement is possible"; "frontier beliefs," such as "each person is responsible for his own well being" and "helping others helps yourself"; "social beliefs," such as "society is a collection of individuals"; and "religious and moral beliefs," such as "God gave men the same birthrights" and "God created nature and human beings." Conspicuously absent is any use of the words "family" and "community," even in vague form.[37] Maybe they are not necessary; or perhaps they are really not "American."

All the same, when McElroy describes recent "troubling signs of . . . cultural deterioration" in America, "family" and "community" are the first two keywords he uses: "In no period of American history . . . have *families* in every class of American society been so disrupted by marital infidelity and divorce . . . , out-of-wedlock pregnancies . . . , abortions and new venereal diseases such as AIDS and herpes"; "[t]he same period has likewise seen a growing disrespect for *community* standards of decency."[38] Are these potent concepts needed after all?

Yes. While one might imagine other ways to gain a sense of affinity and common citizenship among an otherwise divided people, the powerful images surrounding the family and related natural communities seem properly American. Affection for the American home emerged out of the special circumstances of our nation's history. It is an attachment that celebrates human actions bonded to social order, to the creation of new life, and to qualities of abundance and optimism. The metaphor of the American home is certainly more coherent and charged with more meaning and authentic emotion than its rivals crafted in the twentieth century, such as "a nation of nations," neo–Anglo-Saxonism, or the consumption-driven "Wal-Mart civilization."

Moreover, the American self-understanding needs such grounding in social constructs— not to shore up the national security apparatus nor to advance global capitalism, but rather to limit them, to control them, and to restrain their potential abuse of power. As G. K. Chesterton once explained, "this institution of the home is the one anarchist institution." It is "older than law," it is the true "province of liberty," and it is "the only check on the state that is bound to renew itself as eternally as the state, and more naturally than the state."[39] America's global reach, both economic and military, has at least all the trappings of empire, and it holds the ability to disrupt or destroy all that it touches. Only natural and internalized restraints—respect for motherhood, sanctification of the family, concern for the home economy, esteem for the natural communities that shelter families— can hold the modern American corporate state in balance with human values, in domestic matters as well as in foreign adventures and trade. The Reagan administration's concept of a "family impact statement" was a frail approximation of the proper role to be played by such a shared national identity. In addition to its definitional vagueness, its problems were that it did not go far enough and that the permanent government of bureaucrats did not treat it seriously.

What language about family and community might be fit for twenty-first-century Americans? These qualities, at least:

⁰ Affirmation of the family as the natural and irreplaceable human community, one defined as a man and woman living in a socially sanctioned bond called marriage for the purposes of propagating and rearing children, sharing intimacy and resources, and conserving lineage, property, and tradition;

⁰ Recognition that men and women *should be* equal in political and property rights, but *are* different in reproductive, economic, and social functions,[40] differences which must be accommodated in policy and law;

⁰ Encouragement for "deindustrialization" and the return of vital functions to the family circle, with "home schooling" as the most practical and successful recent model;

⁰ Respect for the ancient and still most honorable skills of "housewifery" and "husbandry" and their grounding in a vital home economy;

⁰ Celebration of the birth of new babies and cultural and policy encouragement for the child-rich family; and

⁰ Protection from political interference and economic exploitation for those spontaneous communities—both religious and secular—that nurture and sustain families.

In the industrialized European Union of 2003, these values are openly rejected. A common "democratic socialism" premised on the gender values of equity feminism quietly snuffs out remaining pockets of traditional European family life. One consequence of this post-family environment is the accelerating depopulation of the Old World.

Though its cultural roots lie in Europe, America has always been different. Even in the degraded times of the early-twenty-first century, Americans talk of "marriages," "babies," "mothers," and "fathers" in ways that make sophisticated Europeans cringe. "These are American questions which do not concern us," a Swedish welfare official replied when asked a few years back about his nation's marriage rate.[41] Indeed, these *are* "American questions." With some unnecessary accretions, the qualities listed above once served as "the American way." They should, and they can, again.

Endnotes

PREFACE

1. "Special Report: Results of a Global Survey on Marriage and the Family," conducted in September-October, 1999; sponsored by The Howard Center for Family, Religion and Society and the World Family Policy Center at Brigham Young University; margin of error = ± 1.8 percent.
2. Barry Alan Shain, *The Myth of American Individualism* (Princeton, N.J.: Princeton University Press, 1994).

CHAPTER 1
HOME AND NATION: THE FAMILY
POLITICS OF THEODORE ROOSEVELT

1. Edmund Morris, *The Rise of Theodore Roosevelt* (New York: Coward, McCann & Geoghegan, 1979), 26–28.
2. Numbers from: *Historical Statistics of the United States: Colonial Times to 1970* (Washington, D.C.: U.S. Department of Commerce, Bureau of the Census, 1975): Series A160–71, A172–94, B5–10, B42–48, B67–98.
3. *The Oxford English Dictionary. Second Edition. Vol. XIII* (Oxford, U.K.: Clarendon Press, 1989), 69–70; and *Webster's Third New International Dic-*

tionary (Springfield, Mass.: G & C Merriam, 1969), 1870.

4. Theodore Roosevelt, *The Foes of Our Own Household* (New York: George H. Doran, 1917), 246; hereafter *Foes*.

5. "Review of *Social Evolution* by Benjamin Kidd," *North American Review* (July 1895); in *The Works of Theodore Roosevelt: Memorial Edition, Vol. XIV* (New York: Charles Scribner's Sons, 1924), 111-14; hereafter *Works*.

6. *Works, XIV*, 111. Emphasis added.

7. Theodore Roosevelt, "Twisted Eugenics," *The Outlook* (January 3, 1914); in *Works, XIV*, 173.

8. "Review of *Racial Decay* by Octavius Charles Beale," in *The Outlook* (April 8, 1911); in *Works, XIV*,153.

9. Theodore Roosevelt, "The Woman and the Home [1905]," in *Works, XIV*, 232.

10. *Works, XIV*, 178. Emphasis added.

11. Theodore Roosevelt, *Ranch Land of Argentina and Brazil* [1916]; in *Works, IV*, 76–79.

12. *Works, XIV*, 155.

13. Theodore Roosevelt, *Realizable Ideals: The Earl Lectures* [1911]; originally delivered at the Pacific Theological Seminary; in *Works, XXII*, 600. Emphasis added.

14. Speech originally delivered at the New York State Fair, Syracuse, September 7, 1903; in *Presidential Addresses and State Papers of Theodore Roosevelt. Part Two.* (New York: P.F. Collier & Son, [1904?]), 479, 493.

15. *Works, XXII*, 592.

16. "The Man Who Works With His Hands"; address at the SemiCentennial Celebration of the Founding of Agriculture Colleges in the United States, Lansing, Michigan, May 31, 1907; in *Works, XVIII*, 189.

17. Theodore Roosevelt, *The Great Adventure: Present Day Studies in American Nationalism* [1918]; in *Works, XXI*, 263.

18. *Works, XVIII*, 188. Emphasis added.

19. *Works, XXII*, 593.

20. *Foes*, 246.

21. "Review of Mr. Adam's *The Law of Civilization and Decay*," in *The Forum* (January 1897); in *Works, XIV*, 146. Emphasis added.

22. *Works, XIV*, 158.

23. *Works, XVIII*, 226.

24. *Works, XIV*, 160.

25. *Works, XIV*, 173.

26. *Foes*, 233, 235.

27. *Works, XXII*, 601.

28. *Foes*, 270.

29. *Works, XIV*, 175.

30. *Foes*, 259.

31. *Works, XVIII*, 227.

32. *Foes*, 271.

33. *Works, XXI*, 266.

34. *Foes*, 233-34; *Works, XVIII*, 228. Emphasis added.

35. *Works, XIV*, 175. Emphasis added.

36. *Works, XVIII*, 229.

37. *Foes*, 231, 238.

38. *Works, XVIII*, 284. Emphasis added.

39. *Foes*, 238.

40. John A. Lester, ed., *The Americanism of Theodore Roosevelt* (Boston: Houghton Mifflin, 1923), 69.

41. *Works, XVIII*, 277–78.

42. *Works, XIV*, 161.

43. *Works, XVIII*, 285.

44. *Works, XVIII*, 176, 181.

45. *Works, XVIII*, 188, 191, 197, 225.

46. *Works, XXII*, 599.

47. *Foes*, 241, 252, 264.

48. *Works, XIV*, 167–70.

49. *Works, XVIII*, 225, 284, 289.

50. *Foes*, 250–51.

51. *Works, XIV*, 151–52, 163, 165.

52. *Foes*, 250–51.

53. *Works, XVIII*, 230.

54. *Foes*, 152.

55. *Works, XVIII*, 230.

56. *Foes*, 263.

57. *Works, XIV*, 154, 157.

58. Quoted in Morris, *The Rise of Theodore Roosevelt*, 128.

59. *Foes*, 233–39.

60. Theodore Roosevelt, "Review of *Woman in Science* by H.J. Mozans," *The Outlook*, (January 10, 1914); in *Works, XIV*, 181, 184.

61. *Works, XIV*, 181, 184, 276.

62. *Works, XXII*, 598.

63. *Foes*, 231–39; 254.

64. *Works, XIV*, 180.

65. *Works, XVIII*, 231; *XXII*, 594. Emphasis added.

66. *Foes*, 258; *Works, XIV*, 172.

67. Theodore Roosevelt, "The White Slave Traffic," *The Outlook* (January 18, 1913); in *Works, XVIII*, 290–91.

68. *Foes*, 194–95, 207–8; *Works, XVII*, 178–80, 186–87, 197.

69. *Foes*, 208; *Works, XVIII*, 284–85.

70. *Works, XVIII*, 285.

71. *Foes*, 265–66.

72. *Foes*, 265. Emphasis added.

73. Allan Carlson, *The New Agrarian Mind: The Movement Toward Decentralist Thought in 20th Century America* (New Brunswick, N.J.: Transaction, 2000), chapter 1.

74. A. C. Carlson, "Gender, Children, and Social Labor: Transcending the 'Family Wage' Dilemma," *Journal of Social Issues* 52 (1996), 143–48.

CHAPTER 2
HYPHENATES, *HAUSFRAUS*, AND BABY-SAVING:
THE PECULIAR LEGACY OF GERMAN AMERICA

1. "Wilson Hits 'Hyphenates,'" *Rockford Morning Star*, 15 June 1916, 1.

2. Quotation from June 14, 1916; in Frederick C. Luebke, *Bonds of Loyalty: German-Americans and World War I* (Dekalb: Northern Illinois University Press, 1974), 174.

3. *Rockford Daily Register-Gazette*, 16 June 1916, 1; *Rockford Morning Star*, 16 June 1916, 3; and *Rockford Daily Republic*, 15 June 1916, 1.

4. Philip Gleason, "American Identity and Americanization," in Stephan Thernstrom, ed., *Harvard Encyclopedia of American Ethnic Groups* (Cambridge, Mass.: Harvard University Press, 1980), 31.

5. John Higham, *Send These to Me: Jews and Other Immigrants in Urban America* (New York: Atheneum, 1975), 32–33, 39.

6. Quoted in Kathleen Neils Conzen, "German-Americans and the Invention of Ethnicity," in Frank Trommler and Joseph McVeigh, eds., *America and the Germans: An Assessment of a Three Hundred-Year History* (Philadelphia: University of Pennsylvania Press, 1985), 141; also 131–34; Gleason, "American Identity," 33, 38.

7. Higham, *Send These to Me*, 201–2.

8. On Kallen's background, *see* Higham, *Send These to Me*, 203–6.

9. Horace M. Kallen, "Democracy Versus the Melting Pot: A Study of Ameri-

can Nationality. Part I," *The Nation* 100 (February 18, 1915), 190–91.

10. On this point, *see* Gleason, "American Identity," 44–45; and Higham, *Send These to Me,* 207.

11. Kallen, "Democracy versus the Melting Pot. Part I," 192–93; and "Part II," *The Nation* 100 (February 25, 1919), 217–20. Emphasis added.

12. Horace M. Kallen, *Culture and Democracy in the United States* (New York: Boni and Liveright, 1924), 12–13, 22, 32–35, 58–62; and Horace Kallen, *Cultural Pluralism and the American Idea: An Essay in Social Philosophy* (Philadelphia: University of Pennsylvania Press, 1956), 57–60, 73, 87, 94. Emphasis added.

13. Kallen, *Culture and Democracy*, 18, 31, 53; and Kallen, *Cultural Pluralism and the American Idea*, 74, 92, 97.

14. Kallen, "Democracy versus The Melting Pot," 217–18.

15. Kathleen Neils Conzen, "Germans," in Stephan Thernstrom, ed. *Harvard Encyclopedia of American Ethnic Groups*, (Cambridge, Mass.: Harvard University Press, 1980), 406, 410, 415.

16. Quotation from Geo. Meyer, *The German-American* (October 6, 1890), Madison: The Wisconsin State Historical Society Pamphlet Collection, #57–574. *See also* David Detjen, *The Germans in Missouri, 1900-1918: Prohibition, Neutrality, and Assimilation* (Columbia: University of Missouri Press, 1985), 20–22; John A. Hawgood, *The Tragedy of German-America* (New York: G. P. Putnam's Sons, 1940), 290; Conzen, "German-Americans and the Invention of Ethnicity," 131, 143–44; and U.S. Census Office, *Abstract of The Twelfth Census of the United States. 1900 Statistical Atlas* (Washington, D.C.: Government Printing Office, 1902), Plate 64.

17. Quotations from Detjen, *The Germans in Missouri*, 23, 25–26. Also: Lavern J. Rippley, *The German-Americans* (Boston: Twayne, 1976), 180; and Albert Bernhardt Faust, *The German Element in the United States. Volume II* (Boston: Houghton Mifflin, 1909), 246–49. Symbolic of this cultural schizophrenia among the German-American intellectual elite was the career of George Sylvester Viereck. Born in New York to German parents, his early poetry and books stressed the virtues of German culture and the crudeness of America. He cast Germany and America as seductive women competing for his loyalty [e.g.,: "He returns to She-America, to the source of his vigor and to his 'pristine' mother love."] Backed by wealthy German-Americans, he founded a magazine, *The International*, described as "a vital American periodical with strong German affiliations." Viereck's career would peak in 1914, only to be destroyed by the calamity of World War I. *See* Phyllis Keller, *States of Belonging: German-American Intellectuals and the First World War* (Cam-

bridge, Mass.: Harvard University Press, 1979), 121–61.

18. Carl Wittke, *German-Americans and the World War* (Columbus: Ohio State Archaeological and Historical Society, 1936), 164. Also: Faust, *The German Element in the United States. II*, 198–200.

19. Rippley, *The German-Americans*, 181; and Conzen, "Germans," 416.

20. Detjen, *The Germans in Missouri*, 27.

21. Rippley, *The German-Americans*, 181.

22. Detjen, *The Germans in Missouri*, 28.

23. C. J. Hexamer, "German Achievement in America," *German American Annals* I (January 1903), 46–48.

24. Albert Godsho, *Chronological History of the National German American Alliance of the United States* (Philadelphia: National German-American Alliance, 1911), 3, 32, 37.

25. Quoted in *A Disloyal Combination: The National German-American Alliance and Its Allies* (Westerville, OH: American Issue Publishing, [1918–?]), 4; in Wisconsin State Historical Society Pamphlet Collection, #54–1020.

26. Taken from Don H. Tolzmann, ed., *German-Americans in the World Wars. Vol. II: The World War Experience* (Munich: K.G. Saur, 1995), 395–96.

27. Luebke, *Bonds of Loyalty*, 76–77.

28. Theodore Roosevelt, *America and the World War* (New York: Charles Scribner's Sons, 1916), 65–66, 68–69. A somewhat later and radically different view of Imperial Germany and its war aims can be found in Appendix A ("Why We Are at War: The German Horror") of Roosevelt's *The Foes of Our Own Household* (New York: George H. Doran, 1917), 273–76.

29. Rippley, *The German-Americans*, 182.

30. Keller, *States of Belonging*, 140–45; and Wittke, *German-Americans and the World War*, 7.

31. Rudolf Cronau, *Do We Need a Third War for Independence?* (New York: German American Literary Defense Committee, 1914), 1, 6. Emphasis added. *See also* Keller, *States of Belonging*, 146; Wittke, *German-Americans and the World War*, 14–15; and Rippley, *The German-Americans*, 183.

32. *Address of Dr. C. J. Hexamer to the Mass Meeting at the Academy of Music, Philadelphia, PA., November 24, 1914* (Philadelphia: Graf and Breaninger, [1915]); in Wisconsin State Historical Society Pamphlet Collection, #54–989.

33. Wittke, *German-Americans and the World War*, 10–11.

34. Poem in Frederick Franklin Schroder, *The German American Hand Book . . . 1916–1917* (New York: n.p., 1916): 24. Also: Tolzmann, *German-Americans in the World War*, 404; Hexamer, *German Achievements in America*, 49–52;

and Dr. C. J. Hexamer, *Address* (November 24, 1914), 4.

35. In Schroder, *The German American Handbook*, 105; and originally in Faust, *The German Element in the United States*, 184.

36. Luebke, *Bonds of Loyalty*, 163; and Detjen, *The Germans in Missouri*, 120.

37. For Roosevelt, this was no new obsession. As early as 1897, he reported in a speech: "I stand for the American citizen of German birth or descent, precisely as I stand for any other American. But I do not stand at all for the German-American, or any other kind of hyphenated American." He rejected the "English-American" label as well, arguing that "We Americans are a separate people . . . a new nationality." In a direct rebuke of what later would be called "cultural pluralism," Roosevelt declared: "We are a nation, and not a hodgepodge of foreign nationalities. . . . We must insist on a unified nationality, with one flag, one language, one set of national ideals." In Hermann Hagedorn and John Lester, eds., *The Americanism of Theodore Roosevelt: Selections from His Writings and Speeches* (Boston: Houghton Mifflin, 1923), 201–9.

38. Quoted in Luebke, *Bonds of Loyalty*, 160.

39. Quoted in *A Disloyal Combination*, 10.

40. Detjen, *The Germans in Missouri*, 119–25; Luebke, *Bonds of Loyalty*, 158–64.

41. Luebke, *Bonds of Loyalty*, 178, 184; and Detjen, *The Germans in Missouri*, 122–25.

42. Wittke, *German-Americans and the World War*, 166; Rippley, *The German-Americans*, 184–86; and Luebke, *Bonds of Loyalty*, 190.

43. Hermann Hagedorn, *Prisoners of an Illusion* (reprint from *McClures* magazine, January, 1918) in Wisconsin State Historical Society Pamphlet Collection, #54–1633. *See also*: Robert E. Park, *The Immigrant Press and Its Control* (New York: Harper & Brothers, 1922), 414–17; and Don H. Tolzmann, *German-Americans in the World Wars. Vol. I: The Anti-German Hysteria of World War One* (Munich: K.G. Saur, 1995), 239–40, 268.

44. Park, *The Immigrant Press and Its Control*, 434, 444; Rippley, *The German-Americans*, 185–86; and The Committee on Public Information, *American Loyalty by Citizens of German Descent* (Washington, D.C.: Committee on Public Information, 1917), 5–8.

45. Wittke, *German-Americans and the World War*, 179–95; Rippley, *The German-Americans*, 186–91; Tolzmann, *I: The Anti-German Hysteria of World War One*, 239–44; and *A Disloyal Combination*, 8.

46. The text of Senate hearings on S.3529 is reproduced in: Tolzmann, *II: The World War Experience*, 373–475; also Rippley, *The German-Americans*, 191.

47. Conzen, "Germans," 423.

48. Hawgood, *The Tragedy of German-America*, 297. Some former "German-Americans" founded The Steuben Society in May 1919, to present a new face for Germanism in America by "fostering a patriotic American spirit among all citizens" and educating "the public on the important part played by the Germanic element in the making of America."

49. Theodore Roosevelt, *Letter to the Congress of Constructive Patriotism, The National Security League* (New York: National Security League, [1917]: 1–5; in Wisconsin State Historical Society Pamphlet Collection, #54–825; *see also* Higham, *Send These to Me*, 53.

50. Gleason, "American Identity," 41–42.

51. Higham, *Send These to Me*, 53.

52. Quoted in John F. McClymer, "Gender and the 'American Way of Life': Women in the Americanization Movement," *Journal of American Ethnic History* 10 (spring 1991), 3.

53. Oscar Handlin, *Race and Nationality in American Life* (Boston: Little, Brown, 1957), 175.

54. *A Disloyal Combination*, 13.

55. Jon Gjerde, *The Minds of the West: Ethnocultural Evolution in the Rural Middle West, 1830–1917* (Chapel Hill: University of North Carolina Press, 1997, 252, 261.

56. Philip Gleason, *The Conservative Reformers: German-American Catholics and the Social Order* (Notre Dame, Ind.: University of Notre Dame Press, 1968), 69–83.

57. Gjerde, *The Minds of the West*, 262–63.

58. Gjerde, *The Minds of the West*, 264, 268.

59. Jane Addams, *Twenty Years at Hull-House* (New York: MacMillan, 1910), 233–34.

60. Meyer, *The German-American*, 40; Faust, *The German Element in the United States*, 471; Tolzmann, *II: German-Americans in the World War*, 394; and Luebke, *Bonds of Loyalty*, 65.

61. Gjerde, *The Minds of the West*, 253–60, 264; and Wittke, *German-Americans and the World War*, 4.

62. Faust, *The German Element in the United States*, 463, emphasis added; and Tolzmann, *II: German-Americans in the World War*, 394.

63. Jeraldine R. Kraver, "Restocking the Melting Pot: Americanization as Cultural Imperialism," *Race, Gender & Class* 6 (no. 4, 1999), 68; and Hawgood, *The Tragedy of German-America*, 289.

64. Hawgood, *The Tragedy of German-America*, 289.

65. Gwendolyn Mink, *The Wages of Motherhood: Inequality in the Welfare State, 1917–1942* (Ithaca, N.Y.: Cornell University Press), 9, 25.

66. McClymer, "Gender and the 'American Way of Life,'" 4.

67. Jane Addams, "A Function of the Social Settlement [1899]," in Christopher Lasch, ed., *The Social Thought of Jane Addams* (Indianapolis: Bobbs-Merrill, 1965), 189, 192–93.

68. Addams, *Twenty Years at Hull-House*, 235–47.

69. Addams, *Twenty Years at Hull-House*, 234.

70. Addams, *Twenty Years at Hull House*, chapter 4.

71. Jurgen Herbst, *The German Historical School in American Scholarship: A Study in the Transfer of Culture* (Ithaca, N.Y.: Cornell University Press, 1965), 95–96.

72. Arthur Mann, "British Social Thought and Reformers of the Progressive Era," *The Mississippi Valley Historical Review* 42 (March 1956), 675–76.

73. Frank J. Bruno, *Trends in Social Work, 1874–1956* (New York: Columbia University Press, 1957), 258–60; Linda Gordon, "Social Insurance and Public Assistance: The Influence of Gender in Welfare Thought in the United States, 1890–1935," *American Historical Review* 97 (February 1992), 29; and Mary Jo Deegan, *Jane Addams and the Men of the Chicago School* (New Brunswick, N.J.: Transaction, 1988), 83–85.

74. Frances A. Kellor, *Neighborhood Americanization: A Discussion of the Alien in a New Country and of the Native American in His Home Country*. An address to the Colony Club in New York City, February 8, 1918; Wisconsin State Historical Society Pamphlet Collection, #54–997.

75. Frances Kellor, *Immigration and the Future* (New York: George H. Doran, 1920), 257.

76. Kellor, *Neighborhood Americanization*, 9–10, 19.

77. Molly Ladd-Taylor, "'My Work Came Out of Agony and Grief': Mothers and the Making of the Sheppard-Towner Act," in Seth Koven and Sonya Michel, eds., *Mothers of a New World: Maternalist Politics and the Origins of the Welfare State* (New York: Routledge, 1993), 324; Josephine Baker, M.D., "Why Do Our Mothers and Babies Die?" *The Ladies Home Journal* 39 (April 1922), 32; and "Round Table Conference in Cooperation with The National Study of Methods of Americanization," in *Transactions of the Ninth Annual Meeting. American Association for Study and Prevention of Infant Mortality. December 5–7, 1918* (Baltimore: Franklin Printing, 1919), 230–31, 234.

78. Mink, *The Wages of Motherhood*, 10.

79. Ellen H. Richards, "The Social Significance of The Home Economics Move-

ment," *The Journal of Home Economics* 3 (April 1911), 123–25.

80. Julia Lathrop, "The Highest Education for Women," *The Journal of Home Economics* 8 (January 1916), 3–6.

81. McClymer, "Gender and the 'American Way of Life,'" 12–13.

82. Mink, *The Wages of Motherhood*, 12.

83. Eli Zaretsky, "The Place of the Family in the Origins of the Welfare State," in Barrie Thorne, ed., *Rethinking the Family: Some Feminist Questions* (New York: Longman, 1982), 214–16.

84. Julia Lathrop, "Income and Infant Mortality," *American Journal of Public Health* 9 (April 1919), 273–74.

85. Quoted in Mink, *The Wages of Motherhood*, 48.

86. Quoted in: Joanne L. Goodwin, *Gender and the Politics of Welfare Reform: Mothers' Pensions in Chicago, 1911–1929* (Chicago: University of Chicago Press, 1997), 38. Maternalists, though, were torn on the issue of aiding never-married mothers. The majority thought that aid should be withheld, lest it encourage more illegitimacy. A minority reasoned that "a mother is a mother," and that help should be given. *See also*: Mink, *The Wages of Motherhood*, 33–39.

87. Mary Kingsbury Simkhovitch, *The City Worker's World in America* (New York: Macmillan, 1917), 81.

88. Cora Winchell, "Homemaking as a Phase of Citizenship," *The Journal of Home Economics* 14 (January 1922), 30, 32–33.

89. Virginia Sapiro, "The Gender Basis of American Social Policy," in Linda Gordon, ed., *Women, The State, and Welfare* (Madison: University of Wisconsin Press, 1990), 39.

90. Mink, *The Wages of Motherhood*, 95, 102.

91. Molly Ladd-Taylor, *Mother-Work: Women, Child Welfare, and the State, 1890–1930* (Urbana: University of Illinois Press, 1994), 75–80; and Ladd-Taylor, "'My Work Came out of Agony and Grief,'" 324–25.

92. Ladd-Taylor, *Mother-Work*, 76–88.

93. Mink, *The Wages of Motherhood*, 64–65, 69.

94. Mink, *The Wages of Motherhood*, 78–87, 100; and Addams, *Twenty Years at Hull-House*, 253.

95. Richard A. Meckel, *Save the Babies: American Public Health Reform and the Prevention of Infant Mortality, 1850–1929* (Baltimore: Johns Hopkins University Press, 1990): 147–51; Ladd-Taylor, *Mother-Work*, 89; and Ladd-Taylor, "'My Work Came Out of Agony and Grief,'" 323, 328.

96. Julia Lathrop, *Provision for the Care of the Families and Dependents of Soldiers and Sailors* (New York: Academy of Political Science, 1918), 140–

51; in the Wisconsin State Historical Society Pamphlet Collection, #54–617.

97. Quoted in Ladd-Taylor, *Mother-Work*, 91.

98. Ladd-Taylor, "'My Work Came Out of Agony and Grief,'" 321–28; and J. Stanley Lemons, *The Woman Citizen: Social Feminism in the 1920's* (Urbana: University of Illinois Press, 1973), 154–66.

99. Mink, *The Wages of Motherhood*, 70–71.

100. Ladd-Taylor, "'My Work Came Out of Agony and Grief,'" 329–37.

101. Feminist analysts discussing the victory of the maternalists in scornful ways include: Barbara J. Nelson, "The Origins of the Two-Channel Welfare State: Workmen's Compensation and Mothers' Aid," in Linda Gordon, ed., *Women, the State, and Welfare* (Madison: University of Wisconsin Press, 1990), 132–35, 142; and Sapiro, "The Gender Basis of American Social Policy," 39, 43.

102. Conzen, "Germans," 410; and Sonya Salamon, *Prairie Patrimony: Family, Farming & Community in the Middle West* (Chapel Hill: University of North Carolina Press, 1992).

CHAPTER 3
"SANCTIFYING THE TRADITIONAL FAMILY":
THE NEW DEAL AND NATIONAL SOLIDARITY

1. Lois Scharf, *To Work and to Wed: Female Employment, Feminism, and the Great Depression* (Westport, Conn.: Greenwood Press, 1980), 111, 129.

2. Mimi Abramovitz, *Regulating the Lives of Women: Social Welfare Policy from Colonial Times to the Present* (Boston: South End Press, 1988), 235.

3. Gwendolyn Mink, *The Wages of Motherhood: Inequality in the Welfare State, 1917–1942* (Ithaca N.Y.: Cornell University Press, 1995), 171.

4. Alice Kessler-Harris, *Out to Work: A History of Wage-Earning Women in the United States* (New York: Oxford University Press, 1982), 251.

5. Suzanne Mettler, *Dividing Citizens: Gender and Federalism in New Deal Public Policy* (Ithaca, N.Y.: Cornell University Press, 1998), 214.

6. Winifred D. Wandersee, *Women's Work and Families Values, 1920–1940* (Cambridge Mass.: Harvard University Press, 1981), 101.

7. Scharf, *To Work and to Wed*, 136.

8. Mink, *The Wages of Motherhood*, 171.

9. Jane Humphries, "Women: Scapegoats and Safety Values in The Great Depression," *The Review of Radical Political Economics* 8 (spring 1976), 110.

10. Gosta Esping-Anderson, *The Three Worlds of Welfare Capitalism* (Princeton, N.J.: Princeton University Press, 1990), 23.

11. Allan Carlson, *The Swedish Experiment in Family Politics: The Myrdals*

and the Interwar Population Crisis (New Brunswick, N.J.: Transaction, 1990), especially 195.

12. Lilliam Holmer Mohr, Frances Perkins: "That Woman in FDR's Cabinet!" (Boston: North River Press, 1979), 76.

13. Florence Kelley, "The Family and the Woman's Wage," in Alexander Johnson, ed., Proceedings of the National Conference of Charities and Corrections, Buffalo, N.Y., June 9–16, 1909 (Fort Wayne, Ind.: Fort Wayne Printing, 1910), 119.

14. Kelley, "The Family and the Woman's Wage," 120; and Julia Lathrop, "Standards of Child Welfare," The Annals of the American Academy of Political and Social Science 98 (November 1921), 7–8.

15. Humphries, "Women: Scapegoats and Safety Values in the Great Depression," 105.

16. Kelley, "The Family and the Woman's Wage," 120–21.

17. Ann Shola Orloff, "Gender in Early U.S. Social Policy," Journal of Policy History 3 (no. 3, 1991), 256; also 251–53.

18. Stanley Lemons, The Woman Citizen: Social Feminism in the 1920's (Urbana: University of Illinois Press, 1973), 185.

19. Mohr, Frances Perkins, 190.

20. Linda Gordon, "Social Insurance and Welfare Assistance: The Influence of Gender in Welfare Thought in the United States, 1890–1935," American Historical Review 97 (February 1992), 48. Emphasis added.

21. From: Susan D. Becker, The Origins of the Equal Rights Amendment (Westport, Conn.: Greenwood Press, 1981), 146.

22. Mary Anderson and Mary N. Winslow, Woman at Work: The Autobiography of Mary Anderson (Minneapolis: University of Minnesota Press, 1951), 166–67.

23. Becker, The Origins of the Equal Rights Amendment, 220.

24. Mohr, Frances Perkins, 192; and Anderson and Winslow, Woman at Work, 171.

25. Lemons, The Woman Citizen, 191.

26. Recent Social Trends in the United States: Report of The President's Research Committee on Social Trends (New York: McGraw-Hill, 1933): xlii–xlvi, 661–78, 706. Emphasis added.

27. Lorine Pruette, "The Married Women and the Part-Time Job," The Annals of the American Academy of Political and Social Science 143 (May 1929), 302–6.

28. Stuart Ewen, "Advertising as a Way of Life," Liberation 19 (January 1975), 18.

29. Philip S. Foner, *Women and the American Labor Movement: From World War I to the Present* (New York: Free Press, 1980), 278; also: Frances M. Seeker, "Eleanor Roosevelt and Women in the New Deal: A Network of Friends," *Presidential Studies Quarterly 20* (fall 1990), 711.

30. Gordon Berg, "Frances Perkins and the Flowering of Economic and Social Policies," *Monthly Labor Review 112* (June 1989), 29–30.

31. George Martin, *Madam Secretary: Frances Perkins* (Boston: Houghton Mifflin, 1976), 116.

32. Mohr, *Frances Perkins*, 194.

33. Abramovitz, *Regulating the Lives of Women*, 224.

34. Mary T. Waggaman, *Family Allowances in Various Countries* (Washington, D.C.: U.S. Department of Labor, Bureau of Labor Statistics, 1943), 1.

35. Anderson, *Woman at Work*, 157–158; and Becker, *The Origins of the Equal Rights Amendment*, 177.

36. Eleanor Roosevelt, "Today's Girl and Tomorrow's Job," *Women's Home Companion 59* (June 1932), 12; and Eleanor Roosevelt, "Should Wives Work?" *Good Housekeeping 105* (December. 1932), 212.

37. Mettler, *Dividing Citizens*, 57.

38. Becker, *The Origins of the Equal Rights Amendment*, 150.

39. Gordon, "Social Insurance and Public Assistance," 22–35, 51–54. Emphasis added.

40. Katharine F. Lenroot, "Child Welfare 1930–40," *The Annals of the American Academy of Political and Social Science 212* (November 1940), 1.

41. Anderson and Winslow, *Woman at Work*, 157.

42. Mettler, *Dividing Citizens*, 189.

43. Gordon, "Social Insurance and Public Assistance," 47–49.

44. Mink, *The Wages of Motherhood*, 125, 151, 155.

45. Mettler, *Dividing Citizens*, 45.

46. For example, see: Abramovitz, *Regulating the Lives of Women*, 224, 235.

47. Gordon, "Social Insurance and Public Assistance," 49.

48. Ruth Milkman, "Women's Work and Economic Crisis: Some Lessons of the Great Depression," *Review of Radical Political Economics 8* (Spring 1976), 76, 80, 83.

49. The discussion of New Deal projects focuses on their social and familial aspects; no attempt is made to judge their nature and effectiveness from a political-economic point of view.

50. George E. Paulsen, *A Living Wage for the Forgotten Man: The Quest for Fair Labor Standards, 1933–1941* (Selinsgrove, Penn.: Susquehanna University Press, 1996), 35, 46; Foner, *Women and the American Labor Movement*, 278.

51. Scharf, *To Work and to Wed*, 112, 114, 119; Ware, *Holding Their Own*, 38–39; and Winifred D. Wandersee, "A New Deal for Women: Government Programs, 1933–1940," in Wilbur J. Cohen, ed., *The Roosevelt New Deal: A Program Assessment Fifty Years After* (Austin: University of Texas, 1986), 187–88.

52. Arthur M. Schlesinger Jr., *The Coming of the New Deal* (Boston: Houghton Mifflin, 1958), 362–63.

53. Paul K. Conkin, *Tomorrow a New World: The New Deal Community Program* (Ithaca, N.Y.: Cornell University Press, 1959), 124.

54. Brian Q. Cannon, *Remaking the Agrarian Dream: New Deal Rural Settlement in the Mountain West* (Albuquerque: University of New Mexico Press, 1996), 9; Schlesinger, *The Coming of the New Deal*, 363; Russell Lord, *The Wallaces of Iowa* (Boston: Houghton Mifflin, 1947), 413; and Clarence E. Pickett, *For More Than Bread* (Boston: Little Brown, 1953), 52, 62.

55. Diane Ghirardo, *Building New Communities: New Deal America and Fascist Italy* (Princeton, N.J.: Princeton University Press, 1989), 172, 175, 177.

56. Wandersee, *Women's Work and Family Values*, 96.

57. Ware, *Holding Their Own*, 27.

58. *Current History and Forum*, 1939; in Kessler-Harris, *Out to Work*, 256.

59. Lenroot, "Child Welfare," 10.

60. Mink, *The Wages of Motherhood*, 128; and Ware, *Holding Their Own*, 39.

61. Humphries, "Women: Scapegoat and Safety Values," 107; and Scharf, *To Work and to Wed*, 122.

62. Mink, *The Wages of Motherhood*, 157; Scharf, *To Work and to Wed*, 122; and Ware, *Holding Their Own*, 40.

63. Lenroot, "Child Welfare," 10.

64. Mink, *The Wages of Motherhood*, 158.

65. Mink, *The Wages of Motherhood*, 123.

66. Scharf, *To Work and to Wed*, 123.

67. Mink, *The Wages of Motherhood*, 158–62; Scharf, *To Work and to Wed*, 123. Emphasis added.

68. Doris Campbell, "Counselling Service in the Day Nursery," *The Family: Journal of Social Case Work 24* (March 1943), 29.

69. Scharf, *To Work and to Wed*, 131.

70. Abraham Epstein, *Insecurity: A Challenge to America* (New York: Harrison Smith and Robert Haas, 1933), 101–2. Emphasis added.

71. Grace Abbott, *From Relief to Social Security* (Chicago: University of Chicago Press, 1941), 211.

72. John A. Ryan, *A Living Wage: Its Ethical and Economic Aspects* (New York: Macmillan, 1910).

73. Alice Kessler-Harris, "Designing Women and Old Fools: The Construction of the Social Security Amendments of 1939," in Linda Kerber, Alice Kessler-Harris, and Kathryn Kish Sklar, eds., *U.S. History as Women's History* (Chapel Hill: University of North Carolina Press, 1995), 91, 101.

74. Abramovitz, *Regulating the Lives of Women*, 228, 234–35.

75. Scharf, *To Work and to Wed*, 127–28.

76. Mettler, *Dividing Citizens*, 127.

77. Paul H. Douglas, *Standards for Unemployment Insurance* (Chicago: University of Chicago Press, 1933), 50.

78. Mettler, *Dividing Citizens*, 132.

79. Jane M. Hoey, "Aid to Families with Dependent Children," *The Annals of the American Academy of Political and Social Science 202* (March 1939), 77.

80. Both quotations in: Mink, *The Wages of Motherhood*, 131–32.

81. Hoey, "Aid to Families with Dependent Children," 81.

82. Mink, *The Wages of Motherhood*, 129, 151; Orloff, "Gender in Early U.S. Social Policy," 171; Abramovitz, *Regulating the Lives of Women*, 313–14.

83. Scharf, *To Work and To Wed*, 134; Mettler, *Dividing Citizens*, 191; and Paulsen, "A Living Wage for the Forgotten Man," 50, 92.

84. Janet Hutchison, "Building for Babbit: The State and the Suburban Home Ideal," *Journal of Policy History 9* (no. 2, 1997), 202.

85. James Mason, *History of Housing in the U.S., 1930–1980* (Houston, Tex.: Gulf, 1982): 13; and Mohr, *Frances Perkins*, 184.

86. Hutchison, "Building for Babbitt," 187.

87. Mink, *The Wages of Motherhood*, 135; Kessler-Harris, "Designing Women and Old Fools," 90; and Mettler, *Dividing Citizens*, 99.

88. Orloff, "Gender in Early U.S. Social Policy," 271.

89. Mink, *The Wages of Motherhood*, 136.

90. Kessler-Harris, "Designing Women and Old Fools," 104.

91. Kessler-Harris, "Designing Women and Old Fools," 93.

92. Larry Witt, "Never a Finished Thing: A Biography of Arthur Joseph Altmeyer—The Man FDR Called 'Mr. Social Security,'" at http://www.ssa.gov/history/ajabiocl.html: chapters 1 and 5.

93. A litany found in: Kessler-Harris, "Designing Women and Old Fools," 90, 93–94, 98–100, 105.

94. Mettler, *Dividing Citizens*, 100.

95. Mink, *The Wages of Motherhood*, 150.

96. Kessler-Harris, "Designing Women and Old Fools," 105. Emphasis added.

97. Quoted in Kessler-Harris, "Designing Women and Old Fools," 87.

98. Wandersee, "A New Deal for Women," 186.

99. Milkman, "Women's Work and Economic Crisis," 82.

100. Mink, *The Wages of Motherhood*: 163; and Martin, *Madam Secretary*, 458.

101. Mink, *The Wages of Motherhood*, 165; and Foner, *Women and the American Labor Movement*, 349.

102. Emma O. Lundberg, "A Community Program of Day Care for Children of Mothers Employed in Defense Areas," *Child 6* (January 1942), 153.

103. Mettler, *Dividing Citizens*, 215.

104. Wandersee, *Women's Work and Family Values*, 122.

CHAPTER 4
LUCE, *LIFE*, AND THE "NEW AMERICA"

1. John Courtney Murray, SJ, *We Hold These Truths: Catholic Perspectives on The American Proposition* (New York: Sheed and Ward, 1960), 87, 118–19.

2. Lovell Thompson, "Eden in Peril," *Pacific Spectator* 4 (spring 1950), 200, 210; and Ernest van den Haag, "A Dissent from the Consensual Society," in Norman Jacobs, ed., *Culture for the Millions? Mass Media in Modern Society* (Princeton, N.J.: Van Nostrand, 1961), 56.

3. Edward Shils, "Mass Society and Its Culture," in Jacobs, *Culture for the Millions?*, 1–27.

4. Gary D. Gaffield, "'To Speak and Act Boldly in the Cause of God': Profession and Practice in American Journalism, 1815–1845," *Journal of Popular Culture* 15 (fall 1981), 16.

5. Stephen C. Holder, "The Family Magazine and the American People," *Journal of Popular Culture* 7 (Fall 1973), 264–79; and James Playsted Woods, *The Curtis Magazines* (New York: Ronald Press, 1971), 204–5, 233–34.

6. Stephen Baker, *Visual Persuasion* (New York: McGraw-Hill, 1961).

7. Robert T. Elson, *Time, Inc.: The Intimate History of a Publishing Enterprise, 1923–1941* (New York: Atheneum, 1968), 278.

8. Republished in book form: Henry R. Luce, *The American Century* (New York: Farrar & Rinehart, 1940), 3–40.

9. John Chamberlain, *A Life With the Printed Word* (Chicago: Regnery Gateway, 1982), 69.

10. Robert Elson, *The World of Time, Inc., Volume II* (New York: Atheneum, 1973), 253.

11. Memorandum, Henry Luce to Joseph Thorndike, 8 September 1947; in *The John Shaw Billings Papers*, The South Caroliniana Library, Columbia, S.C., Time-Life-Fortune Collection (hereafter *JSB*), Box II, Folder 101. Emphasis in original.

12. Memorandum, Henry Luce to Joseph Thorndike, 23 March 1948, *JSB*, Box II, Folder 110; and Henry Luce to Planning Committee, 15 August 1949, *JSB*, Box II, Folder 131.

13. Memorandum, Henry Luce to Joseph Thorndike, 1 March 1948, *JSB*, Box II, Folder 108, 1.

14. Letter, Henry Luce to Joseph Thorndike, 8 January 1949, Time, Inc. Archives-New York (hereafter *TA*), 1.

15. Memorandum, Henry Luce to Senior Editors, 16 July 1945, *JSB*, Box I, Folder 60, 1.

16. Henry Luce, "Preliminary Thoughts [January 1958]," *TA*, Section 3, 2.

17. Marginal comments by Henry Luce, on Memorandum, Joseph Thorndike to Mr. Longwell, 30 June 1946, *TA*, 2. Emphasis in original.

18. John K. Jessup, ed., *The Ideas of Henry Luce* (New York: Atheneum, 1969), 6, 9, 28, 318, 381–83; and interview by the author with Clare Boothe Luce, Washington, D.C., September 1984. Emphasis in originals.

19. Memorandum by Henry Luce, "*Life* plans [1944]," *JSB*, Box II, Folder 66, 4–5.

20. Memorandum, Henry Luce to Joseph Thorndike, 28 October 1948, *JSB*, Box II, Folder 119, 12.

21. Henry Luce, "Report to His Staff [22 June 1938]," in Jessup, *The Ideas of Henry Luce*, 267.

22. Henry Luce, "What Makes a Responsible Press?" *Pacific Spectator* 7 (summer 1953), 261.

23. Memorandum, Willi Schlamm to Henry Luce, [May 1945], *JSB*, Box I, Folder 5–6, 1, 4, 7, 11, 20–21.

24. Memorandum, Henry Luce to Joseph Thorndike, 28 October1948, *JSB*, Box II, Folder 119, 8.

25. Memorandum, Henry Luce to "Mr. Heisbell" and Joseph Thorndike, 23 November 1948, *JSB*, Box II, Folder 119, 5.

26. Memorandum by Henry Luce [January 1958], *TA*, Section 3, 1.

27. Memorandum, Henry Luce to Joseph Thorndike, 8 September 1947, *JSB*, Box II, Folder 101, 1.

28. Henry Luce, "The Great Liberal Tradition," address at Temple University, Philadelphia, Penn., 18 June 1953; in Jessup, *The Ideas of Henry Luce*, 124–28.

29. Henry Luce, address to the Duke Divinity School, Durham, N.C., 12 February 1946; in Jessup, *The Ideas of Henry Luce*, 285–89.

30. Henry Luce, address at Southern Methodist University, 19 April 1951; and address at St. Louis University, 16 November 1955; in Jessup, *The Ideas of*

Henry Luce, 154–58, 167.

31. Memoranda, including handwritten marginal comments, Henry Luce to Russell Davenport and Russell Davenport to Henry Luce, both 14 July 1948, *JSB*, Box II, Folder 115.

32. Interview by the author with Edward Thompson, 11 December 1984, Hudson Valley, New York.

33. Murray, *We Hold These Truths*, 23, 31, 42, 74, 80–82, 86–89; and John Murray Cuddihy, *No Offense: Civil Religion and Protestant Taste* (New York: Seabury Press, 1978), 71, 76–77, 90–91.

34. "For Yale, a Thomist," *Time* (13 August 1951); cover, *Time* (12 December 1960); and John Courtney Murray, SJ, "Special Catholic Challenges," *Life* (26 December 1955), 145–46.

35. Henry Luce, address to the Yale Divinity School, 12 February 1946; in Jessup, *The Ideas of Henry Luce*, 290.

36. Henry Luce, address to the Ohio Bankers Association, Cleveland, 10 November 1937; in Jessup, *The Ideas of Henry Luce*, 229–30.

37. Henry Luce, "A Speculation About 1980," *Fortune* (December 1955).

38. Memorandum, Henry Luce to John Shaw Billings, 8 March 1946, *JSB*, Box II, Folder 75.

39. Memorandum by Henry Luce, "Rough Notes on a Radical Revision of *Fortune*," 13 February 1948, Box II, Folder 107, 9–10, 60–67.

40. Memorandum, Henry Luce to Ralph D. Paine, 11 May 1945, *JSB*, Box I, Folder 55, 1–2, 5–6.

41. Memorandum, Henry Luce to "Mr. Heiskell," 25 September 1946, *TA*, pp. 8–10.

42. "Script for *Life* Picturama: 'The New America'," 18 November 1947; Letter by Shepard Spink and attached advertising copy, 29 July 1948; and *The New America*, brochure [1947–?], all in *TA*.

43. Letter, Dwight Eisenhower to Henry Luce, 20 March 1947; and Memorandum, Shepard Spink to Messrs. Luce, Larsen, and Block, 9 September 1947; in *TA*.

44. Letter, Sen. Charles W. Tobey to Henry Luce, 21 March 1947; Memorandum #2521, Shepard Spink to "All *Life* Salesmen," 25 March 1947; and letter, Paul F. Douglas to Henry Luce, 25 March 1947, emphasis added; all in *TA*. And W. Ward Marsh, "*Life*'s 'New America' Should Carry Its Hope to All U.S.," *Cleveland Plain Dealer* (13 September 1947).

45. News Release, "From *Life*," 30 November 1948, in *TA*.

46. Memorandum, Henry Luce to Joseph Thorndike, 8 September 1947; and Draft Introduction to *Life book on Western Civilization [1947]; both in JSB*,

Box II, Folder 105. The final episode in this series, "The American Proposition," appeared only in the published volume.

47. Evelyn Waugh, "The American Epoch in the Catholic Church," *Life* (19 September 1949): 135ff.

48. "Rocketing Births: Business Bonanza," *Life* (16 June 1958): 83ff.

49. Margaret Mead, "She Has Strength Based on a Pioneer Past"; The Editors, "Woman, Love and God"; and Robert Coughlan, "Changing Roles in Modern Marriage," in *Life* (24 December 1956), 26–28, 36, 73–75, 109–16.

50. "A *Life* Round Table on the Pursuit of Happiness: Eighteen Prominent Americans Reinterpret in Modern Times A Great Jeffersonian Right," *Life* (6 September 1948), 99ff.

51. "Christianity: Special Issue," *Life* (26 December 1955).

52. Henry Luce, "Good Architecture is Good Government," address to The American Institute of Architects, 16 May 1957; in Jessup, *The Ideas of Henry Luce*, 274–76, 279.

53. "FHA in Suburbia," *Architectural Forum* 107 (September 1957), 160–61.

54. "Cornerstone for a New Magazine," *House & Home* 1 (January 1952), 107.

55. "House Builders By Size: 4,000 Homes Per Year," *Architectural Forum* 90 (April 1949): 83–93; and "New Levitt Houses Break All Records," *House & Home* 1 (Feb 1952), 98–102.

56. "Toward a Million New Homes a Year [advertisement]," *House & Home* 1 (March 1952), 180–81.

57. "Remodeled 1910 Cottage Overlooks San Francisco Bay," *House & Home* 1 (January 1952), 115.

58. "Charles-Edouard Jeanneret Le Corbusier," *Architectural Forum* 58 (November 1935), 454–55; "The Miesian Superblock," *Architectural Forum* 106 (March 1957), 127–33; and "A Portfolio of Work by Bertrand Goldberg," *Architectural Forum* 84 (March 1946), 107ff.

59. Mary Mix Foley, "The Debacle of Popular Taste," *Architectural Forum* 106 (Febuary 1957), 140ff.

60. "A Traditional Home in the Modern Idiom," *House & Home* 1 (January 1952), 108–15.

61. "Outdoor Living Popular with Everyone," *House & Home* 8 (October 1955), 116–29; and "What Lies Ahead for Home Building?" *House & Home* 1 (January 1952), 138–39.

62. Letter, Henry Luce to Leo Burnett, 13 October 1955, in *TA*.

63. Notes on a talk by Henry Luce, transcribed by Jim Pitt, 2 February 1954, in *TA*.

64. Gerald Holland, "The Golden Age is Now," *Sports Illustrated* (16 August 1954), 46ff.

65. Letter, Henry Luce to Leo Burnett, 18 October 1955, in *TA*.

66. Memorandum ["Confidential and Restricted"], Henry Luce to Mr. Larsen, 6 December 1956, *TA*.

67. "People's Success Story," *Life* (26 December 1960), 20.

68. Otto Friedrich, *Decline and Fall* (New York: Harper & Row, 1969, 1970), 13.

69. Memorandum by Henry Luce, "Preliminary Thoughts," [January 1958], Section 1, 4, Section 6, 4; in *TA*.

70. Memorandum, John Shaw Billings to Henry Luce [1945], *JSB*, Box II, Folder 70, 9.

71. Henry Luce, "Preliminary Thoughts."

72. Interview by the author with Edward Thompson, 11 December 1984.

73. Henry Luce, "The American Pilgrimage," address to the Chicago YMCA, 23 January 1962; and Henry Luce, Testimony before the U.S. Senate Subcommittee on National Policy Machinery, 28 June 1960; in Jessup, *The Ideas of Henry Luce*, 132, 136.

74. Henry Luce, "Preliminary Thoughts," Section 3, 3; Section 4, 1–2.

75. Interview (phone) by the author with John Chamberlain, 30 May 1985; and Chamberlain, *A Life with the Printed Word*, 66, 70–71.

76. Richard M. Weaver, *Ideas Have Consequences* (Chicago: University of Chicago Press, 1948, 1984), 92–112.

CHAPTER 5
COLD WAR AND THE "AMERICAN STYLE"

1. Max Weber, "Der Nationalstaat und die Volkswirtschaftspolitik," in *Gasämmelte Politische Schriften*, ed. J. Winckelmann (Tubingen, 1981), 1–25. From: Rainer C. Baum, *The Holocaust and the German Elite: Genocide and National Suicide in Germany, 1871–1945* (Totowa, N.J.: Rowman and Littlefield, 1981).

2. Eric Larrabee, "David Riesman and His Readers," in Seymour M. Lipset and Leo Lowenthal, eds. *Culture and Social Character: The Work of David Riesman Reviewed* (New York: Free Press, 1961), 404.

3. Clyde Kluckhohn, "Mid-Century Manners and Morals," in Richard Kluckhohn, ed. *Culture and Behavior: Collected Essays of Clyde Kluckhohn* (New York: Free Press, 1965), 323–35. Originally appeared in *Twentieth Century Limited* (1950) and *The New Republic* (1950).

4. David Riesman (with Nathan Glazer), *The Lonely Crowd: A Study of the Changing American Character* (New Haven, Conn.: Yale University Press, 1950).

5. William H. Whyte, *The Organization Man* (New York: Simon & Schuster, 1954).

6. Geroid Tanquary Robinson, "The Ideological Combat," *Foreign Affairs* (July 1949), 525–39.

7. Both lectures published in: Reinhold Niebuhr, *The Irony of American History* (New York: Charles Scribner's Sons, 1952), 16, 139–40.

8. J. Robert Oppenheimer, "Theory versus Practice in American Values and Performance," in Elting E. Morison, ed., *The American Style: Essays in Value and Performance* (New York: Harper & Brothers, 1953), 111–23.

9. Arthur Schlesinger Jr., "Our Country and Our Culture," *Partisan Review 19* (September 1952): 592.

10. Reprinted in George F. Kennan, *American Diplomacy, 1900–1950* (Chicago: University of Chicago Press, 1951), 128.

11. John Foster Dulles, "The Church's Role in Developing the Bases of a Just and Durable Peace," Chicago, May 28, 1941, 2, 8; in the John Foster Dulles Papers, Box 20, Princeton University Library; acceptance speech on receiving the Peace Medal of St. Francis of Assisi from the National Third Order of St. Francis, February 20, 1952, Dulles Papers, Box 306.

12. Dulles, "The Church's Role in Developing the Bases of a Just and Durable Peace," 25–26; and printed text, John Foster Dulles, "To the Members of the Commission to Study the Bases of a Just and Durable Peace," September 18, 1941, Dulles Papers, Box 20.

13. John Foster Dulles to Roswell P. Barnes, May 8, 1946, Dulles Papers, Box 29.

14. John Foster Dulles, "Freedom through Sacrifice," address delivered at the Presbyterian General Assembly, Atlantic City, N.J., May 24, 1946, under the auspices of the Presbyterian Restoration Fund, Dulles Papers, Box 293.

15. John Foster Dulles, "Our Spiritual Heritage," address at The New York Herald Tribune Forum, October 21, 1947, Dulles Papers, Box 294. *See also* John Foster Dulles, *The Christian Citizen in a Changing World*, a document prepared for the Study Department Commission of the World Council of Churches for use at the First Assembly of the WCC, Amsterdam, Holland, August 22–September 4, 1948, Dulles Papers, Box 284.

16. John Foster Dulles, "The Strength of Diversity," address to the anniversary banquet of The Temple, Cleveland, Ohio, May 18, 1950, Dulles Papers, Box 301.

17. John Foster Dulles, "On Unity," address to the Military Chaplains Association, February 29, 1952, Dulles Papers, Box 306.

18. From: Robert H. Ferrell, ed., *The Eisenhower Diaries* (New York: W. W. Norton, 1981): 143; John L. Gaddis, *Strategies of Containment: A Critical*

Appraisal of Postwar American National Security Policy (New York: Oxford University Press, 1982), 143; "Second Inaugural Address," *Public Papers of the Presidents: Dwight D. Eisenhower, 1957* (Washington, D.C.: Government Printing Office, 1958), 62; and "Address at U.S. Naval Academy Commencement, June 4, 1958," *Public Papers of the Presidents: Dwight D. Eisenhower, 1958* (Washington, D.C.: Government Printing Office, 959), 454–55.

19. Daniel Yankelovich, *New Rules* (New York: Bantam, 1981, 1982), 120.

20. Talcott Parsons, *The Social System* (New York: Free Press, 1951), 188.

21. Talcott Parsons, "An Outline of the Social-System," in Parsons, et al, eds., *Theories of Society: Foundations of Modern Sociological Theory, Volume I* (New York: Free Press, 1961), 39 (emphasis added), 73. *See also* Talcott Parsons, *Structure and Process in Society* (New York: Free Press, 1960), 236, 242.

22. Talcott Parsons and Winston White, "The Link between Character and Society," in Seymour Martin Lipset and Leo Lowenthal, eds., *Culture and Social Character: The Work of David Riesman Reviewed* (New York: Free Press, 1961), 116–17.

23. Parsons and White, "The Link between Character and Society," 100–101; Parsons, "An Outline of the Social System," 57.

24. Daniel P. Miller and Guy E. Swanson, *The Changing American Parent: A Study in the Detroit Area* (New York: John Wiley & Sons, 1958), 201; Clyde Kluckhohn, "Shifts in American Values," *World Politics 11* (January 1959), 258–60; Dennis W. Brogan, "Unnoticed Changes in America," *Harper's* (February 1957); and Seymour Martin Lipset, "A Changing American Character?" in Lipset and Lowenthal, eds., *Culture and Social Character*, 148–50, 157–58.

25. William J. Goode, *World Revolution and Family Patterns* (New York: Free Press, 1963), 19, 368–69, 380.

26. Max Millikan, "Preface," in Elting E. Morison, ed., *The American Style: Essays in Value and Performance* (New York: Harper & Brothers, 1958), vii.

27. Published as Walt H. Rostow, "The National Style," in Morison, *The American Style*, 246–313.

28. George F. Kennan, *Realities of American Foreign Policy* (Princeton, N.J.: Princeton University Press, 1954), 47–48, 99, 107–9, 118.

29. Philip E. Jacob, *Changing Values in College* (New York: Harper, 1957); and Caroline Bird, "The Unlost Generation," *Harper's Bazaar* (February 1957).

30. David Riesman, "Commentary: The National Style," in Morison, *The American Style*, 358–68.

31. David Riesman and Nathan Glazer, "The Lonely Crowd: A Reconsideration in 1960," in Lipset and Lowenthal, eds., *Culture and Social Character*, 419–58.

32. Walt W. Rostow's concluding remarks, in Morison, *The American Style*, 415–16.

33. Wilbur J. Cohen, "Memorandum for Honorable Theodore C. Sorensen," September 12, 1961, plus attachment, Theodore Sorensen Papers, Box 34, John F. Kennedy Library, Boston.

34. John McNaughton to McGeorge Bundy, September 28, 1961, John F. Kennedy Papers, National Security Files, Box 273, Kennedy Library; and Gaddis, *Strategies of Containment*, 233.

35. Walt W. Rostow, "The Domestic Base of Foreign Policy," a speech before the biennial convention of the League of Women Voters, Minneapolis, Minn., May 3, 1962, Sorensen Papers, Box 38.

36. Marcus Raskin to McGeorge Bundy, October 17, 1961, Kennedy Papers, National Security Files, Box 295, Document #3.

37. Memorandum, John F. Kennedy to Robert McNamara, August 29, 1961, Kennedy Papers, National Security Files, Box 295. Kennedy's initiative seems to have derived from a conversation between press secretary Pierre Salinger and private defense analyst Roy H. Hoopes Jr. *See* letter, Hoopes to Pierre Salinger, August 20, 1961, Kennedy Papers, White House Central Files, Box 595.

38. Draft, Letter from the President to "My fellow Americans" and draft, "What You Should Know and What You Can Do. How to Survive Attack and Live for Your Country's Recovery," [October 1961?] Kennedy Papers, National Security Files, Box 295, Documents #2 and #7.

39. John Kenneth Galbraith to John F. Kennedy, November 9, 1961, Kennedy Papers, National Security Files, Box 295, Document #8.

40. Marcus Raskin memoranda dated May 19, July 7 and October 13, 1961, Kennedy Papers, National Security Files, Box 295.

41. Marcus Raskin memoranda to McGeorge Bundy, October 23, 1961; to Carl Kaysen, November 15, 1961; to Bundy, November 20, 1961; October 13, 1961; in Kennedy Papers, National Security Files, Box 295.

42. Gaddis, *Strategies of Containment*, 200 fn.

43. S/P Draft, "Basic National Security Policy," March 26, 1962, Lyndon B. Johnson Papers, Vice-Presidential National Security File, Box 7, Lyndon B. Johnson Library, Austin, Tex. Emphasis added.

44. Letter and attachment, George K. Tanham to Walt W. Rostow, September 21, 1961; Memorandum for the President, "Program of Action for Vietnam,"

July 17, 1961; in Kennedy Papers, National Security Files, Box 193. *See also* W. W. Rostow to Robert McNamara, May 2, 1966, Johnson Papers, National Security Files: Agency File, "Dept. of Defense, 6/65," vol. 111, Box 12.

45. McGeorge Bundy to Lyndon B. Johnson, February 7, 1965, Johnson Papers, National Security Files, "National Security Council History," Box 40, Document #22; and Walt Rostow to Robert McNamara, September 29, 1966, Johnson Papers, National Security Files, "National Security Council History: Manila Conference and Presidential Asian Trip," vol. II, tab E, Box 45.

46. Quotations from Gaddis, *Strategies of Containment*, 204. Emphasis added.

47. Arthur Schlesinger Jr. to Theodore Sorensen, January 2, 1963; in Kennedy Papers, National Security Files, Box 327 (emphasis added). *See also* Walt Rostow to Lyndon B. Johnson, July 28, 1967, Harry McPherson Files, Box 55, Johnson Library.

48. Yankelovich, *New Rules*, 91–94.

49. See: "What Happens When Americans Stop Dreaming in Color" *The Economist*, 16 October 1982.

50. Yankelovich, *New Rules*, 94.

51. Interview with Theodore C. Sorensen, April 15, 1964, interview #3, Oral History Collection, Kennedy Library.

52. Notations from "Norman Cousins" (transcript of phone conversation?), n.d. [June 1963]; Sorensen Papers, Box 72; and draft comments, with notation "From Attorney General," n.d. [June 1963]; Sorensen Papers, Box 75.

53. "TCS—1ˢᵗ draft, 6/11/63" Sorensen Papers, Box 73.

54. Karl Kaysen to the Secretary of State and the Undersecretary of State, with attachment, "TCS—2ⁿᵈ draft, 6/7/63," in Kennedy Papers, National Security Files, Box 305. The final draft did drop the phrase suggesting that "conflicts of ideology" do not "last forever," retaining the remainder of the sentence.

55. Memorandum, Thomas L. Hughes (Director of Intelligence and Research) to Dean Rusk, "Khrushchev Sets Terms for Relaxation of Tension in Reaction to President's American University Speech," June 15, 1963; incoming telegram #348, Rivkin (Luxembourg) to Dean Rusk, June 25, 1963; incoming telegram #3124, Kohler (Moscow) to Dean Rusk, June 11, 1963; and "Text of Khrushchev on Kennedy Speech," June 14, 1963; in Kennedy Papers, National Security Files, Box 305.

56. Transcript, "Washington Report," as broadcast on CBS Television, June 16, 1963, in Kennedy Papers, National Security Files, Box 295, Document #1.

57. Arthur Schlesinger Jr., to Theodore Sorensen, January 2, 1963, Kennedy Papers, National Security Files, Box 327.

58. A reproduction of the "Moynihan Report" and the text of President Johnson's

speech are found in Lee Rainwater and William L. Yancey, eds., *The Moynihan Report and the Politics of Controversy* (Cambridge, Mass.: M.I.T. Press, 1967), 39–132.

59. Interview with Harry McPherson, tape #6, March 24, 1969, Oral History Collection, Johnson Library.

60. Frank Riessman, "In Defense of the Negro Family," reprinted in Rainwater and Yancey, *The Moynihan Report and the Politics of Controversy*, 475; Staples quotation from Christopher Lasch, *Haven in a Heartless World: The Family Besieged* (New York: Basic Books, 1977), 158; and Ray L. Birdwhistell, "The American Family: Some Perspectives," *Psychiatry* (August 1966), 203–12.

61. "Changing Families in a Changing Society," Report of Forum 14, White House Conference on Children and Youth, 1970. *See also* Allan Carlson, "Families, Sex and the Liberal Agenda," *The Public Interest* (winter 1980), 73–79.

62. Robert McNamara to Lyndon Johnson, October 14, 1966, Johnson Papers, National Security Files, "National Security Council History: Manila Conference and Presidential Asian Trip," vol. II, tab E, Box 45; Interview with John Roche, July 16, 1970, Oral History Collection, Johnson Library; and Lyndon Johnson to the Secretaries of State and Defense, Director of the Bureau of the Budget, January 31, 1968, Johnson Papers, National Security Files, "National Security Council History," Box 47.

63. Gaddis, *Strategies of Containment*, 240–41. John McNaughton to Robert McNamara, July 13, 1965, plus attachment; and "Summary Notes of 553rd NSC Meeting," July 27, 1965; in National Security Files, "National Security Council History," Box 43, documents #386 and #426. *See also* "The Case against Further Significant Increases in U.S. Forces in Vietnam," March 3, 1968, Johnson Papers, National Security Files, "National Security Council History," Box 49.

64. Interview with Harry McPherson, March 24, 1969, Tape #5, Oral History Collection, Johnson Library.

65. Walt Rostow to Dean Rusk, January 31, 1968, Johnson Papers, National Security Files, "National Security Council History," Box 49.

66. "The Case against Further Significant Increases in U.S. Forces in Vietnam," March 3, 1968, Johnson Papers, National Security Files, "National Security Council History," Box 49; and "Minutes. The Cabinet Meeting of April 3, 1968," 2, Johnson Papers.

67. Walt Rostow to Lyndon Johnson, plus attachment, Richard Helms to Johnson, November 15, 1967, Johnson Papers, National Security Files Intelligence File, Box 3.

68. Richard Helms to Lyndon Johnson, September 4, 1968, plus attachment, "Restless Youth," Johnson Papers, National Security Files Intelligence File, Box 3.

69. George McGhee to Dean Rusk, January 17, 1969, with attachment, "Report of the Student Unrest Study Group:" 7, Johnson Papers, National Security Files: Intelligence File, Box 3.

70. *Public Papers of the Presidents: Richard Nixon 1971* (Washington, D.C.: Government Printing Office, 1972): 219–22.

71. *Public Papers of the Presidents: Richard Nixon 1970* (Washington, D.C.: Government Printing Office, 1971), 117; and Henry Kissinger, *White House Years* (Boston: Little, Brown, 1979), 192.

72. Kissinger, *White House Years*, 191.

73. Henry Kissinger, "The Moral Foundations of Foreign Policy," in *American Foreign Policy*, 3rd Edition (New York: W. W. Norton, 1977): 200–203, 208–9.

74. James Earl Carter, "Commencement Address to the University of Notre Dame, May 22, 1977," *Public Papers of the Presidents: James Earl Carter, 1977, vol. 1* (Washington, D.C.: Government Printing Office, 1977): 954–62.

75. Gaddis, *Strategies of Containment*, 346.

76. "Changing Realities of Family Life," *Listening to America's Families: The Report of the White House Conference on Families* (Washington, D.C.: WHCF, 1980), 159.

CHAPTER 6
FROM MATERNALISM TO REAGANISM AND BEYOND

1. The full debate appears in *The Congressional Record: Proceedings and Debates of The 88ᵗʰ Congress. Second Session* (volume 110, part 2), February 8, 1964: 2577–87. For guidance through this memorable dialogue, I am grateful to Paul Adam Blanchard's, "Insert the Word 'Sex'—How Segregationists Handed Feminists a 1964 'Civil Rights' Victory against the Family," *The Family in America* 12 (March 1998), 1–8.

2. Donald Allen Robinson, "Two Movements in Pursuit of Equal Employment Opportunity," *Signs: Journal of Women in Culture and Society* 4 (no. 3, 1979), 427.

3. J. E. Buckley, "Equal Pay in America," in Barrie O. Pettman, ed., *Equal Pay for Women: Progress and Problems in Seven Countries* (Bradford, U.K.: MCB Books, 1975), 47.

4. "*Weinberger* v. *Wiesenfeld*: 1975," available at *http://www.gale.com/free-resources/whm/trials/www.htm* .

5. Noted in Alice Kessler-Harris, "Designing Women and Old Fools: The Construction of the Social Security Amendments of 1939," in Linda K. Kerber, Alice Kessler-Harris, and Kathryn Kish Sklar, eds.,*U.S. History as Women's History: New Feminist Essays* (Chapel Hill: University of North Carolina Press, 1995), 88.

6. From the reproduction of *The Negro American Family: The Case for National Action*, found in Lee Rainwater and William L. Yancy, eds., *The Moynihan Report and the Politics of Controversy* (Cambridge, Mass.: M.I.T. Press, 1967), 75.

7. Carole Pateman, "The Patriarchal Welfare State," in Amy Gutmann, ed., *Democracy in the Welfare State* (Princeton, N.J.: Princeton University Press, 1988), 231–60.

8. Frances Fox Piven, "Ideology and the State: Women, Power and the Welfare State," in Linda Gordon, ed., *Women, The State and Welfare* (Madison: University of Wisconsin Press, 1990), 251–64.

9. Data from: U.S. Department of Commerce, Bureau of the Census, *Current Population Reports*, Series P-60, 1951–2000.

10. For a more complete discussion of this issue, see: Allan C. Carlson, "Gender, Children, and Social Labor: Transcending the 'Family Wage' Dilemma," *Journal of Social Issues* 52 (no. 3, 1996), 137–61.

11. Gary Becker, "A Theory of the Allocation of Time," *Economic Journal* 75 (1965), 493–517; and Gary Becker, *A Treatise on the Family* (Cambridge, Mass.: Harvard University Press, 1981).

12. Among feminist historians, only Gwendolyn Mink fully acknowledges the great import of the 1964 Civil Rights debate and its aftermath. She writes: "The crucial political decision was The Civil Rights Act of 1964. . . . Still loyal to its maternalist heritage in 1964, the Women's Bureau initially opposed applying Title VII's prohibition on employment discrimination to women. Only after the sex discrimination amendment passed the House of Representatives did The Women's Bureau sign on in support. This shift arguably marked the end of maternalism." In Gwendolyn Mink, *The Wages of Motherhood: Inequality in the Welfare State* (Ithaca, N.Y.: Cornell University Press, 1995), 179n.

13. "News Conference, January 29, 1981," in *Public Papers of the Presidents: Ronald Reagan, 1981* (Washington, DC: Government Printing Office, 1982), 57 [hereafter, *Papers: Reagan*].

14. "Commencement Address at the University of Notre Dame, May 17, 1981," in *Papers: Reagan, 1981*, 434.

15. "The Evil Empire: President Reagan's Speech to the House of Commons,

June 8, 1982,"available at *http://www.townhall.com/hall_of_fame/reagan/speech/empire.html* .

16. "Commencement Address at the University of Notre Dame," 434.

17. "Proclamation of National Family Week, Nov 3, 1981," in *Papers: Reagan, 1981*, 1012.

18. Ronald Reagan, "Remarks at a Presentation Ceremony for the 1983 Young American Medals for Bravery, August 28, 1984," in *Papers: Reagan, 1984*, 1202.

19. "Remarks to the Student Congress on Evangelism, July 28, 1988," in *Papers: Reagan, 1988–89*, 992.

20. Ronald Reagan, "Remarks at a Luncheon with Community Leaders in Chicago, Illinois, September 30, 1988," in *Papers: Reagan, 1988–89*, 1252.

21. Ronald Reagan, "Remarks on Signing the National Hispanic Heritage Week Proclamation, September 13, 1988," in *Papers: Reagan, 1988–89*, 1158–59.

22. Working Group on the Family, *The Family: Preserving America's Future* (Washington, D.C.: Domestic Policy Council, Executive Office of the President, 1986), 6.

23. Working Group, *The Family*, 44–45. Emphasis in original.

24. Working Group, *The Family*, 13–14. Emphasis in original.

25. Dennis R. Fox, "The Reagan Administration's Policy on Using the Family to Advance Capitalism," paper presented at the 1988 Convention of the Law and Society Association, Vail, Colorado; available at *http://www.uis.edu/~fox/papers/reagan-family.htm*.

26. In the interests of full disclosure, this author made such an attempt himself—in retrospect, not a very effective one—in Allan Carlson, "The Family and Liberal Capitalism," *Modern Age* 26 (Summer/Fall 1982): 366–71.

27. Chilton Williamson Jr., *The Immigration Mystique: America's False Conscience* (New York: Basic Books, 1996), 198.

28. Williamson, *The Immigration Mystique*, 201.

29. Peter Brimelow, *Alien Nation: Common Sense About America's Immigration Disaster* (New York: Random House, 1995), 216–18.

30. Arthur M. Schlesinger Jr., *The Dismantling of America: Reflections on a Multicultural Society* (New York: W. W. Norton, 1992), 124–25.

31. Bill Ong Hing, *To Be an American: Cultural Pluralism and the Rhetoric of Assimiliation* (New York: New York University Press, 1997), 4–5, 180–91.

32. Nathan Glazer, *We Are All Multiculturalists Now* (Cambridge, Mass.: Harvard University Press, 1997), 18. Emphasis added.

33. Jody Heymann, *The Widening Gap: Why America's Working Families Are in Jeopardy and What Can Be Done About It* (New York: Basic Books, 2000), 5–6.

34. Stewart Friedman and Jeffrey Greenhaus, *Work and Family: Allies or Enemies? What Happens When Business Professionals Confront Life Choices* (Oxford, U.K.: Oxford University Press, 2000), 6–7.

35. Theda Skocpol, *The Missing Middle: Working Families and the Future of American Social Policy* (New York: W. W. Norton, 2000), 161.

36. For an example of such strategizing, see Allan Carlson and David Blankenhorn, "The Solution to Everything," *The Weekly Standard* (December 14, 1998).

37. John Harmon McElroy, *American Beliefs: What Keeps a Big Country and a Diverse People United* (Chicago: Ivan R. Dee, 1999): summarized on 227–28.

38. McElroy, *American Beliefs*, 223.

39. G. K. Chesterton, "What's Wrong With the World," and "The Superstition of Divorce," in *Collected Works*, vol. IV (San Francisco: Ignatius Press, 1987), 67, 256.

40. This is not a statement of ideology, but the lesson of contemporary social science, which—despite the best efforts of some to suppress the research—continues to discover that women and men are innately and importantly different in behaviors. See, most recently: Lloyd B. Lueptow, Lori Garovich-Szabo, and Margaret B. Lueptow, "Social Change and the Persistence of Sex Typing: 1974–1997," *Social Forces* 80 (2001), 1–35; J. Richard Udry, "Biological Limits of Gender Construction," *American Sociological Review* 65 (2000), 443–57; Martin VanCreveld, "A Woman's Place: Reflections on the Origins of Violence," *Social Research* 67 (2000), 825–46; Shawn L. Christiansen and Rob Palkovitz, "Why the 'Good Provider' Role Still Matters," *Journal of Family Issues* 22 (January 2001), 84–106; and Pamela Wilcox Rountree and Barbara D. Warner, "Social Ties and Crime: Is the Relationship Gendered?" *Criminology* 37 (1999), 789–810.

41. An anecdote told the author by Dr. David Popenoe of Rutgers University.

Index